LUIGI PIRANDELLO
CONTEMPORARY PERSPECTIVES

EDITED BY
GIAN-PAOLO BIASIN AND
MANUELA GIERI

Luigi PIRANDELLO

CONTEMPORARY PERSPECTIVES

UNIVERSITY OF TORONTO PRESS
Toronto Buffalo London

© University of Toronto Press Incorporated 1999
Toronto Buffalo London
Printed in Canada
ISBN 0-8020-4387-9

Printed on acid-free paper

Toronto Italian Studies: Major Italian Authors
General Editors: Massimo Ciavolella and Amilcare A. Iannucci

Canadian in Publication Data

Biasin, Gian-Paolo
   Luigi Pirandello: contemporary perspectives
   (Toronto Italian studies. Major Italian authors)
   Includes bibliographical references.
   ISBN 0-8020-4387-9
   1. Pirandello, Luigi, 1867–1936 – Criticism and interpretation.
   I. Gieri Manuela. II. Title. III. Series.

PQ4835.I7Z53497 1999   852'.912   C98-931427-8

This volume was published with the financial assistance of the Emilio Goggio Chair in Italian Studies, University of Toronto.

University of Toronto Press acknowledges the financial assistance to its publishing program of the Canada Council for the Arts and the Ontario Arts Council.

To Gian-Paolo Biasin
and
Maurizio Grande
in memoriam

Contents

ACKNOWLEDGMENTS ix
CONTRIBUTORS xi

Section 1: Introduction

1 Pirandello at 360 Degrees   GIAN-PAOLO BIASIN and MANUELA GIERI   3
2 Scenes and Texts: Perspectives in Pirandellian Criticism   FRANCA ANGELINI   23

Section 2: Structures

3 Pirandello's Quest for Truth: *Sei personaggi in cerca d'autore*   DONATO SANTERAMO   37
4 Pirandello and the Theatre-within-the-Theatre: Thresholds and Frames in *Ciascuno a suo modo*   MAURIZIO GRANDE   53
5 Families of Characters and Families of Actors on the Pirandellian Stage   PAOLO PUPPA   64
6 The Making and Unmaking of Language: The Rhetoric of Speech and Silence   MARIA ANTONIETTA GRIGNANI   77

Section 3: Meanings

7 Laughter and Political Allegory in Pirandello: A Reading of 'C'è qualcuno che ride'   ROMANO LUPERINI   107

8 Pirandellian Nakedness ROBERT DOMBROSKI 125
9 Eros and Solitude in Pirandello's Short Stories
  CORRADO DONATI 139

Section 4: Innovations

10 Enacting the Dissolution of the Self: Woman as One, No One, and One Hundred Thousand DANIELA BINI 163
11 Regicide, Parricide, and Tyrannicide in *Il fu Mattia Pascal*: Stealing from the Father to Give to the Son THOMAS HARRISON 189
12 Pirandello in the Discursive Economies of Modernity and Postmodernism WLADIMIR KRYSINSKI 214

Acknowledgments

We wish to extend our warmest gratitude to all collaborators who matched their intellectual stature with their generosity and enduring patience and in so doing made possible the publication of this volume. A special thought goes to Maurizio Grande, who left us sadly too early in his journey through life. His work will remain with us as an invaluable legacy, and his memory as a constant inspiration.

We give deep-felt thanks to the translators, including Paul Kottman, whose work could not be included at the last moment for causes beyond our control. Their work has ensured the transmission of ideas from one culture to another without betraying the original – an indispensable task in the cross-cultural circulation of ideas.

Particular recognition goes to the readers of the University of Toronto Press who read and approved the manuscript. Our sincere and wholehearted appreciation is extended to the editor, Ruth Pincoe, who has been an invaluable partner and at times a true accomplice, with her attentive and inquisitive remarks and her suggestions for improving and polishing the manuscript. Our gratitude also goes to Ron Schoeffel and Anne Forte, whose relentless efforts have made publications in Italian Studies a wonderful reality at the University of Toronto Press.

We are extremely grateful to all our friends and colleagues on our respective campuses, who, even without being directly engaged in discussions of Pirandello's work, have contributed powerfully to the intellectual atmosphere that led to the conception of this critical anthology.

Finally, our unqualified gratitude goes to all those scholars who have paved the way for the development of new avenues in Pirandellian criticism, and also to those who are now working to build a new understanding of the rich and ever-changing Pirandellian text.

Toronto, 23 August 1998

No longer two but one, I feel so lonely. Deep sorrow accompanies me as I write these few lines alone. Today Gian Paolo has left his family, his friends, his students and colleagues, and me.

Today is the day that our Pirandello project came to its conclusion. In the past few weeks we corrected the galleys, and this morning I delivered them to the press. Today is also the day Gian Paolo died – an unfortunate but momentous coincidence for me.

A renowned professor of Italian literature at the University of Berkeley and one of the most original and lively intellectuals in the areas of Italian and comparative studies, Gian Paolo brought warmth and light to both my personal and my professional life from our first meeting in the fall of 1986. He immediately gave me the encouragement so deeply needed at the beginning of a new journey as I was starting out in my academic career. Since then he never failed to give me support and advice in hard times, and he always rejoiced with me in good times. Most important, he never ceased to be an inspiration to me as a scholar and as a person.

Today Gian Paolo leaves me with the same light and warmth, and with a tremendous legacy. The illness that was progressively consuming his body never touched his spirit. Until the very last day, he worked with the same enthusiasm and joy that characterized his entire life. Everybody who was fortunate enough to meet him knows that his academic accomplishments were splendidly matched by his unparalleled human qualities. This is Gian Paolo's legacy to me, and to all of us.

For this, and for much more, I can only say thank you, thank you for being such an inspiring colleague and a dedicated friend. I shall always carry you with me.

M.G.

Contributors

FRANCA ANGELINI is professor of Italian dramatic literature at the University of Rome 'La Sapienza.' She is the editor of the series *Il teatro e spettacolo* for Laterza, and she has published extensively on modern and baroque theatre. Her many contributions to Pirandellian studies include *Il teatro del novecento da Pirandello a Fo* (1976; new edition 1990), *Serafino e la tigre: Pirandello tra scrittura, teatro e cinema* (1990), and *Il punto su Pirandello*, a collection of essays edited in 1992.

GIAN-PAOLO BIASIN was professor of Italian studies at the University of California at Berkeley. He wrote numerous books on contemporary Italian literature and culture, both in Italian and in English. *The Flavors of Modernity: Food and the Novel* (1995) received the Presidential Book Award of the American Association for Italian Studies. His recent book, *Le periferie della letteratura: Da Vega a Tabucchi*, was published by Longa in Ravenna.

DANIELA BINI is professor of Italian at the University of Texas at Austin. She co-edited *Italiano in Diretta* (1989), but she established her reputation as a scholar with her studies on Leopardi, *A Fragrance from the Desert: Poetry and Philosophy in Giacomo Leopardi* (1983) and the pioneering *Michelstaedter and the Failure of Language* (1992). Her most important book, it seems, is her latest, *Pirandello and His Muse: The Plays for Marta Abba* (1998).

ROBERT DOMBROSKI is Distinguished Professor of Italian at the City University of New York. He has written extensively on Gadda, Pirandello, Manzoni, intellectuals and Fascism, and Gransci. His most recent

xii Contributors

book, *Properties of Writing: Ideological Discourse in Modern Italian Fiction* (1994), was awarded the Modern Language Association Howard R. Marrano and the Aldo and Jeanne Scaglione Prizes for Italian Literary Studies.

CORRADO DONATI is associate professor of Italian at the University of Trento. He has made an extensive contribution to the field of Italian modern narrative, and he has also published at length on the literary journals of the early twentieth century. In the field of Pirandellian studies, he has published numerous articles and three major volumes: *La solitudine allo specchio: Luigi Pirandello* (1980), *Bibliografia della critica pirandelliana (1962–1981)* (1986), and *Il sogno e la ragione: Saggi pirandelliani* (1993).

MANUELA GIERI is associate professor of Italian and cinema studies at the University of Toronto, where she teaches Italian cinema and modern theatre, Italian women's literature, as well as literary and film theory. After co-authoring *La Strada: Federico Fellini, Director* (1987), she has contributed to Italian cinema and cultural studies with her book *Italian Contemporary Filmmaking: Strategies of Subversion* (1995). She has also published articles on Pirandello, Fellini, and Italian women writers.

MAURIZIO GRANDE was professor of cinema and theatre at the University of Siena and theatre critic for the journal *Rinascita*. He was a scholar of esthetics and semiotics and studied the nature of poetic, theatrical, and film language; his book on the subject – *Introduzione alla semiologia dello spettacolo* was published in 1990. A great connoisseur of one of Italy's contemporary theatrical protagonists, Carmelo Bene, he made substantial and inspirational contributions to the fields of Italian drama – especially with the volume *La riscossa di Lucifero: Ideologie e prassi del teatro di sperimentazione in Italia* (1985) – and cinema – especially with *Abiti nuziale e biglietti di banca: La società della commedia nel cinema italiano* (1986) and *Il cinema di Saturno* (1992).

MARIA ANTONIETTA GRIGNANI is professor of history of the Italian language at the University of Pavia. She has edited critical commentaries of ancient texts including *Navigatio Sancti Brendani* (1975, second edition 1992). In the field of Italian twentieth-century studies, she has published extensively on Vittorio Sereni, Umberto Saba, Beppe Fenoglio, Carlo Emilio Gadda, and Eugenio Montale. Some of her most impressive essays are collected in *Prologhi ed epiloghi* (1987) and *La vita della foresta* (1987).

THOMAS HARRISON is associate professor of Italian at the University of California at Berkeley where he teaches Italian culture and cinema. He was editor of *Nietzsche in Italy* in 1988 and subsequently wrote two intriguing books: *Essayism: Conrad, Musil, and Pirandello* (1992) and *1910, the Emancipation of Dissonance* (1996).

WLADIMIR KRYSINSKI is professor of comparative and Slavic literatures at the Université de Montréal. His numerous and notable publications include *Carrefours de signes: Essais sur le roman moderne* (1981), *Le paradigme inquiet: Pirandello et le champ de la modernité* (1989), and *La novela en sus modernidades: A Favor y contra Bajtin* (1997).

ROMANO LUPERINI is professor of modern and contemporary Italian literature at the University of Siena. He directs *Allegoria*, the journal of literary theory, methodology, and criticism. With books such as *Il novecento: apparati ideologici, ceto intellettuale, sistemi formali nella letteratura italiana contemporanea* (1981) and *L'allegoria del moderno: saggi sull'allegorismo come forma artistica del moderno e come metodo di conoscenza* (1990), he has contributed greatly to the studies of modern and contemporary Italian literature and culture. He has also published influential essays on Verga, Montale, and Pirandello.

PAOLA PUPPA is both an associate professor of theatre at the Universities of Venice and Feltre and a playwright. As a scholar, he has published extensively in literary and theatrical journals, and he is the author of numerous entries on theatre in the *Treccani Encyclopedia*. Among his numerous books are several devoted to Pirandello: *Fantasmi contro giganti* (1978), *Dalle parti di Pirandello* (1987), and *La parola alta* (1993).

DONATO SANTERAMO is assistant professor at Queen's University where he teaches Italian language, and modern and contemporary Italian literature and theatre. He has published numerous articles on Italian theatre, Pirandello, and the modern and contemporary Italian novel. He has also published in the field of general and applied semiotics; he is the co-author of *Deictic Verb Constructions: Observations on Computational/Literalist vs. Experiential Approaches to Semantics* (1994) and *Per un approccio vichiano nella didattica* (1992).

SECTION 1
INTRODUCTION

1

Pirandello at 360 Degrees

GIAN-PAOLO BIASIN AND MANUELA GIERI

With a paradox that Pirandello might have liked, since paradox was a treasured intellectual concept for him, our introduction to this critical anthology begins with a discussion of names that are not included within it; the first is Glauco Cambon, the editor of a 1967 anthology of critical essays in English that could be considered the antecedent of this present volume. In order to introduce current trends and innovations in Pirandellian criticism, it is first necessary to survey – albeit briefly – the itineraries that critics have followed so far. Their achievements have indeed made possible the contemporary views and contributions.

Among Italian writers of the twentieth century, Pirandello is undoubtedly one the most studied, yet he remains mysterious and strangely distant, inviting ever more investigation and interpretation. His life, almost perfectly divided between the century of candlelight and that of electricity, and his varied texts – literary (poetry, short story, novel), theatrical (drama and comedy), essays (philosophical, aesthetic, philological, interpretive), and personal (letters, confessions, memoirs) – continue to be a seemingly inexhaustible source for widely different readings and for successive generations of readers.

Today it would be almost impossible to read Pirandello with virgin eyes. To start with, we approach him knowing a lot (or is it really a lot?) about his life. The first biography, by Federico Vittore Nardelli, *L'uomo segreto* (1932), to which Pirandello himself contributed a great amount of information and gave a sort of official sanction, was taken up and judiciously used by Gaspare Giudice for his *Pirandello* (1963), which remains the most comprehensive and authoritative biography to date in Italian. Enzo Lauretta's *Luigi Pirandello: Storia di un personaggio fuori di chiave* provides a fascinating view of the Sicilian society and culture that bred Pirandello. Nino Borsellino's *Ritratto e immagini di Pirandello* (first published in 1979 under the title *Immagini di Pirandello*) is an excellent biographical-critical profile in Italian, while Walter Starkie's *Luigi Pirandello, 1867–1936* is perhaps the best-known introduction to Pirandello's life and work in English. But this wealth of biographical studies should not induce the conviction that everything worth saying has been said. The flow of informative material on and by Pirandello seems endless, particularly as far as his letters are concerned; there is, for example, his correspondence with Nino Martoglio (edited by Sarah Zappulla Muscarà), that with Gabriele D'Annunzio (edited by Eurialo De Michelis), and most notably, the letters between Pirandello and Marta Abba, on which Pietro Frassica based his remarkable *A Marta Abba, per non morire*. This correspondence has now been published in its entirety in Italian (*Marta Abba. Caro Maestro ...*, edited by Pietro Frassica, and *Lettere a Marta Abba*, edited by Benito Ortolani) and partially in English (*Pirandello's Love Letters to Marta Abba*, edited by Benito Ortolani). There is also a fine and thorough article by Daniela Bini that comments on the importance of these letters.

Aside from and beyond biography, our knowledge of Pirandello is enhanced (and complicated) by the enormous array of critical readings and assessments of his texts. In *Bibliografia della critica pirandelliana, 1962–1981* Corrado Donati provides a detailed and comprehensive overview of recent criticism and proposes to group it into three major trends: historicist, psychoanalytic, and stylistic. The inevitable simplifications of this classification have the great advantage of clarity (but in less able hands than Donati's, such simplification could flatten the interplay between different methodologies that is always present in the best critics). Starting with Donati's classification and proceeding from it, there seems to be little doubt that a major contribution to Pirandellian studies was made by historicist, or to be more precise, sociological and ideological, criticism. This should come as no surprise, given two well-known cultural facts. First, modern Italian culture has been dominated by idealistic, Crocean philosophy, and Croce's polemic against Pirandello certainly helped to keep the latter's fame live and influential. Second, in the postwar years, the spiritual dialectics of the Hegelian–Crocean idealism were easily turned into Marxist, materialistic dialectics for the purpose of literary criticism, particularly under the aegis of Lukàcs and Gramsci. No wonder, then, that the influence of such criticism lasted well into the 1980s, and that Pirandello was a prime object of study, analysis, and contrasting interpretations for a number of critics including: Carlo Salinari and Arcangelo Leone de Castris in the 1960s; Renato Barilli, who continued his investigation well into the 1980s; Roberto Alonge, Lucio Lugnani, Claudio Vicentini, Giorgio Bàrberi Squarotti, and Robert Dombroski in the 1970s and onward; and also Romano Luperini, Gigi Livio, and Gian Franco Venè.

A major shift in Pirandellian criticism in the early 1960s was especially due to Leone de Castris's groundbreaking work, *Storia di Pirandello* (1962). This historicist study came only two years after Salinari's reflection on Italian decadentism and in particular, on Pirandello's place and role within it. Over the years, no consensus has emerged as to whether Pirandello was only 'the conscience of Italian decadentism' and of the crisis of bourgeois society and its values, or whether he projected that crisis onto a universal and ahistorical plane, whether he interpreted and adhered to the negative ideology of Fascism (as Pirandello the man undoubtedly did), or instead proposed a radical criticism of it from within (as his texts and the vision of the world they propose seem to affirm). What is undisputably important is that, despite their contrasting interpretations, the sociologically and ideologically oriented critics have indeed examined Pirandello's *oeuvre* with a totalizing view of his works, both in themselves and against the necessary background of Italian and European history and the history of ideas. It is also important to mention Renato Barilli's long-lasting study of Luigi Pirandello's contribution to Italian and European cultural history. This far-reaching approach has undoubtedly opened new avenues to Pirandellian criticism by placing the Sicilian's *oeuvre* in an open dialogue with the lives and works of other major cultural figures.

The rich and fertile cultural background defined by a generally historicist approach is the focus of other quite valuable studies. Graziella Corsinovi's *Pirandello e l'espressionismo*, Wladimir Krysinski's *Il paradigma inquieto: Pirandello e lo spazio comparativo della modernità*, Anthony Caputi's *Pirandello and the Crisis of Modern Consciousness*, Thomas Harrison's *Essayism*, *Pirandello nel romanzo europeo* by the late and beloved Giancarlo Mazzacurati, and Franco Zangrilli's *Linea pirandelliana nella narrativa contemporanea*. Undoubtedly, the historicist critics have extensively explored the 'public' content and context of Pirandello's works, laying the ground for much subsequent criticism. Our readers will certainly appreciate the latest developments in the readings and interpretations offered in this anthology – a clear indication of the strength and vitality of the historicist, both in Italy and the United States, even when it is presented under the label of 'new historicism.'

No matter how philosophical, ideological, or intellectual an author may be, and Pirandello undoubtedly possessed these qualities to a high degree, the other direction in which a text or a corpus of texts can and should be read is the interior one. Psychological and psychoanalytic criticism is often allied or intertwined with a sociological, thematic, or stylistic approach, as is evident in Gian-Paolo Biasin's treatment of the Pirandellian 'antihero' in 'Moscarda's Mirror,' and in Manuela Gieri's discussion of Pirandello's narrative within and beyond modernism. Such criticism has exerted a considerable influence and produced some memorable books. For example, Giovanni Macchia's *Pirandello o la stanza della tortura* is an elegant and refined reading of Pirandello's anguished and tortured characters by a critic armed with the tools of psychology, symbolism, style, and European culture, whose aim is to discover the most secret meanderings of human motivations and expressions. Or consider Giacomo Debenedetti's *Il romanzo del Novecento*; in a chapter on *Il fu Mattia Pascal* Debenedetti argues, with intellectual subtlety coupled with an impassioned participation verging on moralism, that the Pirandellian protagonist is incapable of achieving his own epiphany – that is, the protagonist fails to see his innermost self and to resolve his existential crisis by really changing himself, so that the epistemological project of the novel remains incomplete.

Other critics use a more decidedly psychoanalytic approach: Jean-Michel Gardair, Neuro Bonifazi, Paolo Puppa, Elio Gioanola (perhaps the most strictly technical of all), Jean Spizzo, Edoardo Ferrario, Jennifer Stone, and Anna Meda are among those who have applied psychoanalytic categories (taken mostly from Freud but also from Jung and Binswanger) to Pirandellian texts, with excellent interpretive results. Still others, such as Antonio Illiano, explore the metapsychic dimension of Pirandello's texts. Yet no critic seems to show an interest in Lacanian criticism for an interpretation of Pirandello's texts – a somewhat surprising situation, given the wide contributions of structuralism to contemporary thought. (On the other hand, Jacques Derrida seems to have had little to do with Pirandellian criticism as a whole: only an essay by David McDonald seems worth mentioning.)

The stylistic approach was and still is particularly vigorous in Italy, given the lasting influence of Crocean aesthetic sensibility. The range includes: proud philological and textual studies; Leo Spitzer's essays, published in the 1950s (not on Pirandello, but Ulrich Leo's 'Pirandello Between Fiction and Drama,' written at Toronto, should be noted); continuing interest in the history of the language and the *questione della lingua*, including the place and function of dialects; renewal and revitalization brought about by the grafting of structuralism and semiotics onto the pre-existing critical tradition. In Pirandellian criticism, stylistic concerns are present even in the sociological, ideological, psychological, and psychoanalytic works already mentioned, but a comprehensive study of Pirandello's style is still missing (notwithstanding the promising title of Filippo Puglisi's *Pirandello e la sua lingua*). Sectorial studies abound and are generally quite successful – an indication of the complexity and variety of Pirandello's texts. Indeed, it is not easy to assimilate the language and rhetoric of a short story, an essay, a drama. One of the most memorable studies in the field is Marziano Guglielminetti's 'Il soliloquio di Pirandello' in his volume *Struttura e sintassi del romanzo italiano del primo novecento*. As the title suggests, Guglielminetti traces narrative techniques used by Pirandello in his novels (indirect free speech, authorial commentary, dialogue, syntax, verbal tenses, and addresses) and in so doing he traces Pirandello's subversion of the naturalistic code, the author–character and author–reader relationships, the implicit disparity between fictional and theatrical language, and the tension between spoken words and 'interior silence.' Maria Antonietta Grignani's latest volume on Pirandello is a remarkable contribution to this area of study.

Benvenuto Terracini's analysis of Pirandello's pre-grammatical expression (especially in the character of Madama Pace in *Sei personaggi*) effectively shows how a stylistic device reveals the refusal of a character by the author. Giovanni Nencioni's study of the use of interjection in Pirandello's plays links the study of style with that of staging, a link that is particularly evident in Giuseppe Bartolucci's and Franco Fido's analyses of stage directions. Maria Luisa Altieri Biagi's study *La lingua in scena* compares the language of the *novelle* with that of the one-act plays; her skilful analysis takes up some insights by Nencioni and provides a valuable model for understanding the profound differences that distinguish the 'spoken' language of fiction from the 'spoken' language of theatre, and distinguish both of them from actual spoken language.

Stylistic criticism, including a sophisticated use of rhetoric and a continuous interrelation with other methodologies (as demonstrated in this anthology) is crucial for contemporary developments: on the one hand it is the indispensable precursor for a semiotic approach to Pirandello's texts, such as the one proposed by Cesare Segre with models of Pirandello's 'theatrical communication' or Umberto Eco's treatment of 'Pirandello ridens'; on the other hand it opens the way for the study of the 'language' that is most properly theatrical: the staging and the production of a play, the interpretive role of the great directors, the theories of playing, the costumes, lights, and stage props. In this context there is an ever increasing number of studies including: two clever contributions by Riccardo Scrivano in his *Finzioni teatrali* (he has also edited a useful critical anthology, *Letteratura e teatro*); Roberto Tessari's attention to Pirandello's tension between writing and directing; Richard Sogliuzzo's study of Pirandello as director; Alessandro D'Amico and Alessandro Tinterri's treatment of Pirandello as *capocomico*; and Claudio Meldolesi's critical systematization of Pirandello's theatrical productions. Finally, a much awaited re-thinking of Luigi Pirandello's often contradictory yet constant work in and for the theatre, but also and especially of his contribution to the development of modern and contemporary theatricality has come with Claudio Vicentini's outstanding volume *Pirandello: Il disagio del teatro*.

The new developments of the historicist approach to Pirandello's life and work have also produced, after decades of indifference and/or disdain, a growing critical attention to the relationship between Pirandello and the cinema. After Maurizio Del Ministro's pioneering work, quite slowly at first and now more and more decidedly, scholars are paying due attention to a long neglected segment of Pirandello's contribution to modernity. Notable examples are the many valuable essays collected in the proceedings *Pirandello e il cinema* (edited by Enzo Lauretta), and the analysis of a Pirandellian humoristic mode in Italian cinema from Pirandello to Fellini, Scola and the directors of the new generation in the recent book by Manuela Gieri, *Contemporary Italian Filmmaking: Strategies of Subversion*; Gavriel Moses's focus on the 'cinematographic novel' in *The Nickel Was for the Movies* is the last but not the least stage of an interest nourished for decades. Unquestionably, all recent studies of Pirandello's work for, on, and in the cinema have profited enormously from the publication of Francesco Càllari's *Pirandello e il cinema*, a work which includes a complete collection of Pirandello's theoretical and creative writings on the cinema, and also from the publication of two excellent volumes by Nino Genovese and Sebastiano Gesù unified under the title *La musa inquietante di Pirandello: il cinema*.

Finally, feminist and gender criticism, as the newcomer on the scene, has brought about some of the most innovative and original interpretations of Pirandellian texts and the vision of the world they convey. By highlighting the female viewpoint and the treatment of female characters by a male Sicilian author, these studies have opened up a whole new chapter in Pirandellian criticism. Aside from essays dealing with single texts, Luciana Martinelli's *Lo specchio magico: Immagini del femminile in Luigi Pirandello* and Maggie Gunsberg's *Patriarchal Representations: Gender and Discourse in Pirandello's Theatre* are undoubtedly the most powerful and provocative studies in this field, and as our anthology shows, they have laid the groundwork for further inquiries. In fact, the final section of this volume is devoted to such innovative approaches to Pirandello's work, including Daniela Bini's 'Enacting the Dissolution of the Self: Woman as One, No One, and One Hundred Thousand' and Thomas Harrison's 'Regicide, Parricide, and Tyrannicide in *Il fu Mattia Pascal*: Stealing from the Father to Give to the Son.'

Bini's discussion focuses on the dissolution of the male *logos* via the empowerment of female discourse. 'In giving voice to women, Pirandello accomplishes the goal of his male characters,' one which they constantly attempt to fulfill through humoristic reflection, that is, 'the defeat of logical discourse, the unveiling of the fallacy of words.' Where male characters denounce the entrapping nature of words and language, Bini observes, female characters deconstruct logic and language by building their discourse on nuances of the voice, silence, and body and facial expressions. This challenging specification of female discourse is explicated in Pirandello's plays on the theatre/life controversy – *Sei personaggi in cerca d'autore* [*Six Characters in Search of an Author*, 1921] and *Ciascuno a suo modo* [*Each in His Own Way*, 1927] – but also in one of the plays he wrote especially for Marta Abba, *Trovarsi* [*To Find Oneself*, 1932]. Bini places the meeting with Marta Abba at the centre of a major twist in Pirandello's development, since with the actress 'lending her body and soul to his characters, Pirandello was to succeed in defeating the philosophical discourse of the male *logos* and ascertaining woman's positive force in the world.' As Pirandello himself wrote in 1934, the mystery of any artistic birth is the same as that of any natural birth; thus, woman is the perfect metaphor for life and art. As previously noted, Bini's study is powerfully grounded in recent feminist studies, such as Gunsberg's and Martinelli's texts, but it is also basically inspired by phenomenological philosophy.

Harrison's essay is not directly inscribed within a feminist or gender-oriented approach, but is certainly indebted to the generalized critique of patriarchal society pursued by new historicist and cultural studies. Although he deals primarily with one novel, *Il fu Mattia Pascal* [*The Late Mattia Pascal*, 1904], Harrison provides us with a new model for discussion of the male subject in a radically modernist text, since, as he states, 'what is at stake is a vision of modernity, where Orestes becomes Hamlet, and Hamlet turns into the self-knowing Oedipus.' Moving from a celebrated passage (where Paleari tells Mattia about a marionette theatre that is about to perform the tragedy of Orestes and wonders what would happen if the paper sky were torn apart in the very moment Orestes lifts his hand against the tyrant), Harrison proceeds to a close analysis of the novel as it exemplifies modernity – that is, 'the epoch of the antihero, of the perplexed, self-conscious Pirandellian character.' According to Harrison, what is at work in *Il fu Mattia Pascal* is not a myth of restoration, such as that of Orestes, but a myth of implacable rivalry – between fathers and sons, and between brothers – the myth of Oedipus. Even though at first he reacts as Hamlet would, Mattia ultimately decides to act as the avenging Orestes. Yet, 'the tyrannical/tyrannicidal syndrome is broken ... not when Orestes turns into Hamlet, but when Hamlet turns into Oedipus,' that is, 'when he realizes that tyranny is not a feature of the *other* male, but a principle in which they all [males] participate.' At the end of the story, resigned to his non-identity, Mattia is now 'an Oedipus appeased outside the order of all literal, historical accomplishment.' Thus, Harrison concludes that there are reasons – thematic and rhetorical – to interpret *Il fu Mattia Pascal* as a text which 'leaves ancient, patriarchal logic permanently disrupted.'

Our volume is divided into four sections, entitled respectively 'Introduction,' 'Structures,' 'Meanings' and 'Innovations.' In the first section, Franca Angelini's chapter offers a broad overview of the renewed interest in Pirandello's *oeuvre* beginning in 1993, the year in which copyright of his works expired. Since then, productions of his plays, editions of his texts and scholarly activity have flourished at an incredible pace. Angelini limits her discussion to the years 1993–4, and focuses on productions and editorial initiatives 'that avoid routine, fashion, or the anxiety of unmotivated subversion.' Participating in a general move from the theatre of the actor-artist to the theatre of the director-artist, the history of the staging of Pirandello's works records a growing interest of the great Italian *metteurs en scène*, such as Giorgio

Strehler, Luca Ronconi, Mario Missiroli, Leo De Berardinis and Nanni Garella, especially for two texts which Angelini defines as 'canonical': *Sei personaggi in cerca d'autore* and *I giganti della montagna* [*The Mountain Giants*, 1936]. Angelini's detailed analysis of these productions is of utmost interest for a non-Italian audience, as she pointedly lists the variants brought to the original texts and to their earlier and more famous stagings. Angelini's mapping of recent Pirandellian *mises en scène* by some of the most thought-provoking Italian directors also qualifies as a valid contribution to the study of contemporary Italian theatre.

The final section of her essay is devoted to editions and criticism. First she rightly singles out the publications of Pirandello's works by Mondadori, Einaudi, and Garzanti as they are sustained by a rigorous philological commitment which aims at accounting for the numerous and important textual variants. Unquestionably, such editions contribute enormously to scholarly work in this field, a work whose most characteristic feature is now, Angelini states, a visible preference for documents over global interpretations and philosophical perspectives. She also mentions a notable exception, Romano Luperini's critical work on the development of the theme of allegory in modernity and its application to Pirandellian texts insofar as such a theme is connected to Pirandello's theory of humour and thus to the impossibility of the tragic in his narrative and theatrical works. Angelini then rightly mentions the renewed interest in Pirandello's biography, especially prompted and inspired by the recent publication of his letters to Marta Abba, as well as a flourish of studies on Pirandello's complex relationship with the cinema, and with the theatre of his time.

The essay that opens the second section of the volume, Donato Santeramo's 'Pirandello's Quest for Truth: *Sei personaggi in cerca d'autore*,' focuses on the investigation of Luigi Pirandello's contribution to modern theatricality. Santeramo moves from an initial acknowledgment of the main themes of theatrical debate in the early twentieth century, that is, the hiatus between the written text and its *mise en scène*. Such debate gave rise to a generalized discussion of the nature of artistic representation but also, and more importantly, of the complex relationship between art and truth and the possibility of producing convincing signification in a world which had lost all certainties. Basically, then, at the turn of the century theatrical debates developed according to two main perspectives, one centred on the idea of 'theatre as spectacle' and leading to the rise of the director, and the other focusing on the notion of 'theatre as dramatic text' and leading to an emphasis on the role of the author. Pirandello actively participated in these debates taking the side of the text, and, thus, of the author, in an effort to define 'the function of drama as an artistic means of creating signification.' Following the suggestions offered to contemporary criticism by such works as Claudio Vicentini's *Pirandello: Il disagio del teatro*, Santeramo proceeds to a valuable discussion of Pirandello's controversial relationship with the theatre in general, and with the staging of a written work in particular, since 'his theoretical writings until 1936 display a kind of suspicion ... towards the very concept of theatricality. In contrast, his plays written after 1918' became an experimental laboratory for his investigation of the dissonant relationship between the written text and the *mise en scène*. *Sei personaggi in cerca d'autore* is closely discussed and taken to be the breaking point in Pirandello's dramatic production as well as a first significant attempt to explore the boundaries between fiction and reality. *Sei personaggi* progressively becomes a forum for the conflict between the author's subjective stance and the Characters' fables presented as objective and true. On the one hand it testifies to the impossibility of finding 'a single source of discourse and an unambiguous instance of signification.' On the other hand, by submitting the Characters' story and the author's refusal to acknowledge their tragedy to 'a radical process of estrangement,' the play sanctions the definitive deconstruction of the typical structure of bourgeois drama.

The complex relationship between text and performance – the rapport between reality and its theatrical representation but also that between the realistic nature of theatre and the theatrical nature of reality – is at the centre of Maurizio Grande's far-reaching and groundbreaking study of the second play of the trilogy, an essay entitled 'Pirandello and the Theatre-within-the-Theatre: Thresholds and Frames in *Ciascuno a suo modo*.' Grande argues that in the dramaturgical writing of the trilogy 'the play between *fiction* and *simulation*' is so pronounced that they become barely distinguishable. Furthermore, the metatheatrical nature of the three plays erases the boundaries between theatrical illusion and illusionistic reproduction of reality, and makes *simulation* indiscernible from *illusion*. The issue then becomes to establish the way in which Pirandello 'orchestrates the relationship between fiction and simulation' in the theatrical illusion and in its metatheatrical reflection, and thus neutralizes simulation and magnifies fiction. In so doing, Pirandello makes of '*metatheatrical simulation* the most external frame of dramatic game playing, a frame which leads us to the innermost threshold of fiction: the *illusion of reality*.'

Grande then proceeds to draw a convincing analogy between theatrical simulation and game playing. Yet, theatre cannot be reduced to the logic of simulation, since theatre is characterized not only by the suspension of disbelief but also by the suspension of dramatic fiction, that is simulation which then becomes *non-game*: 'the symbolic pact which regulates theatrical fiction makes ... simulation ... assume the nature of suspended game and illusory reality.' Given the significant role played by the paradoxical form of simulation that is the device of the 'theatre within the theatre,' Grande argues that 'Pirandello's metatheatre strengthens theatrical illusion and pushes it to the limits allowed by the game between fiction and reality, and the game between simulation and truth, placing theatre at a new frontier of illusion, that of *hallucination*.' With *Ciascuno a suo modo*, Pirandello 'aims at erasing the boundaries between theatre and life.' Metatheatre, being 'the script of an impossible performance,' is then 'life that mirrors itself in the theatre and ... transcends any illusion of reality.' Yet, 'when metatheatre forces theatre to mirror itself in life, then theatrical illusion again becomes the reflection of another illusion, to infinity.' This is how, according to Maurizio Grande, Pirandello moves beyond the avant-garde and becomes a 'classic,' that is, 'the prophet of a world in which nature cannot 'hold up a mirror to art,' any more than art can duplicate nature.'

In his essay 'Families of Characters and Families of Actors on the Pirandellian Stage,' Paolo Puppa takes us on a mesmerizing journey through the complexity of Pirandello's work, ultimately focusing on his theatre and especially on the development of the dramatic character. In his writing on the theatre Pirandello displays a true phobia for the transposition of a text onto the stage, since he perceives any translation to be a betrayal of the original creation of the poet. Yet, characters constantly oscillate between the harmonious identity received by their creator, and a neurotic urge to rebel and find fulfilment outside the text, in the body of the actor. However, according to Pirandello, the actor/interpreter is an inadequate *medium* for the type of character who finds a desperate and impotent answer to his or her nightmarish and hellish experience in flights into fantasy and madness, and is persecuted by recurring impulses to suicide. Ultimately death is wished for as a release to the *beyond*, 'that is, the only form of indemnity or compensation ... Before climbing onto (or descending upon) the stage, the victim is relieved' of all bonds, *disembodied* and 'turned into a mysterious shadow.' It is the appearance of such ectoplasmatic creatures that signals Pirandello's entrance into the world of theatre, and his protagonists become philosophical *raisonneurs*, that is, *epic* subjects, anti-heroes of a *dialectic* theatre.

Puppa argues that 'the *dialectic* theatre owes its irresistible tendency towards *metatheatrical* solutions to the disturbed presence of its logical reasoner.' In fact, the development from stage to metastage is parallel to the genesis of the character of the philosopher. *Sei personaggi in cerca d'autore* is the climatic stage of a progressive annihilation of theatre achieved through a neurotic reasoning on theatre itself. In the two subsequent moments of Pirandello's metatheatre, *Ciascuno a suo modo* and *Questa sera si recita a soggetto*, 'what is emphasized is the lack of symmetry in the internal passages,' and 'strident ruptures at all levels' prevail. Yet with the progressive silencing of the *raisonneur*, the author-father is finally condemned to sterility. Pirandello's word becomes 'poetic' and the scene corresponds to a religious practice whose new *minister* is now the female actor. With words that uncannily echo the stances of Harrison and Bini in this present volume, Puppa concludes that, as 'all traces of a patrilinear heritage are erased,' Pirandello's stage becomes a place of mediation for 'a metaphoric pregnancy.' The character as author now coincides with the author as character who becomes an 'offspring of his own creation.'

The study of the Pirandellian subject's discursive strategies, that is, the use of language and rhetoric in narrative texts, is the focus of Maria Antonietta Grignani's essay 'The Making and Unmaking of Language: The Rhetoric of Speech and Silence.' The title alludes to Roman Jakobson's study of the 'specular relations between language at its birth in a child and that in the state of dissolution in various forms of aphasia,' and is taken here as a metaphor for the themes and rhetoric of the object at hand. Being thoroughly conscious of its own precariousness and that of language, the Pirandellian subject may decide to break 'the discursive pact that organizes linguistically the instance of communication among the I/you demarcators,' and then reach an aphasic stage where silence prevails. Grignani pointedly explains the reasons why it is now not only possible but urgent and useful to analyse Pirandello's persuasive speech with the tools provided by neorhetorical studies. While in periods in which rhetoric corresponded to constituent harmony there was no space for humour, now that scholars of rhetoric investigate 'the techniques of advancing reasons for and against a given topic of discussion and the argumentative efficacy of rhetorical figures,' Pirandello becomes a suitable writer insofar as he is a 'philosophical author.' His writing is characterized by a constant juxtaposition of sentiment and reflection which produces images associated by contrast, and a comprehensive dismantling of the naturalistic model caused by 'digression as a perpetual flight from the linearity of the story.' As the novel form is profoundly disturbed by the appearance of the *raisonneur*, which corresponds to the triumph of repartee enunciation and theatralization of speech, naturalism is finally overcome.

The soliloquy of Pirandello's autodiegetic narrators ultimately leads to silence, a condition which stands for an 'absence from oneself, an emptying out of the values of life, and a hallucinatory perception of reality outside the measures of history and human reason, an enormous lacuna in the principle of cohesion of the *I*.' Such a situation of dispossession and suspension is due to the death of correspondence between nature and subject. Some of the narrative texts of Pirandello's final years thematize this ecstatic but also horrific suspension, and thus rely on syntactic and stylistic solutions that are removed from persuasive logic. Yet, in her *persuasive* and far-reaching study, Grignani paves the way for a thorough investigation of the ways in which Pirandello becomes a protagonist of the definitive pillorying of classical rhetoric and the establishment of 'a counter-rhetoric as the art of unmasking and persuasion.'

All four essays included in the second section of the volume deal with diverse aspects of the fundamental structures of Pirandello's narrative and dramatic texts, as they progressively pursue a subversion and/or a dissolution of traditional discursive strategies. As one of the protagonists of the tormented passage from the nineteenth to the twentieth century and, thus, to modernity, Pirandello participated in and eventually contributed to the overcoming of the debates activated by the avant-garde movements. The themes and motifs of his 'modernist revolution' are the focus of the third section of our volume; these essays are mostly inspired by historicism and, in Donati's work, by psychoanalysis.

Marked by a fundamentally materialist and historicist approach, both Luperini's and Dombroski's essays recognize in Pirandello a representative of those conservative bourgeois artists who, at the turn of the century, eventually came to pursue a form of anarchist utopia through which they wanted to achieve a critical and alternative perspective, and thus be truly 'realist.' In 'Laughter and Political Allegory in Pirandello: A Reading of "C'è qualcuno che ride"' Romano Luperini continues the groundbreaking work he initiated with his volume *L'allegoria del moderno* and discusses the allegorical structure of a short story whose theme is laughter. Drawing abundantly from the rich background of stylistic criticism, Luperini moves from the acknowledgment of the mimetic and thematic character of a title that creates a suspension of meaning, and proceeds to an analysis of Pirandello's peculiar use of language signalling the danger of laughter insofar as it represents a rupture in the social pact, a true 'betrayal.' Narration originates in the direct witnessing of unfolding facts by the narrating subject, and is thus open. The narrator shares the community's unknowing condition, but is also estranged and detached from it. In this particular position, the narrating voice has a critical function, and has the ability to raise doubts and suspend meaning. Customarily, 'the handling of defamiliarization through the figure of incomprehension' aids authors in placing human beings 'in a state of allegory,' and unmasking the 'false, ill conventionalism of social relationships.' Through a close analysis of the text, Luperini successfully proves that 'the allegorical suspension of meanings, pursued by the narrating voice through the figure of incomprehension, does not reach any explicit reintegration of meaning, and yet demands a hermeneutic effort from the reader.' The tale is certainly constructed as an allegorical apologue, but, as always happens in the twentieth century, the allegory remains enigmatically void and yet constantly demands interpretation. In the end, the search for the meaning of both the disturbance provoked by the family's laughter and the apologue remains open. On the one hand, the short story exemplifies Pirandello's overcoming of the poetics of humour, and on the other it provides a critique of the repressive nature of civilization. Insofar as 'C'è qualcuno che ride' exposes 'the mechanism through which society unifies and excludes those who are different,' it is a 'political allegory."

At the turn of the century a wave of anti-modernism developed all over Europe and thus also in Italy, especially in the works of writers such as Pirandello and D'Annunzio. Robert Dombroski considers this event in the prefatory stage of his essay, 'Pirandellian Nakedness,' a basically materialist study of Pirandello's critique of modernity as it is exemplified in particular by a dramatic work, *Enrico IV* [*Henry IV*, 1921]. According to Dombroski, in Pirandello's vision modern tragedy begins with the moment of dispossession experienced by human beings as they become lost in the labyrinth and surrounded by the mystery of life. Thus, his characters share a condition of nakedness and self discovery. Yet, the kind of subject that Dombroski investigates in his essay is one realized via the embodiment of a modern consciousness in the persona of a mad king. It is thus necessary to approach the issue of nakedness from a different perspective, and to propose 'the existence of a sub-text or allegorical register,' or, in Frederic Jameson's words, 'a "political unconscious" at the base of *Enrico IV*'s aesthetic ideology.' Written to dramatize the condition of nakedness that translates into the question of modernity, '*Enrico IV* can be most usefully read as an allegory of capitalist economic development' insofar as it successfully captures both the sense of psychological disorientation and the great emancipation resulting 'from being released from the feudal confines of a pre-capitalist past.' Henry's fall 'into the madness of modernity activates a tremendous emancipation; he becomes literally bigger than life and capable of acting beyond all moral boundaries within a realm of absolute possibility.' Yet, 'how can the play's allegorical register contain two thoroughly opposing impulses? ... how can the hero be both radical and iconoclastic?' To explain this paradox, Dombroski proceeds to an engaging discussion of the Pirandellian character in its tragi-comic, that is humoristic nature, since, as he states, 'humour diverts attention from human nakedness.'

The last essay of the third section of the volume is a psychoanalytic study of Pirandello's short stories, and especially of the role eros plays in the complex *Weltanschauung* that stands at the foundation of the author's poetics. Donati's study, 'Eros and Solitude in Pirandello's Short Stories,' focuses primarily on the relationship between affection and sexuality in the wealth of cases offered by Pirandello's short narratives, cases which indeed find correlatives in Pirandello's novels and plays. In order not to generate the error of reducing the theme of Eros to sexuality, it is imperative to remember that in Pirandello's works 'vital and sexual impulses touch and interact, activating and/or negating themselves in the impulses to death.' The critic observes that this issue generally falls within the boundaries of the relationship between individual and collectivity, a relationship which is always oppositional for the Pirandellian character who incessantly tries to escape the many social 'prisons' created by conventions and appearances. The character's rebellion does not manage to disintegrate the very structure of the world; the only choices are to reintegrate oneself, to be marginalized forever in madness, or to enact a narcissistic defence through estrangement or through the 'philosophy of farness.' This is the field in which eros brings its subversive strength into play. Through a close analysis of several short stories, Donati concludes that in Pirandello, eros is a transgressive force that only operates 'in the atemporal space that encloses a person between death in life and the surrender to the boundless evanescence of nothingness.' In general terms, then, the place of eros is the place of Pirandello's 'most severe critique of a society that ... hides its own failure behind the irrevocable condemnation of any form of pleasure.'

The fourth section of the volume includes the essays by Daniela Bini and Thomas Harrison that we have previously discussed, and concludes with Wladimir Krysinski's 'Pirandello in the Discursive Economies of Modernity and Postmodernism,' an engaging investigation of Luigi Pirandello's theatrical and narrative work as it stands on the gateway between modernity and postmodernity. More precisely Krysinski ventures into an outline of postmodern re-readings and true reappropriations of the Pirandellian textual body. In the conclusion of his stimulating contribution, Krysinski also provides a concise and yet challenging panorama of the aftermath of Pirandello's theatrical innovations on the contemporary scene.

Although our volume is divided into four separate sections, it is clear from all the essays that Pirandello's textual structures are meaningful, that his meanings are always and rigorously structured and often innovative, and that his innovations go to the very heart of artistic and social structures. Thus, all the essays eloquently testify that Pirandello's *oeuvre* is not an isolated island in the turbulent ocean of western culture with its criss-crossing currents of modernity and post-modernity. After powerfully helping to establish modernism on the Italian cultural scene, today Pirandello continues to be present in mysterious and challenging ways. Within the folds of his work, explored in its entirety and from an impressive array of critical approaches at 360 degrees, ever new messages and meanings are discovered, enriching both the Pirandellian texts and the intellectual and human lives of his readers.

WORKS CITED

Alonge, Roberto. *Pirandello tra realismo e mistificazione.* Naples: Guida, 1972.
Altieri Biagi, Maria Luisa. *La lingua in scena.* Bologna: Zanichelli, 1980.

Angelini, Franca. *Serafino e la tigre. Pirandello tra scrittura teatro e cinema.* Venice: Marsilio, 1990.
Bàrberi Squarotti, Giorgio. *Le sorti del 'tragico'.* Ravenna: Longo, 1978.
Barilli, Renato. *La barriera del naturalismo.* Milan: Mursia, 1964.
– *La linea Svevo-Pirandello.* Milan: Mursia, 1972.
– *Pirandello. Una rivoluzione culturale.* Milan: Mursia, 1986.
Bartolucci, Giuseppe. *La didascalia drammaturgica.* Naples: Guida, 1978.
Biasin, Gian-Paolo. 'Moscarda's Mirror.' In *Literary Diseases. Theme and metaphor in the Italian Novel.* Austin: University of Texas Press, 1975.
Bini, Daniela. 'Il carteggio Luigi Pirandello – Marta Abba.' *Italica* 72, 2 (Summer 1995): 356–66.
Bonifazi, Neuro. 'Il paradiso perduto di Pirandello.' In *Il racconto fantastico da Tarchetti a Buzzati.* Urbino: STEU, 1971.
Borsellino, Nino. *Ritratto e immagini di Pirandello.* 1979; Bari: Laterza, 1991.
Càllari, Francesco. *Pirandello e il cinema. Con una raccolta completa degli scritti teorici e creativi.* Venice: Marsilio, 1991.
Cambon, Glauco, ed. *Pirandello: A Collection of Critical Essays.* Englewood Cliffs, NJ: Prentice-Hall, 1967.
Caputi, Anthony. *Pirandello and the Crisis of Modern Consciousness.* Urbana: University of Illinois Press, 1988.
Corsinovi, Graziella. *Pirandello e l'espressionismo.* Genoa: Tilgher, 1979.
D'Amico, Alessandro, and Alessandro Tinterri, eds. *Pirandello capocomico.* Palermo: Sellerio, 1987.
Debenedetti, Giacomo. *Il romanzo del Novecento.* Milan: Garzanti, 1971.
De Castris, Arcangelo Leone. *Storia di Pirandello.* 1962; Bari: Laterza, 1984.
– *Il decadentismo italiano: Svevo, Pirandello, D'Annunzio.* Bari: De Donato Editore, 1974.
Del Ministro, Maurizio. *Pirandello: scena, personaggio e film.* Rome: Bulzoni, 1980.
De Michelis, Eurialo. 'D'Annunzio e Pirandello.' In *Roma senza lupa: Nuovi studi sul D'Annunzio.* Rome: Bonacci, 1976.
Dombroski, Robert. *L'esistenza ubbidiente. Letterati italiani sotto il fascismo.* Naples: Guida, 1984.
– *Properties of Writing. Ideological Discourse in Modern Italian Fiction.* Baltimore: Johns Hopkins University Press, 1994.
Donati, Corrado. *Bibliografia della critica pirandelliana 1962–1981.* Florence: La Ginestra, 1986.
Eco, Umberto. 'Pirandello ridens.' In *Sugli specchi.* Milan: Bompiani, 1985.
Ferrario, Edoardo. *L'occhio di Mattia Pascal.* Rome: Bulzoni, 1978.

Fido, Franco. 'The Overbearing Author in the Stage Directions of *Maschere Nude*.' In *Pirandello 1986*, edited by Gian-Paolo Biasin and Nicolas J. Perella, 45–58. Rome: Bulzoni, 1987.

Frassica, Pietro. *A Marta Abba per non morire*. Milan: Mursia, 1991.

– ed. *Marta Abba. Caro Maestro ... Lettere a Luigi Pirandello (1926–1936)*. Milan: Mursia, 1994.

Gardair, Jean-Michel. *Pirandello: Fantasmes et logique du double*. Paris: Larousse, 1972.

Genovese, Nino, and Sebastiano Gesù, eds. *La musa inquietante di Pirandello: il cinema*. 2 vols. Palermo: Bonanno Editore, 1990.

Gieri, Manuela. 'From Pascal to Moscarda: Pirandello's Narrative within and beyond Modernism.' *Forum Italicum* 22, 2 (Fall 1988): 176–86.

– *Contemporary Italian Filmmaking: Strategies of Subversion. Pirandello, Fellini, Scola, and the Directors of the New Generation*. Toronto: University of Toronto Press, 1995.

Gioanola, Elio. *Pirandello la follia*. Genoa: Il Melangolo, 1986.

Giudice, Gaspare. *Pirandello*. Turin: UTET, 1963.

Grignani, Maria Antonietta. *Retoriche pirandelliane*. Naples: Liguori, 1993.

Guglielminetti, Marziano. *Struttura e sintassi del romanzo italiano del primo novecento*. Milan: Silva, 1964.

Gunsberg, Maggie. *Patriarchal Representations. Gender and Discourse in Pirandello's Theatre*. Oxford: Berg, 1994.

Harrison, Thomas. *Essayism. Conrad, Musil, and Pirandello*. Baltimore: Johns Hopkins University Press, 1992.

Illiano, Antonio. *Metapsichica e letteratura in Pirandello*. Florence: Vallecchi, 1982.

Krysinski, Wladimir. *Il paradigma inquieto. Pirandello e lo spazio comparativo della modernità*. Translated by Corrado Donati. Naples: Edizioni Scientifiche Italiane, 1988.

Lauretta, Enzo. *Luigi Pirandello. Storia di un personaggio fuori di chiave*. Milan: Mursia, 1980.

– ed. *Pirandello e il cinema. Atti del convegno internazionale*. Agrigento: Centro Nazionale di Studi Pirandelliani, 1978.

Leo, Ulrich. 'Pirandello between Fiction and Drama.' In *A Collection of Critical Essays*, edited by Glauco Cambon, 83–90. Englewood Cliffs, NJ: Prentice-Hall, 1967.

Livio, Gigi. 'Il periodo grottesco del teatro pirandelliano.' In *Il teatro in rivolta*. Milan: Mursia, 1976.

Lugnani, Lucio. *Pirandello: Letteratura e teatro*. Florence: La Nuova Italia, 1970.

Luperini, Romano. *L'allegoria del moderno. Saggi sull'allegorismo come forma artistica del moderno e come metodo di conoscenza.* Rome: Editori Riuniti, 1990.

Macchia, Giovanni. *Pirandello o la stanza della tortura.* Milan: Mondadori, 1981.

Martinelli, Luciana. *Lo specchio magico: Immagini del femminile in Luigi Pirandello.* Bari: Dedalo, 1992.

Mazzacurati, Giancarlo. *Pirandello nel romanzo europeo.* Bologna: Il Mulino, 1987.

McDonald, David. 'Derrida and Pirandello: A Post-Structuralist Analysis of *Six Characters.' Modern Drama* 20 (1976): 421–36.

Meda, Anna. *Bianche statue contro il nero abisso.* Ravenna: Longo, 1993.

Meldolesi, Claudio. *Fondamenti del teatro italiano. La generazione dei registi.* Florence: Sansoni, 1984.

– 'Un teatro di doppie trasmutanti nature: quattro esempi di messinscena pirandelliana.' In *Pirandello 1986*, edited by Gian-Paolo Biasin and Nicolas J. Perella, 89–115. Rome: Bulzoni, 1987.

Moses, Gavriel. *The Nickel Was for the Movies.* Berkeley: University of California Press, 1995.

Nardelli, Federico Vittore. *L'uomo segreto. Vita e croci di Luigi Pirandello.* Milan: Mondadori, 1932.

Nencioni, Giovanni. 'L'interiezione nel dialogo teatrale di Pirandello.' *Studi di grammatica italiana* 6 (1977): 227–63.

– 'Parlato-parlato, parlato-scritto, parlato-recitato.' *Strumenti critici,* 10, 29 (1976): 1–56

Ortolani, Benito, ed. and trans. *Pirandello's Love Letters to Marta Abba.* Princeton: Princeton University Press, 1994.

– ed. *Lettere a Marta Abba.* Milan: Mondadori, 1995.

Puglisi, Filippo. *Pirandello e la sua lingua.* Bologna: Cappelli, 1962.

Puppa, Paolo. *Dalle parti di Pirandello.* Rome: Bulzoni, 1987.

– *Fantasmi contro giganti: Scena e immaginario in Pirandello.* Bologna: Pàtron, 1978.

Salinari, Carlo. *Miti e coscienza del decadentismo italiano.* Milan: Feltrinelli, 1960.

Scrivano, Riccardo. *Finzioni teatrali da Ariosto a Pirandello.* Messina: D'Anna, 1982.

– ed. *Letteratura e teatro.* Bologna: Zanichelli, 1983.

Segre, Cesare. 'La comunicazione teatrale in Pirandello.' In *Pirandello 1986*, edited by Gian-Paolo Biasin and Nicolas J. Perella, 75–87. Rome: Bulzoni, 1987.

Sinicropi, Giovanni. 'L'espressione pregrammaticale in Pirandello.' *Lingua nostra* 34, 4 (1973): 120–3.
Sogliuzzo, A. Richard. *Luigi Pirandello Director: The Playwright in the Theater.* Metuchen, NJ: Scarecrow Press, 1982.
Spizzo, Jean. *Pirandello: Dissolution et génèse de la représentation théatrale. Essai d'interprétation psychanalytique de la dramaturgie pirandellienne.* Paris: Les Belles Lettres, 1986.
Starkie, Walter. *Luigi Pirandello, 1867–1936.* Berkeley: University of California Press, 1967.
Stone, Jennifer. *Pirandello's Naked Prompt: The Structure of Repetition in Modernism.* Ravenna: Longo, 1989.
Terracini, Benvenuto. *Analisi stilistica: teoria, storia, problemi.* Milan: Feltrinelli, 1966.
Tessari, Roberto, ed. *Pirandello tra scrittura e regia.* 'Quaderni di teatro' 34. Florence: Vallecchi, 1986.
Vené, Gian Franco. *Pirandello fascista.* Milan: Sugar, 1971; Venice: Marsilio, 1981.
Vicentini, Claudio. *L'estetica di Pirandello.* Milan: Mursia, 1970.
– *Pirandello. Il disagio del teatro.* Venice: Marsilio, 1993.
Zangrilli, Franco. *Linea pirandelliana nella narrativa contemporanea.* Ravenna: Longo, 1990.
Zappulla Muscarà, Sarah, ed. *Pirandello/Martoglio.* Catania: CUECM, 1985.

2

Scenes and Texts: Perspectives in Pirandellian Criticism

FRANCA ANGELINI

Scenes

In 1993 Pirandello's copyright expired; this is one reason why productions of his plays and, especially, editions of his books have followed one upon another at a frantic pace. But such activity is not necessarily a sign of vitality. It can happen, in fact, that quantity does not correspond to quality, that the race for production and publication is concerned more with an appealing name than with the necessity of confronting a classic author of the twentieth century such as Pirandello, whose works are much studied but far from exhausted. Such an excessive offering can also provoke reactions of rejection – healthy reactions, that are certainly more fruitful than a formal, unconsidered homage. It can happen then that critics may elude the homage, expressing indifference to Pirandellian drama and sometimes even boredom in confronting texts that are overly used by directors, actors, critics, and scholars.

Given the danger that Pirandello may be not only used but also consumed and wasted, given the indiscriminate flowering of new, not always controlled and philologically reliable, editions, and given critical proposals in search of originality and novelty at any price, I will restrict my brief overview in two ways. First, I will limit my analysis to the years, 1993–4, and second, I will point out and reflect upon only productions and editorial initiatives that avoid routine, fashion, or the anxiety of unmotivated subversion.[1]

I will start with the productions, convinced as I am that they reach the public most directly and that they have an essential function in spreading an image, modifying a commonplace, and giving international status to a writer. The writer in our case – Pirandello – has been confined by past criticism within the narrow limits of nineteenth- and early twentieth-century Italian culture, among verismo, anti-verismo, and irrationalism. To be more specific, it may be surprising that a catalogue of western literary texts of any period might deny a relevant place to Pirandello as narrator, but it would be unthinkable in an analogous – imaginary – catalogue of theatrical texts of our century. Dramaturgy of the twentieth century would be unthinkable without his name, because his prestige with the public and the strength of his inventions endure to the present, and the 'scandal' of the situation represented in his works can still be modern, at least in part. I wish to maintain then – pending verification – that in the two years under examination, the major novelties have come from Pirandellian productions, just as, in the past, they came from productions directed by his contemporaries – Georges Pitoeff, Max Reinhardt, and Rudolf Beer, among others. Such productions were destined to influence literary criticism and to mould the image of the playwright with the public.

The first consideration concerns the present interest for Pirandellian theatre, in Italy, on the part of 'great' directors, rather than younger ones, and consequently, the choice of canonical texts such as *Sei Personaggi in cerca d'autore* [*Six Characters in Search of an Author*, 1921] and *I giganti della montagna* [*The Mountain Giants*, 1937] rather than texts that are considered minor and seldom performed. In 1993 there were three prestigious productions of *Sei Personaggi* – by Franco Zeffirelli, Mario Missiroli, and Nanni Garella (not to mention one in China where this text was still unknown).[2]

Zeffirelli's October 1993 production was based on a desecrating determination (not far from Anatoly Vasiliev's by now famous 1987 production,[3] but with less theatrical ingenuity) aimed at an amusing modernization of the text.[4] Zeffirelli re-wrote the first part of the play, imagining that the actors, dressed in the casual way of young people, speak about the facts of the day heard on television and then start rehearsing not *Il gioco delle parti* [*The Rules of the Game*, 1918] but *I giganti della montagna* (a text that, as we shall see, became a favourite of Italian directors the following year). Along the same modernizing and desecrating line, the actors' moments of 'theatricality' make fun of the great Italian directors, from Luca Ronconi to Gianfranco Cobelli, from Giancarlo Nanni to Massimo Castri, all are teased for their stylistic tics and formal characteristics. In the first part of the play the amusement and irony prevail over the Pirandellian text, and widen an original structure (which did allow such evasions, since Pirandello himself was polemic against the theatre of his time). In the second part, tragedy wins, and with it today's actors win too, thanks to a knowledge acquired also through so many years of Pirandellian practice.

From the highest treason to the utmost fidelity: for his production, Nanni Garella chose the original 1921 edition of the play (rather than the customary 1925 edition), where the dialogue is more harsh and many stage directions are different.[5] Garella gives masks to the six characters as suggested also by Pirandello in the 1925 edition; these ghastly masks with a strong expressionistic mark imprint a mythic, classical value on the drama. At the same time Garella prunes the philosophemes, eliminates the cerebral, implied meanings of Pirandellism, and gives back its absolute truth to the conflict.

By contrast, Missiroli focussed on the identity of truth and fiction and the crisis of modern values and convictions; he also marks out a line in Italian bourgeois theatre, having the actors try out not *Il giuoco delle parti* but the beginning of Carlo Goldoni's *Smanie della villeggiatura*.[6] The first act is entirely replaced by Goldoni's dialogues, with the Six Characters breaking into them, that is, breaking into a performance that is already concluded (rather than one that is being rehearsed). This allows the immediate and even visual comparison between the eighteenth-century scene and the naked stage of a theatre in the 1920s. The reason for this choice is stated by the director himself:

I chose the *Villeggiatura* because I wanted the Sicilian-Italian language of Pirandello to be grafted onto and to react against the Italian-Venetian language of Goldoni ... I was interested in staging through the theatre two centuries, the twentieth and the eighteenth, the latter being distant enough in time to allow us to utilize a costume comedy, but also already intellectually modern. Finally, eliminating that first act allowed me to cut the noisy chattering of the actors who are rehearsing, the inside talk and the talk through quotes typical of all milieus.[7]

As we can see, every director in his own way re-thinks that part of Pirandello's text which the playwright himself had already thought of as a scene open to variations and which was in fact varied in the productions of many directors who were his contemporaries. In Missiroli's case, the novelty consists of the elimination of the 'rehearsal' in which the actors introduce themselves, and the choice instead of a comparison between two different theatres. These two theatres, however, have something in common – their modernity; both criticize their respective contemporary societies, of which the dialectal-national language (Italian-Venetian and Italian-Sicilian) is the most evident point of comparison.

The Mountain Giants

If 1993 was the year of *Sei Personaggi*, 1994 was the year of *I giganti della montagna*, the script chosen by Giorgio Strehler for his third drama production[8] (after those of 1947 and 1966) and chosen as well, as their first encounter with Pirandello, by Leo de Berardinis and Luca Ronconi. Outside Italy, this same play was also chosen by Cesare Lievi for a production in Hamburg and by Bernard Sobel for a Parisian production with the great Maria Casarès.

Critical considerations of the reasons for such a recurrent choice should begin by proposing conjectures based on the productions and on the statements made by the directors. There seems to be no doubt that historical analogies induce Italian directors and actors to propose again and again the historical, pessimistic Pirandellian view not only of the destiny of the theatre but of human beings in their relationship with art, poetry, and aesthetic vision.

One further aspect of the modernity and contemporary relevance of *I giganti della montagna* is that it is an open and not concluded text. This openness is partly the result of the author's death, but is even more the result of the structural impossibility that a text so open in its themes and so infinitely interpretable be closed and confined in a conclusion and a univocal meaning. In fact there is no doubt that both Countess Ilse and her co-protagonist and partial antagonist Cotrone can be placed in contrasting positions, and both of them have a good baggage of rights and wrongs. Cotrone is right and wrong when he isolates himself from the world and from society, as Ilse is right and wrong when she maniacally repeats a poetry text by a young lover who is dead – just as dead both poets and authors are also dead in this text that could well be considered postmodern. And what about the Giants? They are crude and brutal, but they nevertheless build worlds, preferring new and cheap shows to poetry. These shows could be yesterday's sport events or today's television shows; they are 'obscene' shows – that is, shows *outside* the scene – that are favoured by the masses.

I am intentionally simplifying and listing some of the irreconcilable positions proposed by Pirandello's text in order to demonstrate its infinite interpretability – just as classic and modern myths cannot be interpreted in just one sense. This aspect is certainly an important explanation for the success of *I giganti* among the great Italian directors of today. The other reason lies in the singular analogies between the 1930s of the Pirandellian text and the 1990s, analogies that concern the relationship between poetry and theatre and between theatre and society. In fact the actress Ilse and the actor-director-wizard Cotrone establish a relationship of *comparison* or *competition* rather than one of *conflict*; the comparison is based not only on the difference between the institutional, traditional theatre of Ilse's 'cart' and the private, mental, visionary theatre that anybody can create through the wizard-like power of imagination, but also on the obstinate presence of Ilse in the world, even if she has been rejected by it. Cotrone, on the other hand, acts in aristocratic isolation, without following the performance rules that, though criticized and criticizable, form the essence of the theatrical institution. The comparison then is between a theatre for society and an individualistic theatre, destined only for its own pleasure and consumed in aristocratic isolation.

Pirandello doesn't choose, doesn't decide; he limits himself to listing the constitutive elements of the two theatres and their conflict with the rude world of the Giants, a world that is at the same time both archaic and, in a modern way, mechanicistic. But even this outline I just proposed can be modified; the perspective can change to suggest other differences and other comparisons. It is exactly this aspect, the infinite interpretability of the text together with the modernity of the conflict, that makes this script interesting for today's scenes. The continuing significance of *I giganti* lies, in sum, in the bad conditions for the Italian theatre of today, crowded out by sport games and television. (In fact cinema might have been the 1930s equivalent of television.)

From these premises I can develop a brief analysis of the productions of Strehler, Ronconi, and Leo De Berardinis. Between the 1966 production and the 1994 production by Strehler there is first of all the same contrast as that between the Ilse of Valentina Cortese and that of Andrea Jonasson; Cortese was gifted with every charm and affectation (*'birignao'*) of the 'great actress' of historical Italian memory; by contrast Jonasson's Isle is more severe in a modern way and lacks narcissistic concessions.

In the 1966 production the end of the epoch of the 'great actor' was central; in fact, the play ended with an iron curtain that crushed the cart of the comedians on which Ilse and her company were travelling. The 1994 production underlines the character of legacy given to Pirandello's text, and makes of it the summa of Strehler's vision of the theatre as well – a vision that combines both the reasons of Ilse's theatre of poetry and words and the reasons of Cotrone's theatre of pure vision and magic lights. The former doesn't want to give up talking to human beings and society and 'being-there' in the world; the latter finds a metaphysical space, away from human beings, aristocratically self-referential and sullenly self-sufficient. Both are also Strehler's theatres, cultivated by him through his long career against the Giants, to whom we can attribute different names and functions, but who, in any case, represent the obtuse reasoning of economic and political power, afraid of the critical force contained in a theatre made for human beings. At the end of the play, a dead Ilse is carried into the audience by her art companions. This ending can be interpreted in different ways, but seems to affirm the necessity of communion between theatre and society.

The staged Salzburg production by Luca Ronconi is very different.[9] The choice of an isolated, disused factory distances the representation of Cotrone's magic world in time and space. The characters appear on the scene, marked by weariness and time, as if they had escaped a disaster and miraculously survived. Here, too, the scenic play of the protagonist is central, because she appears simultaneously as a 'great actress' (of the Russian rather than the Italian school) and as a person sharply identified and involved with her drama.

The director Ronconi, who has always preferred other archetypes of twentieth-century dramaturgy, from Ibsen to Schnitzler, made an interesting statement concerning his first production of a Pirandello script:

Io – dichiara il regista – che mi sono sempre sottratto alle interpretazioni ... sostanzialmente negative della 'via italiana' a Pirandello, ho accettato ... proprio perchè l'approccio al suo teatro è mediato da una lingua straniera. Il luogo dove lo spettacolo si svolge – un ex-fabbrica di sale in un'isola sul fiume – l'ho scelto io perchè mi è sembrato ideale per rispettare la struttura frammentaria di un testo che pur centrato sul teatro e la sua essenza, si svolge fuori dal palcoscenico.

I, who have always avoided the substantially negative interpretations of the 'Italian approach' to Pirandello, have accepted ... exactly because the approach to his theatre is mediated by a foreign language. As for the place where the performance takes place – a former salt factory in an island on the river – I chose it because it seemed to me ideal in order to respect the fragmentary structure of a text that, even though it is centered on the theatre and its essence, takes place outside the stage.

Ronconi, unlike Cesare Lievi, refuses the ending added by Pirandello's son Stefano Pirandello, because he respects the integrity of the work left unfinished at the author's death. This decision brings the whole play within an autobiographical sphere which characterizes – according to Ronconi – all Pirandello's later works. For Ronconi, then, the writer's love for Marta Abba is central, as is the homage to the actress that he lovingly translated into the play. Marta Abba or Eleonora Duse? Which of the two actresses was the model for Ilse? Or was it both of them, the close Abba, and the divine Duse, who always avoided interpreting Pirandello's plays?

The problem arises mainly when we consider the Berardinis production of *I giganti*;[10] the extraordinary acting performance by Leo de Berardinis *en travesti*, reaching trance and transfiguration on stage, had a strong emotional impact on the public. The production notes point out three reading levels in Pirandello's work: the Ilse-Cotrone juxtaposition, Cotrone's magic, and the Giants. 'My attempt,' writes the director-actor, 'has been that of absorbing Pirandello's pages by adhering to them and making them my own, so much my own that, as an actor, I chose Ilse's figure and made her become tragic, for a kind of biographical identification. Biography in depth, to be sure. For years I have firmly believed in the strength of poetry among people, be they giants or human beings, in spite of any derision.'[11] And in an interview Berardinis clarifies the idea that guided him to his identification with Ilse, starting from the model of Eleonora Duse: 'Ten years after the death of the actress, and after the "decline of the great actor" and the advent of the director as supreme artist of the scene had been announced, this image is still very alive in Pirandello. The Ilse of *I giganti* preserves many traits of it ... The following history of the theatre witnesses a progressive distancing from the figure of the actor-artist.'[12] Leo de Berardinis asserts the primacy of poetry and of the actor-director. He sees Pirandello as the one who, aware of the decline of this epoch, announced with *I giganti* the transition to another theatre (perhaps Ronconi's or Strehler's?).

Books: Editions and Criticism

The strong influence that productions of this kind have on the work of historians and critics is evident, but for the publishing industry the most important phenomenon is represented by the great quantity of Pirandello texts that were published when the copyright expired.

Since there are too many recent editions to list here, I will simply point out the most important ones, published by Einaudi, Garzanti, and Mondadori, that all met an immediate success among the reading public. In the past two years *Il fu Mattia Pascal* [*The Late Mattia Pascal*, 1904] has been a bestseller in Italy.[13]

As we saw in regard to *Sei personaggi*, it is time for the critic of both narrative and theatre to face the problems of variants in different editions; by now a philological study must (or should) accompany any edition of Pirandello's works, even an inexpensive one intended for the common reader. Let me single out, among the most important ones, the Mondadori editions of the novels and short stories edited by Mario Costanzo with introductions by Giovanni Macchia, and of the plays edited by Alessandro d'Amico.[14] The dialect plays have been edited by Sarah Zappulla Muscará for the Bompiani publishing house, and by Gaspare Giudice for Garzanti. All these editions are sustained by an arduous philological commitment, and are aimed at rendering readable the dialectal texts and at documenting the numerous drafts of the theatrical texts in Italian. We can consider this commitment as the distinctive mark of the most recent Pirandellian criticism, a criticism which prefers documents to global interpretations, philosophical perspectives, and the so-called 'Pirandellisms.'

An important exception is the critical work of Romano Luperini on the theme of the allegory of the modern that he applies to the Pirandello's works. His analysis starts from the problem of the loss of aura, as Walter Benjamin called it, which characterizes modernity. According to this point of view 'art can realize its objectives of knowledge and analytical deconstruction only by adapting itself to the degraded reality by which it is surrounded and by positing itself, at the same time, as the mirror and the critical conscience of that same reality.'[15] The theme of allegory is connected with the theory of humour as the consciousness of a loss of 'universal meaning' of the world; therefore it is connected to the impossibility of the tragic in Pirandello's work and in modern theatre in general – hence the *deconstructive* and *destructuralizing* character of the Pirandellian conception of art.

On the side of document-oriented criticism, by contrast, I should point out the research on Pirandellian biography, on the letters that the playwright exchanged with friends, with Marta Abba, with men of theatre, and with contemporary political figures. These letters document complex relationships, that can now be seen with unprejudiced eyes, not in a Manichean way, but with close attention to Pirandello's various attitudes, often difficult and conflictual, towards the vast world of 'others.' As for the biographies, there are two remarkable approaches by M.L. Aguirre d'Amico – *Vivere con Pirandello* and *Album Pirandello*[16] – which offer new perspectives and points of view, particularly the first one, which is mostly dedicated to the two women of Pirandello's family, his wife and his daughter, both differently marked by a life close to and in the shadow of a man of genius.

The publication of Pirandellian letters has been stimulating new critical perspectives for quite a time. Those published by Alfredo Barbina, Sarah Zappulla Muscarà, and Elio Providenti[17] have cast light on Pirandello's years of studies in Bonn, his sentimental and family life, and his first contacts with the world of literature and theatre. His letters to Marta Abba, edited by Pietro Frassica,[18] outline a very complicated love relationship between the old, adoring playwright and his pupil, Marta Abba. She was capable of inspiring Pirandello with many female characters for his last plays, but she was unable to take upon herself the role of 'divine' that both of them desired.

Half-way between document and critical indication are the volumes dedicated to the relationship between Pirandello and the cinema. This complex relationship, after the initial rejection documented by the novel *Si gira ...* [*Shoot!*, 1915–16], later re-titled *Quaderni di Serafino Gubbio operatore* [*Notebooks of Serafino Gubbio, Cameraman*, 1925–6], adheres in an increasingly convinced way to the numerous linguistic possibilities of the cinema.[19] After these researches the judgment on the relationship between the playwright and the cinema can perhaps be radically reversed. In fact cinematic productions of Pirandellian texts have profoundly marked the history of the cinema, with the first sound-musical film in Italy, *La canzone dell'amore* [*Love Song*, 1930], an adaptation of the short story 'In silenzio' ['In Silence,' 1923], and with the 'international use' of his texts that became possible – for example, the French productions of

Il fu Mattia Pascal by M. L'Herbier and P. Chenal, and the superb 1932 interpretation of *Come tu mi vuoi* [*As You Desire Me*] by Greta Garbo.

Let me turn from Pirandello's personal relationships and his relationships with contemporary culture to those often conflictual relationships with the theatre of his time.[20] They were, as we know, far from linear, made of an unsuppressable vocation for the stage and a similarly unsuppressable refusal of its laws and conventions, all of which were regularly subjected to criticism and deconstruction. At this point I can return to the theatre of the directors with which my brief and far-from-exhaustive analysis began, and I can draw some provisional conclusions. I understand why the most recent productions have preferred not the Pirandello of existential plays and 'minor' works, but the Pirandello of the plays on the theatre, which present the most comprehensive criticism of the laws of representation and at the same time affirm their unsurpassable truth and poetry.

This conviction concerns us directly and involves the theatre of the last twenty years. The hypotheses of transferring the theatre into immediate time and place(s), the happenings and the experiences of the Living Theatre (also dreamed of by Pirandello), are contained in an experience which is fundamental for us even though that too may no longer be relevant. Other theatres remain; that of the actors-artists (according to the definition of Leo de Berardinis), or that of the Characters in search of an author, or that of Countess Ilse and Cotrone (which could also be, aside from the visionary quality of a single individual, the modern magic of the cinema). The already existing theatre also remains, with its limits and its dependence on society's laws and rules, together with the theatre of Utopia, which must not die.

That is why in recent years Italian actors and directors alike have favoured the Pirandellian plays dealing with the theatre; and above all that is why they return with insistence to the text that deals with the problem of art in an epoch of loss of aura, in an epoch of reproduction and mass media, that is, to *I giganti della montagna*.

Translated by Maria Rita Francia Biasin

NOTES

1 For the most recent years see Romano Luperini, *Introduzione a Pirandello* (Bari: Laterza, 1992), and Franca Angelini, *Il punto su Pirandello* (Bari:

Laterza, 1992). These volumes offer detailed information about less recent critical tendencies, which are here omitted for reasons of space.
2 This interesting 1993 production took place in Beijing. Similarly attuned to Dave Stamper's song sung by the step-daughter, *Prends garde à Tchou-Thin-Tchou*, it evoked liberty-style *chinoiseries* of the 1920s, thanks also to the costumes. The production was quite formal (the child dies of a gun shot bending his head three times), and was able to neutralize the scandal and the disturbing elements such as the incestuous situation created by the attraction of the step-daughter for the Father.
3 The Russian director Anatoly Vasiliev later produced a more modest version of *Ciascuno a suo modo* at the Centro Teatro Ateneo in Rome with young Italian actors alternating their roles.
4 *Sei personaggi*, staged October 1993 at the Teatro Manzoni in Milan; directed by Franco Zeffirelli, with Enrico M. Salerno, Barbara Buccellato, G. Zanetti, and R. Bianchi.
5 *Sei personaggi*, staged November 1993 at the Teatro Testoni in Bologna; with Virginio Gazzolo, Patrizia Zappa Mulas, Emanuela Grimaldi, and Roberto Trifirò, and with Garella himself in the director's role. Pirandello's 1921 text is available in the volume edited by Guido Davico Bonino (Turin: Einaudi, 1993).
6 *Sei personaggi*, staged November 1993 at the Teatro Argentina in Rome; with Gabriele Lavia, Monica Guerritore, Gianrico Tedeschi, and Marianella Laszlo.
7 Missiroli made this statement to the journalist Stefania Chinzari for the newspaper *L'unità*, 7 November 1993.
8 *I giganti della montagna*, staged March 1994 at the Piccolo Teatro of Milan; with Andrea Jonasson, Franco Graziosi, Giulia Lazzarini, Tino Carraro, Giancarlo Dettori, Lino Troisi, Anna Saia, and Enzo Tarascio.
9 Staged July 1994 in a former salt factory in Perner-Ilsen; with Jutte Lampe, Walter Schmidinger, Wolf Redl, and Sebastian Mirow.
10 Staged in 1993 and subsequently at the Teatro Argentina in Rome in January–February 1994; with Antonio Campobasso, Marco Sgrosso, Elena Bucci, and Donato Castellaneta, and with Leo de Berardinis as Ilse.
11 This statement can be found in the playbill of the Teatro Argentina for the 1993–4 season.
12 See *Quaderni di Santarcangelo* 1 (1994): 7.
13 The best editions of this novel are the Garzanti (edited by Nino Borsellino and Giorgio Patrizi), the Mondadori (edited by Marziano Guglielminetti and L. Nay), and the Einaudi (edited by Giancarlo Mazzacurati). All three contain critically relevant readings. See also Franca Angelini, 'Miti

moderni e miti classici nel *Fu Mattia Pascal*,' *Rivista di studi pirandelliani* (11 December, 1993): 7–15.
14 To date only two volumes of the *Maschere nude* [*Naked Masks*] have been published – one in 1986 and another in 1993 – containing the plays written between 1898 and 1923.
15 Luperini, 'L'atto del significare allegorico in *Sei personaggi* e in *Enrico IV*,' *Rivista di studi pirandelliani*, 6/7 (June–December 1991): 9. See also Guido Guglielmi, 'L'allegoria in Pirandello' in *Ironia e negazione* (Turin: Einaudi, 1974).
16 Both published by Mondadori, Milan, in 1989 and 1993 respectively.
17 Alfredo Barbina, ed., *Lettere d'amore di Luigi a Antonietta* (Rome: Bulzoni, 1986); Sarah Zappulla Muscarà, ed., *Carteggi inediti* (Rome: Bulzoni, 1980); *Lettere da Bonn* (Rome: Bulzoni, 1984); *Epistolario familiare giovanile (1886–1889)* (Florence: Le Monnier, 1986), and *Lettere giovanili da Palermo e da Roma* (Rome: Bulzoni, 1993).
18 Pietro Frassica, ed., *A Marta Abba per non morire* (Milan: Mursia, 1991).
19 See especially Lucio Lugnani, *Pirandello: Letteratura e teatro* (Florence: La Nuova Italia, 1970) and *L'infanzia felice e altri saggi su Pirandello* (Naples: Liguori, 1986); Franca Angelini, *Serafino e la tigre* (Venice: Marsilio, 1990); Francesco Càllari, *Pirandello e il cinema* (Venice: Marsilio, 1991). Claudio Camerini edited Pirandello's film script for *Acciaio* (Turin: ERI, 1990) and Rossano Vittori edited the screenplay for *Sei Personaggi* (Florence: Liberoscambio, 1984).
20 See the recent volume by Claudio Vicentini, *Pirandello: Il disagio del teatro* (Venice: Marsilio, 1993).

SECTION 2
STRUCTURES

3

Pirandello's Quest for Truth: *Sei personaggi in cerca d'autore*

DONATO SANTERAMO

The hiatus between the text and its *mise en scène*, the dichotomic relationship between the stagnant text and the dynamic, ever changing staging, was at the centre of the debates on and around the theatrical event at the beginning of the twentieth century. Such debate, far from being merely a formal discussion on the nature of representation, encouraged significant aesthetic speculation on theatre in particular and on art in general, as it investigated the relationship between art and truth and the possibilities of creating signification in a world that had lost the certainties of experience.[1] According to Peter Szondi the modern theatrical age, in particular the period from 1880 to 1950, is characterized by the introduction of an 'epic element' in drama. In its first phase modern dramatists such as Ibsen, Chekhov, and Maeterlinck pursued the negation of the *hic et nunc* within intersubjective relationships. However, at this point the 'epic element' was to be produced at the level of content only; the structure of the play maintained that of traditional dramaturgy.[2] At the turn of the century, however, the core of the debate focused on two principal perspectives: theatre as spectacle, which led to the rise of the figure of the director, and theatre as dramatic text, the author's standpoint.

Significantly, Luigi Pirandello was at the centre of this debate as he tackled the issues from the latter perspective and focused on textuality. While he was surely aware of the philosophical implications such a discourse could bring about, Pirandello continuously challenged his own assumptions, as the internal dialogue between his artistic production and his essays denotes. It is a dialogue that never achieves a true resolution. In fact, one can detect the spectacle/text controversy in Pirandello's endeavour as he reflected on the nature of the theatre by favouring the text over the performance in his essays while questioning and investigating the *zona franca* offered by the stage in many of his plays. Though he sought to answer the questions related to theatre as drama, his goal, similar to the project of those who focused on theatre as spectacle, was to define and determine the function of drama as an artistic means of creating signification.[3] This task became exceptionally intricate because of the complete failure of speculations of both the naturalist and symbolist movements, a failure which had led to the complete annihilation of the entire theatrical apparatus.[4] Thus, Pirandello's viewpoints on the theatre amalgamate both the proposed theoretical hypothesis and the empirical stage experimentation in the theatre at the turn of the century as spectacle and as dramatic text.

In 1908 Pirandello published an essay entitled 'Illustratori, attori e traduttori' [*Illustrators, Actors, and Translators*],[5] an elaboration of an essay he had written in 1899, 'L'azione parlata' [*The Spoken Action*].[6] In both essays, he fiercely opposed any 'interpretative' action whatsoever by the director or the actor. He disputed the artistic validity of the *mise en scène* by arguing that there is an irredeemable dissonance between the text written by the author and its staging. In 'Illustratori, attori e traduttori,' he stated that, if sometimes the *mise en scène* of a text is better than the written text itself, it is only because the written text was of no value in the first place. Pirandello also maintained in that same essay that if one wants the original and not a mere *translation* of the text onto the stage, one must turn to the *commedia dell'arte* and its 'canovacci,' that is, 'sketches in embryo.' He concluded his essay by affirming that the *commedia dell'arte* is nevertheless a trivial form that lacks the ideal simplification and concentration common to every superior work of art.[7] The text, therefore, was central for Pirandello at this stage of his life and career, and the written word here is considered to be the supreme and absolute *auctoritas*. A playwright's text is considered an authentic artistic creation, whereas the staging of that text is seen, by Pirandello, as only a mawkish and unnecessary product.

However, Pirandello's attitude towards the theatre was quite different only a few years earlier. In a letter sent to his family from Rome in November of 1887 he wrote: 'Oh il teatro drammatico! Io lo conquisterò. Io non posso penetrarvi senza provare una viva emozione, senza provare una sensazione strana, un eccitamento del sangue per tutte le vene.'[8] [Oh, the dramatic theatre! I shall conquer it. I cannot enter it without experiencing a vivid emotion, without feeling a strange sensation, an arousal of the blood throughout my veins.] This statement is not surprising if one considers that Pirandello had written plays, which he later destroyed, at a very early stage of his career. In fact, his initial artistic efforts were almost completely devoted to the theatre. *La gente allegra* [*Happy People*] and *Le popolane* [*The Common Women*], were written when he was in his twenties (both were destroyed); and *L'epilogo* [*The Epilogue*], *Il nibbio* [*The Kite*], and *Scamandro*, although not staged until many years later, were written between 1891 and 1899. Yet, from 1899 to 1916, Pirandello did not write anything for the theatre except for *Lumie di Sicilia* [*Lights in Sicily*, 1910], *Il dovere del medico* [*The Doctor's Duty*, 1911], and *Cecè* (1913), all of which are considered stage adaptations rather than plays. On the contrary, during this period he composed many short stories[9] and, in 1904, he published what is considered his narrative masterpiece, *Il fu Mattia Pascal* [*The Late Mattia Pascal*]. He also completed his essay on humour, *L' umorismo* [*On Humour*, 1908], a work that is pivotal for an understanding of his aesthetics and is considered his philosophical testament.

It is noteworthy that the sixteen years in which Pirandello the playwright was dormant are the same years in which the crisis of the two leading European theatrical aesthetics, naturalism and symbolism, reached its peak. Pirandello's theoretical starting point in 'L'azione parlata' and 'Illustratori, attori e traduttori' coincides with that of the naturalists. In fact, he continuously insisted on the validity and necessity of the written text. However, as he explored the possibilities of the stage, he came to realize that the impasse such a conception of the theatre would create had to be overcome. This awareness coincided with an understanding of the impossibility of creating narrative works capable of producing meaning.[10]

It has also been argued that Pirandello's attack on theatre in 'Illustratori, attori e traduttori' was triggered by the fact that his early theatrical works had all been turned down by producers and directors, and that his disposition towards the theatre was a personal vendetta against the theatrical entourage that had refused to stage his plays.[11] It is important to note, however, that even in 1925, after he had received international acclaim, he reiterated everything he had written in 'Illustratori, attori e traduttori.' While in Paris for the staging of *Sei personaggi in cerca d'autore* [*Six Characters in Search of an Author*, 1921], in an interview given to the daily newspaper *Le Temps*, he explained that he still believed that the staging of a play is always a betrayal of the original – that is, of the text as the author conceived it – and that the *mise en scène* is not in itself a work of art.[12] What is extremely startling is that Pirandello, from 1916 onwards, had devoted practically his entire artistic production to the theatre and he would continue to do so until his death.

Pirandello was not unique in trying to find a resolution to the theoretical impasse the theatre was facing throughout Europe.[13] As a matter of fact, at the beginning of this century, all the various theories of the stage investigate and reveal the contrast between three aesthetic domains: the artistic elaboration of the text by the author, the interpretation of the director, and the interpretation of the actor. Significantly, while in Italy, Edward Gordon Craig, one of the first theorists to address these contrasts, was drawing the most extreme consequences from the distinction between theatre as spectacle and theatre as work of art.[14] However, his starting point was not the dramatic text. Instead, he insisted on the importance of the visualization/inspiration of the text, which should give life to a 'performance text,' thus creating an original work of art that will have only a 'thematic relationship with the dramatic text.'[15] There is a statement in Pirandello's 'Illustratori, attori, traduttori' that is a confutation of Craig's thesis: 'Per quanto l'attore si sforzi di penetrare nelle intenzioni dello scrittore, difficilmente riuscirà a vedere come questo ha veduto, a sentire il personaggio come l'autore l'ha sentito, a renderlo sulla scena come l'autore l'ha voluto.'[16] [No matter how much the actor tries to penetrate into the writer's intentions, he will unlikely be able to see as the writer did, to feel the character as the author did, to realize the character on the stage as the author wanted.]

As Umberto Artioli observes in his study *Il ritmo e la voce: Alle sorgenti del teatro della crudeltà*, even though both thinkers insist on the necessity of an *auctor*, Craig believes that such a role is played by the director, and the *enemies* are the text and the actors, whereas for Pirandello the *auctor* is the dramatist himself.[17]

However, in 1936, Pirandello wrote an introductory essay to Silvio D'Amico's *Storia del teatro italiano* that presents great incongruities with respect to his previous writings on the theatre:

Il Teatro non è archeologia. Il non rimettere le mani nelle opere antiche, per aggiornarle e renderle adatte a nuovo spettacolo, significa incuria, non già scrupolo degno di rispetto. Il Teatro vuole questi rimaneggiamenti, e se n'è giovato incessantemente, in tutte le epoche in cui era più vivo. Il testo resta integro per chi se lo vorrà rileggere in casa, per sua cultura; chi vorrà divertircisi andrà a teatro, dove gli sarà ripresentato mondo da tutte le parti vizze, rinnovato nelle espressioni non più correnti, riadattato ai gusti dell'oggi.

E perchè questo è legittimo?

Perchè l'opera d'arte, in teatro, non è più il lavoro di uno scrittore ... ma un atto di vita da creare, momento per momento, sulla scena, col concorso del pubblico.[18]

[Theatre is not archaeology. Not to manipulate antique texts in order to actualize them and turn them into a new spectacle is a sign of neglect and should not be regarded as respectable behaviour. Theatre demands manipulation and has incessantly profited from it in every age in which it was more lively. The text remains intact for those who want to read it at home for personal pleasure; those who want to enjoy themselves will go to the theatre, where the text will be presented cleansed of withered parts and unfashionable terms, and adapted to contemporary taste.

And why is this legitimate?

Because the work of art in the theatre is no longer the work of a writer ... but an act of life to be created, moment by moment, on the stage and together with the spectators.]

Significantly, this essay was written after his experience as *capocomico* at the Teatro d'Arte from 1925 to 1928, an episode which would prove to be a decisive factor in his dramatic production.[19] Only a few months before his death Pirandello redeems the stage, as he states that those who expect complete fidelity to the text from its staging should stay at home and read it. His closing statement is startling; he maintains that the work of art in the theatre is no longer the work of a writer but an act of life to be created, moment by moment, on the stage and in collaboration with the audience. In this last segment, he implicitly maintains that the two works – the text and the *mise en scène* – belong to two different realms of art, and are both to be considered, legitimately *art*. In this essay, he asserts (just as Craig had) the independence of the *mise en scène* from the text. Pirandello does not go as far as to maintain that the staging of a text is superior to its written form, but he promotes theatre to the level of art and exhorts directors to intervene on the *written* word.

Luigi Pirandello's position towards theatre is thus problematic. His theoretical writings until 1936 display a kind of suspicion towards the very concept of theatricality. In contrast, his plays written after 1918 can be considered the experimental laboratory in which he searches for answers to problems related to the dissonance between the text and its *mise en scène*.[20] In this light, *Sei personaggi in cerca d'autore* can be seen both as the breaking point within Pirandello's dramatic production, and as his first attempt to explore the narrow boundaries between fiction and reality in general and on the stage in particular.

Significantly, Pirandello placed *Sei personaggi in cerca d'autore* at the beginning of his collected theatre, *Maschere nude* [*Naked Masks*], thus denoting its primary role in the development of his artistic vision. In this play, Pirandello explores the impossibility of identifying a single source of discourse and an unambiguous instance of signification of a text. Here, one finds an explicit conflict between the author's subjective stance and the fable that each Character believes to be objective, so that in *Sei personaggi*, more than in the other texts of the trilogy, 'the battle of signatures explodes.'[21] This unresolved conflict extends also to the supposed objectivity of the written text and the subjectivity of author, actors, Characters, and spectators, a conflict which never finds a true resolution in the prevailing Pirandellian text. The absence of a dominant point of view leaves the Characters a prey to their conflicts. The autonomy of the Characters and the refusal of the author to give them life are, according to Romano Luperini, the substance of a 'gnoseological play.' For Luperini, the traditional author, with his capacity to interpret, is forfeited. The Characters are in search of a universal truth which no longer exists, a truth that even the author is unable to assert.[22]

Unlike Craig, Pirandello looked for answers in the text. It is not by chance that in *Sei personaggi in cerca d'autore* the actors and the director are rehearsing *Il giuoco delle parti* [*The Rules of the Game*], a play written by Pirandello himself in 1918. In *Il giuoco delle parti*, the conflict between the individual and society bears the typical structure of traditional bourgeois drama. Pirandello metaphorically annihilates this structure by having the six Characters interrupt a rehearsal which never resumes. As Sergio Colomba observes in his volume *La scena del dispiacere*, in *Sei personaggi* the typical conflictual structure of bourgeois drama between an individual and society is lost. *Il giuoco delle parti* cannot be represented. The Characters' story, as well as Pirandello's renunciation of their tragedy and his refusal to acknowledge it, undergoes a radical process of estrangement which leads to the definitive destruction of the dramatic structure upon which bourgeois drama was based.[23]

Pirandello's insistence on the existence of a text before the arrival of the Six Characters is noteworthy. Before their unexpected appearance, the script of *Il giuoco delle parti* is the main protagonist. *Sei personaggi in cerca d'autore* begins with a few lines exchanged between the director and an electrician; immediately thereafter, there is a stage direction in which the actors are brought onto the stage together with the prompter who is carrying the script of *Il giuoco delle parti*. The stage director indicates the exact point at which he wants the rehearsal to begin, and the prompter is ordered to read the stage directions from the script. The prompter is often interrupted by the director, who makes detailed suggestions about the *mise en scène*. Moreover, when the first actor asks if he has to wear a chef's hat, the stage director's irritated reply is, 'Mi pare! Se sta scritto lì! [indicherà il copione]'[24] [I should say so! It's written there, isn't it?! (pointing to the script)]. As soon as the Six Characters become part of the action, though, the situation changes dramatically; the prompter no longer has to read the script to the actors, on the contrary he merely records on paper the succession of scenes and the Six Characters' lines. In so doing, he inverts the process of theatrical textual creation. At the beginning of the play, with the director's insistence upon representing the text on the stage *ad litteram*, Pirandello mimics the naturalists' attitude towards the *mise en scène* of a written text. By introducing the Six Characters onto the stage, he maps a new possibility for the staging which will no longer be tyrannized by the author's text.

Interestingly in 1923, two years before Pirandello wrote the preface to *Sei personaggi in cerca d'autore*, Antonin Artaud attended the *mise en scène* of the play in Paris and saw that there was no text, as he stated in his review of the performance: 'Au commencement la vie continue. Il n'y a pas de spectacle. Le regard plonge sur la scène jusqu'au fond. Envolé le rideau. Toute la salle est un immense plateau où, pour une fois, le spectateur va assister à la cuisine d'une répétition. Répétition de quoi? Il n'y a pas de pièce. Le drame va se faire devant nos yeux.'[25] [At the beginning life goes on. There is no spectacle. Our gaze plunges into the depth of the stage. The curtain disappears. The theatre is an immense plateau where, for once, the spectator is going to witness the making of a rehearsal. Rehearsal of what? There is no play. The drama is going to unfold before our eyes.] However, the production of a performance text is not created by the Characters themselves, who instead see their exploration fail miserably. Moreover, it is with the appearance of the Six Characters and their unwritten text that problems begin for the actors. While the performance of the pre-existing text, *Il giuoco delle parti*, did not challenge the actors and their acting techniques, once they try to impersonate the Characters they are scorned and deemed inadequate as actors. Pirandello seems to be suggesting here that as theatre moves away from the nineteenth-century bourgeois agenda, new acting techniques are also necessary.[26] In *Sei personaggi in cerca d'autore*, Pirandello points out that a new theatre can only be represented by the Characters themselves. As he writes in the preface added to the play in 1925, the Characters introduced themselves to him. He did not evoke or invent them, they simply appeared from a zone of penumbra – the Pirandellian *oltre* [beyond].

Essi si sono già staccati da me; vivono per conto loro; hanno acquistato voce e movimento; sono dunque già divenuti di per se stessi, in questa lotta, che han dovuto sostenere con me per la loro vita, personaggi drammatici, personaggi che possono da soli muoversi e parlare; vedono già se stessi come tali; hanno imparato a difendersi da me; sapranno ancora difendersi dagli altri.[27]

[They have already detached themselves from me, they live on their own; they have acquired independent voice and movement; in this struggle for their life they had to fight with me, on their own, they have thus become already dramatic characters, who are able to speak and move on their own; they already see themselves as such; they have learned to defend themselves from me; they will be able to defend themselves from others.]

The characters' place of origin is thus, *otherness*. Pirandello had already contemplated the issue of the independence of a character with respect to the author in three short stories, 'Personaggi' ['Characters'], 'La tragedia di un personaggio' ['The Tragedy of a Character'] and 'Colloqui coi personaggi' ['Conversations with Characters'], published respectively in 1906, 1911 and 1915.[28] Each short story begins in the same way, the author, Pirandello himself, is visited by characters who more or less implore him to give them life in some manner. Each of these short stories presents different characters, and provides a pretext for Pirandello to investigate and elaborate on the reasons why a character has the right to live his or her own life. The idea is that the character does not merely follow the plot created by the author, but rather the plot unfolds from the *life* of the character. The characters are ultimately sent away by the author who is not willing to grant them their desire.

In *Sei personaggi in cerca d'autore*, the situation of independence is extreme; not only is a life (that of a character) not to be narrated, but also, there is a multiplication of characters. To be precise, we have six, and five of them insist that their story be represented. There is no dialogic relationship nor any real interaction among the Characters. Any possibility whatsoever of mediation – a fundamental component for the fulfillment of meaningful communication, necessary to achieve interaction amongst characters in a play – is lost in *Sei personaggi in cerca d'autore*.

IL PADRE   Ma se è tutto qui il male! Nelle parole! Abbiamo tutti dentro un mondo di cose; ciascuno un suo mondo di cose! E come possiamo intenderci, signore, se nelle parole ch'io dico metto il senso ed il valore delle cose come sono dentro di me; mentre chi le ascolta, inevitabilmente le assume col senso e col valore che hanno per sé, del mondo com'egli l'ha dentro? Crediamo d'interderci; non c'intendiamo mai![29]

[THE FATHER   But if the evil is entirely here! In the words! We all have a world of things inside; each one of us has his own world of things! And how can we understand one another, Sir, if in the words I utter, I put the meaning and value of things as they are inside me; while the one who listens, inevitably takes them with the meaning and value they have for him, of the world he has inside? We believe we understand one another; but we never do!]

Far from making a merely metaphysical statement, Pirandello is alluding to the possibility, or rather the necessity of overcoming the dualistic nature of *experience*. The extreme subjectivism of the Characters, a mirror of the new *Weltanschauung*, is evident throughout the play as the 'epic relativization' depicts the split of the synthesis between subject and object, which is undoubtedly a qualifying characteristic of *Sei personaggi in cerca d'autore*.[30]

In fact, the Characters are not able to find the author they are looking for – an author in the etymological sense of the word: authority. Thus their play is not performed. What is instead staged are their useless attempts to find a producer of such an unequivocal and definite text.[31] When the *capocomico* asks the Father where the script is, the answer is 'È in noi, signore. Il dramma è in noi'[32] [It is in us, Sir. The drama is in us]. The Father, from his first appearance, insistently attempts to become simultaneously character, actor, and, most importantly, author of what he believes to be the *true* play. He strives to impose his narrative account of what happened and is, in this, opposed by everybody else in the play: the other five Characters, the actors who were rehearsing *Il giuoco delle parti*, the stage director, and most importantly, Pirandello himself, the author of *Sei personaggi in cerca d'autore*. According to the Sicilian playwright, not only can the author no longer be *auctor*, but also, the existence of any *auctor* whatsoever has been forfeited as the unity of interpretation has collapsed. In this play the characters' independence and autonomy from the writer and the text are absolute, since Pirandello is aware that a single source for the creation of signification cannot portray reality.

On the stage this signifying chaos explodes as the actors who were rehearsing *Il giuoco delle parti* are not fit to play the Characters, thus frustrating the *mise en scène*. In fact, as the Characters live a life of their own and feel in a subjective way, so do the actors, who are unable to conciliate themselves with the multiple 'selves' of the Characters. Here one cannot but think of the scene in *Sei personaggi*, in which the director casts the leading actress of *Il giuoco delle parti* as the Stepdaughter. When the actress utters the lines previously narrated by the Stepdaughter, the latter bursts out in laughter and states, 'Ma non dicevo per lei, creda! dicevo per me, che non mi vedo affatto in lei, ecco. Non so, non ... non m'assomiglia per nulla.'[33] [I wasn't talking about you, believe me! I was speaking of myself, whom I cannot see at all in you! That's all. I don't know, you don't ... you aren't in the least like me.] Here again, Pirandello attempts to resolve textually the contradiction presented by the staging of a play. The actors as human beings are conditioned by their psychological, social and material existence. Such characteristics undermine the ability of the actors to feel and essentially to be as the Characters feel and are. With the actual staging this problem is taken to its extreme: actors who are playing actors rehearsing *Il giuoco delle parti*, who want to play the Characters of *Sei Personaggi*, a play which the author does not want to write.

Therefore, at the very core of *Sei personaggi*, one finds the attempt the Characters make as performers to play *Sei personaggi*. They utter their lines first, and by doing so generate the text. Through the negation of a pre-existing text (*Il giuoco delle parti*) and the assertion of the incompatibility between the text and the director, the actors, the Characters, and ultimately between the Characters themselves, Pirandello poses, textually, the problem relating to the creation of a single source of signification. There is however one Character, the Son, who is unwilling to be given a fixed role, 'Non ho proprio nulla, io, da fare qui! Me ne lasci andare, la prego! Me ne lasci andare.'[34] [I've got nothing to do with all this! Let me go, I beg you! Let me go!]. He strongly reiterates this unwillingness to act when, towards the end, the Father asks him to represent the terrible scene in the garden and he answers, 'Io non rappresento nulla! E l'ho dichiarato fin dal principio!'[35] [I shall represent nothing at all! And I've said so from the very beginning!].

Interestingly, in his 1925 'Preface' to the play, Pirandello himself comments on this matter: 'C'è un personaggio infatti – quello che 'nega' il dramma che lo fa personaggio, il Figlio – che tutto il suo rilievo e il suo valore trae dall'essere personaggio non della 'commedia da fare' – che come tale quasi non appare – ma della rappresentazione che io ne ho fatta.'[36] [As a matter of fact there is a character – the one who 'denies' the drama that makes him a character, the Son – that draws his relevance and value from the fact of being a character not of the 'play to be' – which, as such, hardly appears – but of the representation that I have given of it.] Pirandello virtually closes his preface by arguing that he is quite aware of the confusion introduced by the Son and yet, in so doing, he reaffirms the centrality of a character who, as he himself states, has been almost peripheral to the play to be – a character who 'denies the play.'[37]

Pirandello's Son, in a Hamletic manner,[38] refuses his fixed role. He thus tries to subvert the *mise en scène* with his unwillingness to act out his given role. In the play, the Son is unwilling to represent and therefore is the only one of the Characters who interprets the author's intention, which is, in fact, not to give life to the play: 'Io non mi presto! non mi presto! E interpreto così la volontà di chi non volle portarci sulla scena!'[39] [I am not going to lend myself to this! I am not going to! And in this way I interpret the will of the one who did not want to bring us onto the stage!]. Interestingly, by not wanting to represent, the Son renounces his existence, something the other Characters are not ready to do.

Paradoxically, the situation is a complete reversal of that presented in the three short stories ('Personaggi,' 'La tragedia di un personaggio' and 'Colloqui coi personaggi'), where the characters begged the author to give them life; it is also a reversal of the experience of the other Characters in *Sei personaggi* who all insist that they exist as they are, without accepting any sort of compromise. However, despite the Son's reluctance, a play unfolds and swiftly moves towards its problematic ending. It is at the very close of this most controversial play that

Luigi Pirandello (a dramatist repeatedly accused of being incapable of untangling himself from the tyranny of the written text) conjectures the necessity and yet the impossibility of a performance text. At the close of the play *Sei personaggi in cerca d'autore*, at the boy's presumed death, fiction and reality merge on Pirandello's stage:

PRIMA ATTRICE   È morto! Povero ragazzo! È morto! Oh che cose!
PRIMO ATTORE   Ma che morto! Finzione! Finzione! Non ci creda!
ALTRI ATTORI DA DESTRA   Finzione? Realtà! realtà! È morto!
ALTRI ATTORI DA SINISTRA   No! Finzione! Finzione!
PADRE   Ma che finzione! Realtà, realtà, signori! realtà![40]

[ACTRESS   He is dead! Poor boy!
ACTOR   He is not dead! It's fiction! It's only fiction!
ACTORS (*entering from the right*)   Fiction? Reality! Reality! He's dead!
ACTORS (*entering from the left*)   No! Fiction! Fiction!
FATHER   But what fiction? Reality, reality, ladies and gentlemen! Reality!]

As all the Characters leave the stage, the Capocomico aimlessly trying to regain control over the performance, and thus reality, exclaims, 'Finzione! realtà! Andate al diavolo tutti quanti! Luce! Luce! Luce!'[41] [Fiction! Reality! Why don't you all go to hell?! Lights! Lights! Lights!]. Yet, this last attempt to put order into the chaos is doomed to fail; the shadows of the Characters regain access to the stage and the Stepdaughter, who had constantly insisted on representing and not narrating her drama – 'Qui non si narra! Qui non si narra!'[42] [No narrating here! No narrating!] – ultimately leaves the place of representation, the stage, rushes into the orchestra and plunges into the place of narration, the place of history and thus reality.[43]

In *Sei personaggi in cerca d'autore*, Pirandello did not find any answers to the various questions he had posed. Firstly, he tried to solve, at the level of the text, the problem related to the creation of a performance. While the Characters were in search of an author, Pirandello was searching for a resolution to the problem relating to the creation of an absolute and univocal truth to be expressed by the *mise en scène*. By confining himself totally to the written word, he was unable to pose the question at the level of representation. Thus, at this point of his theatrical production, his investigation of truth and creation of signification continue to be central to his artistic production. He continued to investigate these questions in the other two plays of his meta-theatrical trilogy, *Ciascuno a suo modo* [*Each in His Own Way*] and *Questa sera si recita a soggetto* [*Tonight We Improvise*], but the dilemmas brought about by his research not only remain unresolved, they also expand and demand a drastic resolution. In his 1936 introduction to D'Amico's *Storia del teatro italiano* Pirandello established, theoretically, the base to overcome the afflicted state of the theatre; simultaneously, he set forth to unravel the impasse artistically in *I giganti della montagna* [*The Mountain Giants*], only to be hindered by death.

NOTES

1 Walter Benjamin, *Schriften* (Frankfurt: Suhrkamp Verlag, 1955). See also Renato Solmi's 'Introduction' to the Italian translation of the above mentioned text, *Angelus Novus* (Turin: Einaudi, 1962), vii–xliii.
2 Peter Szondi, *Theorie des modernen Dramas* (Frankfurt: Suhrkamp Verlag, 1956).
3 Romano Luperini, *L' allegoria del moderno* (Rome: Editori Riuniti, 1990), 202–48.
4 These two poetics had monopolized theatrical experimentation at the end of the nineteenth century. For a full account of the theatrical controversy between naturalism and symbolism, see Claudio Vicentini, *Pirandello: Il disagio del teatro* (Venice: Marsilio, 1993). Both the naturalist and the symbolist theatre aesthetic based the *mise en scène* on a faithful reproduction of the text onto the stage. For the naturalists the *mise en scène* had to depict the historic and social situation in the play written by the author, making the staging completely dependent upon the written text. The symbolists preached and called for a complete cerebral perception of the *mise en scène*, as they considered the ideal staging to come about totally in the spectator's mind. The words of the author thus were to enable the symbolist spectator to visualize the 'evoked' scene. Both aesthetics were cumbersome as the only way for the spectator to be completely 'taken away by the text' would be to read it.
5 Luigi Pirandello, 'Illustratori, attori e traduttori,' in *Saggi, poesie, scritti varii* (Milan: Mondadori, 1960), 209–24.
6 Luigi Pirandello, 'L'azione parlata,' *Il Marzocco*, 7 May 1899.
7 Pirandello, 'Illustratori, attori e traduttori,' 223–4.
8 Emilio Proventi, *Epistolario familiare giovanile*, *Quaderni della Nuova Antologia* 26 (Florence: Le Monnier, 1986), 22.
9 Even though Pirandello hardly wrote anything for the stage between 1899 and 1916, many of the short stories composed in this period served

as thematic bases for dramatic works written after 1916. See Vicentini, *Pirandello: Il disagio del teatro*.

10 The search for an artistic form which would deliver 'full signification' and the crisis of 'traditional' artistic conventions was the common denominator of the exponents of the avant-garde in Europe. See Corrado Donati, *Il sogno e la ragione* (Rome: Edizioni Scientifiche Italiane, 1993), 155–88; Theodor W. Adorno, *Asthetische Theorie* (Frankfurt: Suhrkamp Verlag, 1970), 162–75; and Luperini, *L'allegoria del moderno*, 3–55.

11 For a detailed account of Pirandello's experiences with the staging of his plays see Claudio Vicentini, 'Il problema del teatro nell'opera di Pirandello,' in *Pirandello e il teatro*, ed. Enzo Lauretta (Palermo: Palumbo, 1985), 9–35.

12 'En confidence,' *Le Temps*, 20 July 1925.

13 In Italy, the futurists themselves actually addressed this problem in their various theatrical manifestos (1913, 1915, 1921) as well as in their *mises en scène*. It is however noteworthy to recall that while they took quite a diverse position, in 1921 Filippo Tommaso Marinetti, the founder of futurism, emphasized the primary role *Sei personaggi in cerca d'autore* played in mediating the subversive futurist positions towards a broad audience, and thus asserting the 'futurist' nature of Pirandello's play. See Filippo Tommaso Marinetti, *Teoria e invenzione futurista* (Milan: Mondadori, 1968), 171.

14 It is certain that Pirandello and Craig met in 1934. Pirandello actually invited Craig to attend an international conference on the theatre that same year. Many, however, sustain that Pirandello often attacked and ridiculed Craig's theories. In particular, the protagonist of *Stasera si recita a soggetto*, the malicious Hinkfuss, is said to be Pirandello's portrayal of Craig. The Englishman also was familiar with Pirandello's work. In fact, in an article entitled 'The Originality of Luigi Pirandello' he attacked the playwright fiercely. Among other things he accused Pirandello of being a 'novelist who uses dramatic form without having any understanding of the theatre.' The article, signed Henry Fhips (one of the eighty-two pseudonyms Craig used) appeared in *The Mask* 12 (1926), 33–6.

15 Edward Gordon Craig, *On the Art of the Theatre* (London: Chelsea, 1911).

16 Pirandello, 'Illustratori, attori e traduttori,' 215.

17 Umberto Artioli, *Il ritmo e la voce: Alle sorgenti del teatro della crudeltà* (Milan: Shakespeare & Co., 1984), 202.

18 Silvio D'Amico, *Storia del teatro italiano* (Milan: Mondadori, 1936), 25.

19 For an accurate account of Pirandello's experience as *capocomico* at the Teatro d'Arte, see Paolo Puppa, 'Pirandello capocomico: repertorio e

Pirandello's Quest for Truth 51

repertori,' *Biblioteca Teatrale* 12 (1989): 37–59; see also A. D'Amico and A. Tinterri, *Pirandello capocomico* (Palermo: Palumbo, 1987). For a portrayal of his aesthetic experience at the Teatro d'Arte see Donato Santeramo, 'Sagra del signore della Nave: simbolo ed allegoria,' in Enzo Lauretta ed., *Pirandello: teatro e musica* (Palermo, Palumbo, 1995), 225–33.

20 However, as stage manager and director at the Teatro d'Arte from 1925 to 1928, Pirandello addressed the problems related to the complex relationship between the written text and the *mise en scène* in a practical way. On this matter, see Puppa, 'Pirandello capocomico: repertorio e repertori,' 51–2.

21 Jennifer Stone, *Pirandello's Naked Prompt: The Structure of Repetition in Modernism* (Ravenna: Longo, 1989).

22 Romano Luperini, 'L'atto del significare allegorico nei *Sei personaggi* e in *Enrico IV*,' *Rivista di studi pirandelliani* 3(6/7) (June–December 1991): 9–19.

23 Sergio Colomba, *La scena del dispiacere. Ripetizione e differenza nel teatro italiano degli anni Ottanta* (Ravenna: Longo, 1984), 173.

24 Luigi Pirandello, *Sei personaggi in cerca d'autore*, in *Maschere nude* (1958; Milan: Mondadori, 1986), 35–116.

25 Antonin Artaud, '*Six personnages en quête d'auteur* à la Comédie des Champs-Elysées,' in *Oeuvres complètes* (Paris: Gallimard, 1980), 142.

26 It is certainly relevant to note here that some of the most important contributions to a contemporary theory of acting were formulated during Pirandello's lifetime, including Konstantin Stanislavsky, *My Life in Art* (London: Bles, 1924) and *An Actor Prepares* (London: Theatre Arts Books, 1936); Adolphe Appia, *La mise en scène du drame wagnérien* (Paris: Léon Challey, 1892) and *L'Oeuvre d'art vivant* (Genève-Paris: Edition Atar, 1921); Edward Gordon Craig, *On the Art of the Theatre* (London: William Heinemann, 1911). Later on, of course, a major contribution came from Bertolt Brecht, particularly with his *Schriften zum Theater: Über eine nicht-aristotelische Dramatik* (Frankfurt am Main: Siegfried Unseld. Suhrkamp Verlag, 1957).

27 Pirandello, 'Preface' to *Sei personaggi in cerca d'autore*, in *Maschere nude*, 37.

28 Pirandello, 'La tragedia di un personaggio,' in *Novelle per un anno* (Milan: Mondadori, 1988), 1/1: 816–24; 'Colloqui coi personaggi,' in *Novelle per un anno* (Milan: Modadori, 1990), 3/2: 1138–53, and 'Personaggi,' ibid., 3/2: 1474–8.

29 Pirandello, *Sei personaggi in cerca d'autore*, 46.

30 Szondi, *Theorie des modernen Dramas*, 61–6; Benjamin, *Ursprung des deutschen Trauerspiels*, 178–97.

31 'Il dramma non riesce a rappresentarsi appunto perchè manca l'autore che essi cercano; e si rappresenta invece la commedia di questo loro vano tentativo.' [The drama cannot be represented precisely because the author they are in search of is lacking; instead, what is represented is the comedy of this vain effort of theirs.] 'Preface' to *Sei personaggi in cerca d'autore*, 40.
32 Pirandello, *Sei personaggi in cerca d'autore*, 59.
33 Ibid., 82.
34 Ibid.
35 Ibid., 109.
36 Pirandello, 'Preface' to *Sei personaggi in cerca d'autore*, 45.
37 Ibid., 45–6.
38 There seems to be a parallel between the Son and Hamlet; the latter refuses to act out his 'given role' and yet, after many hesitations, will 'execute' his 'captious duty.'
39 Pirandello, *Sei personaggi in cerca d'autore*, 114.
40 Ibid., 115.
41 Ibid.
42 Ibid., 65.
43 Manuela Gieri, 'Effetti di straniamento come strategia della messa in scena: appunti e spigolature sulla poetica della scena di Luigi Pirandello,' in Enzo Lauretta, ed., *Pirandello e il teatro* (Milan: Mursia, 1993), 335–42.

4

Pirandello and the Theatre-within-the-Theatre: Thresholds and Frames in *Ciascuno a suo modo*

MAURIZIO GRANDE

Simulation and Fiction

In Luigi Pirandello's so-called theatre-within-the-theatre trilogy – *Sei personaggi in cerca d'autore* [*Six Characters in Search of an Author*, 1921], *Ciascuno a suo modo* [*Each in His Own Way*, 1923], and *Questa sera si recita a soggetto* [*Tonight We Improvise*, 1929] – the play between *fiction* and *simulation* is quite pronounced, to the point where it becomes extremely difficult to distinguish these two aspects of dramaturgical writing. The issue becomes more complex still if one considers that the metatheatrical nature of these works tends to erase the border between 'theatrical illusion' and 'illusionistic reproduction' of reality and life, thereby rendering *simulation* (what we might call the fictitious nature of theatre) indiscernible from *illusion* (the illusory nature of theatre's pragmatic effects). The object here is to analyse the way in which Pirandello 'orchestrates' the relationships between fiction and simulation, both at the level of theatrical illusion and at the level of its 'metatheatrical reflection,' and thus obtains the neutralization of simulation and the magnification of fiction beyond the conventional, statutory limits assigned to them. In this way, Pirandello is able to make of metatheatrical simulation the most external frame of the dramatic game playing, one which leads us to the innermost threshold of fiction: the *illusion of reality*.

In order to understand the nature and the role of metatheatrical simulation it is necessary to examine the categories that (1) identify fiction and simulation at the conceptual level, and (2) uphold the modal and functional distinctions between the two, both in artistic practice in general, and in theatrical practice in particular. First, it is important to state that any act of simulation is a *specification* of the act of fiction, in the most general sense of the term. It may also be said that simulation is a specific aspect of fiction, and that the relationship established between simulation and fiction is one of *inclusion* (as a 'species' is included in a genus). Every work of art is a work of 'fiction,' and this condition itself becomes the nature of theatre, where simulation is the *characteristic* form of dramatic fiction. For this reason it is said that the fictitious reality of the script is transformed into a verisimilar and 'truthful' representation of the real, precisely through the contrivance of simulation (which affects both the art of the actor and the art of staging).

The conceptual category by which theatrical simulation is rendered explicit is the *make-believe* category, that is to say, the same conceptual category of *game playing* in which fiction as such is suspended and then elevated to the status of boundary between the 'true' and the 'false.' Every act is both real, in so far as it is a move in the game, and, at the same time, false, if it is assumed to be a real gesture. Within the game everything must be true: the commitment of the players, the confrontation amongst the opponents, the conquest of the stake, and even the psycho-physical waste exerted in the attempt to gain advantage from one's own actions. Yet, everything must be *simulated*, so that it will not be confused with the actions executed in reality.

Here the paradox of the game becomes evident. The same act (for instance, that of striking an adversary with a physical blow), takes on different meanings in game playing and in life. In the boxing ring, for example, one respects certain rules when striking an opponent, rules which institute and govern the confrontation as an athletic competition. In life, the selfsame act is 'framed' in a different type of situation: the confrontation is simply a confrontation; it is not governed by rules which, if applied, would transform the confrontation into sport (boxing). It stands to reason that the only case in which there is complete simulation is the specific game that is theatre – both the theatre of child's play (with children dressing up as warriors and engaging in a battle that is not a battle, but that must be conducted as though it were a battle proper) and of adults' play (of which the only non-competitive and non-athletic form is theatre). This is the paradox of game playing, on which the 'game of the theatre' is based; it is a game in which make-believe is especially specified in simulation and defined as a special practice of fiction.

But the nature of theatre is not ascribable and cannot be reduced to the logic of simulation. It does not exhaust itself in the contrivance of the game that regulates the two-tiered act of fiction, an act which consists of: (a) *fictitious action* executed according to the rules of dramatic composition; and (b) an *act of simulation* that specifies and actualizes the dramatic fiction within the performance. The nature of theatre implies the willing suspension of disbelief in a manner so as to make the audience willing to accept the artistic devices of fiction as true, and to put in brackets the fictitious nature of the dramatic game. On the other hand, the nature of theatre also includes the suspension of the *specific* condition of the dramatic act of fiction (simulation). Through this suspension, this game of simulation assumes a role of *non-game*, a role of *characteristic illusion* that transcends the nature of fiction. It follows that the symbolic pact which regulates theatrical fiction makes this simulation assume the nature of *suspended game* and *illusory reality*, a nature that transcends both the act of fiction and its specific theatrical modality, simulation (from performance to stage design, from costumes to lighting, from the real objects seen onstage to their metaphorical significations).

In this 'game within a game,' game/non-game of simulation, the device of the theatre-within-the-theatre plays a significant role; it is a paradoxical form of simulation that we may call *metatheatrical simulation*. It is my intention to show that Pirandello's metatheatre strengthens theatrical illusion and pushes it to the limits allowed by the game between fiction and reality and between simulation and truth, placing theatre at a new frontier of illusion, that of *hallucination*.

Mountings and Thresholds

There is no doubt that in the trilogy of the theatre-within-the-theatre there is a play of mountings[1] between the different planes of fiction and simulation, so that the first performance progressively loses the illusory nature guaranteed to it by simulation. Such an unveiling occurs as that first performance becomes the frame for a second performance that presents the *fictitious* nature of the first, thereby revealing theatre as the locus of simulation. And yet, at the moment when the second performance establishes itself as a framework mounted around the first performance and unmasks its essence as simulated reality, the second performance positions itself as an even more powerful illusion, in that it enunciates itself as non-theatre, or rather, as *hyper-theatre* which contains a sort of *hypo-theatre* as a performance (that is to say, a staging) revealed to be a simulation of reality. In this way, the theatrical game enunciates itself at two levels: (1) the staging of a script, that is, the fictitious reality produced by dramatic art; and (2) the simulation, as the specific realization of the dramatic fiction. Thus, the performance that constitutes the second mounting frames the first performance as a mounting of *the drama that is enunciated (and denunciated) as such*,[2] a theatre that is unable to guarantee the suspension of disbelief, and even that of the theatrical game. This never-ending play of mirrors, frames, mountings, levels, reflections, and thresholds of fiction tends to displace the theatrical illusion from the realm of simulation into that of meta-simulation, to the point of rendering the borders between theatre and life indiscernible.

The role of Pirandello's theatre-within-the-theatre is to cross the threshold which separates art and life, and to make the distinction between reality and theatre indiscernible, thereby creating a theatrical illusion that erases the distinction between theatre and non-theatre. It is therefore a radical and paradoxical form of metatheatre, one that does not have either the logical and aesthetic function of rendering theatrical simulation explicit, or the ideological goal of exposing the fictitious or game-like nature of theatre. Furthermore, it is not the objective of this form of metatheatre to strengthen the theatrical illusion, to enunciate metatheatre as hyper-simulation or as a simulation of a simulation (even though the increase in theatrical illusion is the immediate effect of this play of metatheatrical mountings). Metatheatrical simulation has an alternative pragmatic purpose and another aesthetic objective. It has the purpose of prohibiting simulation and the objective of realizing a form of *trans-theatre* which transcends theatrical fiction, and expands it to the point of paradox in the theatrical performance: thus it moves from simulation to reality.

Pirandello's metatheatre, therefore, cannot be explicated by referring to the theatre-which-speaks-of the-theatre, that is, a theatre which dismantles its devices and displays the theatrical condition as a theme of its *metatheatrical simulation*. Pirandello's metatheatre does not expose the theatrical fiction of the theatre; rather, it shows the theatrical fiction that exists in life. But that is not all. Such a theatrical form speaks to us not of the world of performance, but of the way in which we can travel or transit through the performance into reality, by dint of a fiction that exasperates its own contrivance to such an extent that it becomes a *real hallucination.* This is the hallucinatory reality of the everyday 'naked masks,' and of everybody's daily life.

The term theatre-within-the-theatre, in its obvious sense, is not to be confused with the *metatheatrical simulation;* a distinction is needed, therefore, between theatre-within-the-theatre and *metatheatre.* Pirandello's metatheatre is not theatre-within-the-theatre; it is, if anything, theatre *beyond* the theatre, theatre that leads into the paradoxical form of simulation that is life, even when this paradoxical form of simulation (life) is presented on a theatrical stage. It is not a coincidence that in *Ciascuno a suo modo* the stage is continuously shifting, and the extended scene begins to include and define the restricted or primary scene of the theatre, to the point that the distinctions between one scene and the other, between theatre and metatheatre, disappear.

In this manner, Pirandello's metatheatre proceeds to a prodigious play of mountings: theatre within theatre, performance within performance, performance within theatre, theatre within performance. In the end, there is no enunciation of the theatre in the fiction staged; rather, the contrary occurs. Metatheatrical simulation is not placed in the outermost frame of the theatrical fiction, in which the *performance of simulation* is inscribed. Instead, frames and thresholds undergo a radical overturning, so that metatheatre is placed in the innermost mounting, the one in which simulation becomes neutralized by an even more powerful fiction. This particular fiction, in turn, becomes occluded and blocked as fiction, and is reworked into a new theme as true drama–true theatre; it exceeds theatre and enters into life. The theatre thus becomes the place where simulation hides (and suspends) the *make-believe* of the dramatic game playing, while fiction, in turn, constructs metatheatre as a *threshold* between theatre and life.

Finally, the performance, in its integral form of theatre and metatheatre, will be constructed as a *trans-theatrical stage event* in the continuous passage from threshold to threshold, from frame to frame, from mounting to mounting. Initially, the performance is situated in the *innermost mounting* of theatrical simulation – for example the rehearsal of *Il giuoco delle parti* in *Sei personaggi in cerca d'autore* or Palegari's drawing room in *Ciascuno a suo modo*. Then the performance moves to the *intermediary mounting* between theatrical simulation and metatheatre, producing an effect of theatre-within-the-theatre – for example, the entrance of the Six Characters and the ensuing dispute regarding dramatic fiction and theatrical simulation in *Sei personaggi*, or, the first *intermezzo corale* in *Ciascuno a suo modo*, and the overturning of levels of

58   Maurizio Grande

simulation, fiction, and re-simulation. Finally, the performance moves to the *outermost mounting* of theatrical simulation; this mounting includes the other levels, but overturns their positions and meanings. In fact, in the outermost mounting, simulation becomes metatheatre and erases the differences between simulation and reality, so that the level of metatheatre reveals itself to be the innermost mounting and becomes the *threshold* between simulation and reality, between fiction and illusion, between art and life. Metatheatrical simulation transcends fiction, and reveals it to be simulative, to be a specific characteristic of the game of theatre, thus rendering impracticable every *make-believe* in the succession from theatre to life, from reality to illusion, from mirror to reflection. The multiplication of the levels of simulation and of the mountings of theatrical illusion is reflected at a *trans-theatrical* level, one that is indistinguishable from the complete illusion of reality. This complete illusion of reality is the notion of life as hallucination, beyond any possible type of theatre.

Beyond the Threshold

There is often a tendency in common discourse (and also in specialized discourse) to confuse metatheatre and other forms of meta-art, with *metalanguage*, or at least, to assimilate these two forms of semiotic praxis in the figure of *reflection*. The difference between meta-art and metalanguage can be fully understood in the functional distinction between the two practices: metalanguage assumes language as the object of reflection, the field of investigation, or the material to be analysed. On the other hand, meta-art takes art to be a reflection of artistic practices. Thus, the modality of *reflection* is the element which distinguishes meta-art from metalanguage. In metalanguage, reflection on language produces a description of the language-object by means of a series of reformulations of utterances based on the 'principle of equivalence' among the terms as well as among the syntactical modalities of their concatenation. In the case of meta-art, there is no reflection on art for the purpose of reformulating its practices in non-artistic terms; rather, what occurs is the elaboration of a *reflected* art form, in which the artistic practice becomes the theme and the content of the work. Meta-art produces the work as *self-reflexivity of the artistic practice*, as a reflected form of art and of its semiotic conventions, of its style and of its language, to the point of overturning the relationship between form and content. Metalanguage produces a reflection on language as the content of analysis, a transitive reformulation of linguistic codes and mechanisms. Metalanguage is 'transitive' in the same measure as meta-art is 'intransitive.' Metalanguage transits through language by reformulating the meaning of messages on the basis of a possible semantic equivalence of the terms involved. Meta-art impedes the transit from the signs to their referents, making the form of the artistic practice into a *reflection of meaning*, and calling into question the relationship between art and extra-artistic reality, between language and referent, between form and content.

Metatheatre, like any other meta-artistic practice, calls into play the relationship between stage fiction and reality by neutralizing simulation through a multiplication of the levels of simulation, and by producing a series of splittings and doublings of fiction in the various mountings of the theatre. Such mountings then function as *consecutive mirrors* in which the reciprocal images of form-meaning and sign-referent are annulled. The splitting-doubling of simulation becomes the typical content of metatheatre, that is to say, theatre as a reflection which leads beyond the mirror. Metatheatre mounts theatre and simulation (stage fiction) with the reflection of the theatrical form, beyond spectacle as performance (beyond performance as representation) or staging of the script.

At this point the issue is to examine the ways in which Pirandello's work is affected by this short circuit between simulation and fiction, this process by which *performance* positions itself in the outermost frame of the drama, and the *stage event* produced by metatheatre places itself in the innermost threshold between theatre and trans-theatre. In fact, if metatheatre is the reflection of an *interdicted* simulation, then theatre (inasmuch as it is an institution of fiction and simulation) will be the frame and the mirror of such a reflection, making fiction and simulation, signs and things, art and life indiscernible. The trans-theatrical dimension will be opened up by the continuous transit between theatre and metatheatre, leading to the overturning of the condition which constitutes dramatic art itself: instead of having a situation in which the theatre acts as a *mirror of life*, there is one in which life acts as *mirror of theatre*.

What has just been described constitutes the trans-theatrical dimension of Pirandello's theatre, a dimension which will be here exemplified in that play of reflections already implicit in the title of the second work of the trilogy, *Ciascuno a suo modo*.

Life as Mirror Reflection of Theatre

The second play of the theatre-within-the-theatre trilogy is a long debate on the masks reality is able to assume, and on the multiple facets of the truth that subtends human actions. Each individual sees things 'in his/her own way,' so that the different positions are presented as reciprocal and specular, like the obverse and the reverse of an image and its reflection. Reciprocity is characterized by the symmetrical inversion of identity; the 'same' thing seems to be repeated in the other as a doubling of the identity, as *symmetrical to the identical*.

The reflection, the double, and the symmetrical of the identical, do not simply constitute the theme of the contrast between Doro Palegari and Francesco Savio. Twice the two characters find themselves on opposite sides of the same 'truth': on the first occasion, they formulate two different interpretations of Delia Morelli's behaviour; on the following day, they find themselves supporting the opposite to their previous positions, thereby taking each other's place, and thus mirroring each other reciprocally in the Punch-like overturning of their own opinions. The notion of reflection as symmetrical to the identical *is* the theatre; and metatheatre has the task of focusing on it by relegating it to the stage of the 'primary' simulation, that is, the performance that fictitiously reproduces an event which has occurred. In this, metatheatre has several and diverse functions:

1. Metatheatre moves theatrical fiction from 'direct' simulation (the staging of the script), to meta-simulation. For instance, in the first *intermezzo corale*, the fiction is dislocated from the stage to the foyer, so that the script expands to include the mounting of the first simulation within the mounting of the second simulation (the spectators who comment on the performance).
2. By expanding, the script establishes a caesura (but also a diverse continuity) between stage and pit, remounting both in a theatrical fiction that includes the audience, and inaugurating a new game between performance and spectators.
3. Metatheatre is not only the second performance that includes the first as the performance proper; metatheatre is also the *illusion of continuity* between theatre and non-theatre, between art and life, given that there cannot be logical continuity between performances which are mounted one within the other, without jeopardizing the very sense of the theatre as performance. (Nothing prevents one

from continuing the game, and imagining an even more exterior mounting that contains the actual spectators of the first two performances, finally the audience in the real hall, who comment on the game of simulation within simulation, but who inevitably would become fictitious spectators of an even more external mounting of the script, and so on, to infinity.)
4. Metatheatre brings theatrical illusion to an end with an even more potent illusion – life that doubles the theatre (and not the contrary) – and that makes the theatre the place of stage exemplification of the debate on life.
5. Metatheatre makes of the double theatre of simulation a clarification of reality; or, to be more consonant with the Pirandellian thematics, it makes of the theatre the impossible double of a truth that presents itself as a play of mirror reflections.
6. Metatheatre leads one to exit the theatre as illusion, and forces the audience (be they spectators or readers) to question the notion of theatre as a double of reality.
7. Metatheatre shows simulation – both theatrical simulation onstage, and theatrical simulation in life – as a reflection of life. Therefore, everything that Diego Cinci says regarding the *pagliaccetti* [little clowns] that we are, and regarding the game of mirrors in which we either recognize ourselves or disavow ourselves, fixes itself on the boundary between theatre and life, suspending the theatrical fiction, and making the theatre the place where truth is brought into play, and life the place where truth disguises itself with each person's own ways.

Life, like the theatre, is not just a play of reflections and masks. It is a kind of metatheatre into which one enters into and exits from simulation and mendacity, deceit and truth, fiction and reality. Life, at least for Pirandello, seems to exemplify the game playing between theatre and metatheatre, turning itself into a play and a reflection of that play. Life then is fiction and unmasking of fiction, in an interference of mountings and mirrors that reflect the theatrical play of reality, to the point that simulation, fiction and meta-simulation become indistinguishable. (In this manner, once having appeared, the lie, like fiction, cannot but lead to its own enlargement into another more sly, or more naïve, lie, which is, properly speaking, the same thing set as the mounting of truth, and so on to infinity.)

Life is the metatheatre in which one plays the game between illusion and reduction of illusion, between mask and face, between the simulation that we adopt in order to live and lie, and the fiction that the metatheatre dealing with the social debate on the mask exposes as a *mirroring of an illusion*. Masks, therefore, are naked because metatheatre prohibits their theatrical simulation by doubling and overturning such simulation to the point that no theatre is possible but the metatheatrical game on simulation and illusion.

No one will ever know the true, the ultimate motivations behind Delia Morelli–Amelia Moreno's behaviour. Did she bring death to her lover in order to save him from the slow death of passion? or to make him an eternal prey beyond life? or because she was overwhelmed by the love for another man? The play closes on the impossibility of untangling this knot or answering this question (and perhaps on the impossibility of the question as well). And it is not by accident that the play does not close but rather is interrupted at the threshold of the third act which will never be staged because it would simply involve the infinite continuation of the premises of the play.

Metatheatre closes the theatre on its own generous confession of impotence in saying more than it says: truth is only representable, not knowable; the theatre of truth is still and always theatre, – a *simulation of an illusion*. On this beheading of the theatre and of the illusion of truth, metatheatre re-opens and re-closes the curtain several times, shifting boundaries, thresholds, mountings, and frames. The final frame is again a threshold – the threshold between theatre-metatheatre and life – where metatheatre opens up to the unresolved theatre of life, re-starting the game playing of masks and reflections of simulation in *reality*.

Metatheatre, therefore, speaks of the theatre, but not of a theatre of the stage where simulation makes a script believable. Rather it speaks of the script of life mounted inside the double-theatre of performance and metatheatre, which in turn frames that performance on another performance, all the way to the end of illusion on the threshold of the entrance into reality. But reality, too, is still theatre, and the theatre which wants to represent it can only be the metatheatre of that play of masks which is life.

With *Ciascuno a suo modo*, this artful and pathetic melodrama of the impossible truth, Pirandello uncovers all of his cards and aims at erasing the differences between theatre and life, between that theatre which is life, and that life which is theatre. Metatheatre is nothing other than the script of an impossible performance, of a prohibited simulation, of a doubled fiction. Metatheatre is life that mirrors itself in the theatre, and, because of this, it transcends any illusion of reality. But when metatheatre forces theatre to mirror itself in life, then theatrical illusion again becomes the mirror of another illusion, to infinity. It becomes the mirroring of an impossible symmetry between reality and reflection, between the double and the original, between art and the world.

In this way, Pirandello exits from the avant-garde and becomes a classic: he becomes the prophet of a world in which nature cannot hold up the mirror to art, any more than art can duplicate nature. Pirandello becomes the prophet of an era in which the simulacrum dominates, undisputed, over the reality of human relationships. Yet in Pirandello's theatre the simulacrum is not a copy without an original. It is a play of symmetrical reflections that acts as the reality of the simulacrum. It is like an original that allows neither models nor copies, neither reality nor simulation, but only an infinite *hallucination*, beyond any possible illusion.

Translated by Lucia di Rosa

NOTES

1 Translator's note: Maurizio Grande uses the Italian term *incastonamento* here in the sense of 'setting' or 'mounting.'
2 Translator's note: In Italian, the text reads: '*enunciato (denunciato)*.'

5

Families of Characters and Families of Actors on the Pirandellian Stage

PAOLO PUPPA

In the beginning, theatre was largely peripheral to Luigi Pirandello's literary vocation. His conception of the *written* work, or rather of its creation within the author's imagination, existed well outside the sphere of the stage machinery. This fact is not simply due to remnants of idealistic positions. Rather, it can be attributed to the author's siding with contemporary literati in their resistance to the low level of theatrical production, with its obsolete craftsmanship, and to the devalued, commercial nature of the *material* circuit of the theatrical spectacle. From Arrigo Boito to Eduardo Boutet, from the *Scapigliati* to the authors in pre-Raphaelite circles, we see in the period of King Umberto I and in that of Prime Minister Giolitti [that is, at the end of the nineteenth century and the beginning of the twentieth] an obsessive, polemical objection to the world of actors and *capocomici* (theatre company leaders), impresarios and prompters, managers and 'consumers' (audiences), that is, in short, an objection to the spaces in which the mysterious and magical word of the poet is in danger of becoming altered and prostituted.

In Italy just as theatrical reforms were catching hold of the European stage, writers were revolting against the actor, against the actor's free body and against the deformations and narcissistic improvisations of this body. Only much later did Pirandello follow suit, by representing exaggerated and mundane caricatures who are unmindful of the original furor of their creator – of the possessed acquaintance of those phantoms who make up, for instance, the misfit troupe in *Sei Personaggi in cerca d'autore* [*Six Characters in Search of an Author*, 1921]. But there is more. In his theoretical works, from 'L'azione parlata' ['The Spoken Action,' 1899] to 'Illustratori, attori e traduttori' ['Illustrators, Actors and Translators,' 1908], and even to 'Teatro e letteratura' ['Theatre and Literature' 1918], the Sicilian author manifests an explicit phobia toward the passage from written text to stage, where translation (traduzione), is the equivalent of betrayal (tradimento). By definition, theatre will always be unfaithful to the *original* creation of the poet. Consequently, according to Pirandello, the *indefinite* quality of that which is represented on stage must not contaminate the primordial *Urszene* – the hidden and thus, invisible vision of the poetic act.

However, with such a 'spiritualistic allergy,' one cannot avoid a *humoristic* contradiction regarding the very nature of the hidden text prior to its fall onto the natural world of the spectacle. Such a contradiction originates in the clash between a centripetal and a centrifugal phase of the written work. In the centripetal phase, the play is an organon, a structure made up of internal relations and maintaining a dynamic balance that leads one back to its creator or to a severe, ancient, sacred archetype from whose inspiration the *action* of the text has taken shape. In the centrifugal phase, on the other hand, the work seems to be a chaotic force field, in which various characters are propelled into the foreground by an egocentric impulse, each claiming the entire space of the story to be his or her own and expecting to impose his or her own version of the plot on the others.

Who, then, is the originator of the drama in such a case? Is it the creator, that is, the father? Or is it the created, that is, the offspring? Any transposition onto the stage, besides being devalued by idealistic hypotheses, bears the burden of the irremediable aporias of such a fracture. The mandate of the character thus oscillates between the charismatic identity conferred by the author-god within a harmonious and well-disciplined outline, and the neurotic fixation or rebellious compulsion that turns the character into a voice of sorrow, forced to seek realization outside the text, perhaps in the body of an actor. Unquestionably, the character, by isolating himself or herself in a pathetic, foolish ambition of autonomy and shattering his or her relationships with the other dramatis personae, eventually and inevitably decomposes or falls apart. This type of character is a pure and organic *form*, or alternatively, an accumulation of obscure *forces* and ambiguous tensions. He or she is the type of character who offers himself or herself to the bewildered interpreter – the actor – who is thoroughly inadequate as a medium.

Moreover, it may be said that Pirandello urges his actors *to serve* his characters, and not to use them. He presses actors to eliminate their own presence in the evocation of the absent. (These are archaic, shamanistic aspects of Pirandello's gothic-romantic aesthetics.) Pirandello, furthermore, often exposes the risks and obstacles of experiencing a trance state, of embarking on a voyage toward the land of the 'dead.' Suffice it here to cite as examples his metatheatrical short story, 'Il pipistrello' ['The Bat,' 1920], or his play *Questa sera si recita a soggetto* [*Tonight We Improvise*, 1930], to illustrate this point. During the period in which his paradoxical vocations as dramatist and *capocomico* were developing, Pirandello wrote narrative works, from *Il fu Mattia Pascal* [*The Late Mattia Pascal*, 1904] to *Si gira* ... [*Shoot!*], 1915) and *Uno, nessuno e centomila* [*One, Nobody, and One Hundred Thousand*, 1925–6], in which he prompts the monologuing character, the narrating 'I,' to disintegrate and sink into multiformity and indistinctness. This occurs through the apologetic 'multiple personality' seen in paranormal and schizoid states that no actor, no matter how pure, willing, ascetic, and detached from ego he or she may be, could ever successfully portray.[1]

It must be remembered, on the other hand, that in the kind of prehistory it experiences in the short stories, the Pirandellian character is pushed to the margins by the author, overburdened by unbearable situations in an anxious and precarious existence. Squalid, petit-bourgeois décors, merciless hostility displayed by social institutions, poor incomes, excessive responsibility burdening heads of families, unpredictable diseases – everything contributes in a hyper-naturalistic setting to force this *travet*, this insignificant mortal not guaranteed by history, in a time of underdevelopment in the South and proletarization of the lower classes, a time between Adua and the First World War, to 'make his/her exit,' so to speak, tempted by self-destructive gestures. This Pirandellian character succumbs to persecution fantasies, fiendish grudges, foolish ambitions, and flights toward fantasy and madness, and is plagued by recurring provocations toward suicide. All of these constitute the character's desperate and impotent psychological answers to domestic hellishness, to an alienating job, to bureaucratic hierarchy, and to an environment that does not allow the development of any kind of mundane social self-affirmation. From 'Il professor terremoto' ['Professor Earthquake,' 1910] to 'Il treno ha fischiato' ['The Train Whistled,' 1914], from 'La trappola' ['The Trap,' 1912] and 'Tu ridi' ['You Laugh,' 1912] to 'Rimedio: la geografia' ['Remedy: Geography,' 1920], from 'Visitare gli infermi' ['To Visit the Sick,' 1896] to 'La camera in attesa' ['The Room Awaiting,' 1916], we witness a continuous accumulation of affronts and provocations in an increasingly conflictual and uninhabitable society, an accumulation to which perhaps 'La morte addosso' ['With Death On,' 1918] offers the most coherent and liberating solution.

Death is, in fact, the spectre that haunts these ironically macabre pages. Death is wished for one's oppressors or feared for one's loved ones. Death is also at times wished for a useless and cumbersome body, releasing one to the *beyond*, the only form of indemnity or compensation. These short stories function as a kind of metaphysical laboratory, a rite of passage, a way of the Cross marked by derisive and humiliating stations that quickly provoke a tormented disgust for socialized life and motivate a progressive movement away from its values and seductions. Before climbing onto (or descending upon) the stage, therefore, the 'victim' is relieved of all his or her bonds, purged of such funereal ceremonials, *disembodied*, and thereby turned into a mysterious shadow, a bizarre creature that emerges from the author's disenchanted pages (the author on several occasions being disguised as a slothful attorney), a ghost that prowls behind the author's back, pathetic and pusillanimous, prepared to bounce onto an esoteric stage. Often, spectres are evoked by the melancholy of a live person who has been deprived of the loved one. This is the case in 'Notizie del mondo' ['News from the World,' 1901], or 'I pensionati della memoria' ['The Pensioners of Memory,' 1914] or the second 'Colloqui coi personaggi' ['Colloquia with Characters,' 1915].

In any case, such ectoplasmic apparitions generated by torment, by desire, and by the imaginary world of the narrating subject, signalled Luigi Pirandello's official entrance, one which could no longer be postponed, into the world of theatre, with an explicitly transcendental choice. Such an event took place in the years of world carnage, and of global mourning when human losses were weighing heavily upon an entire generation. This period is also well within romanticism, with borrowings from an archaic peasant culture, in an atmosphere of the *fantastic* stirred by expressionist winds that endowed the term 'fantastic' with the meaning Todorov intended – that of suspension of judgment. In fact, Pirandello's petulant shadows are born of an author who is ideologically dissociated between a scientific, positivistic upbringing and repeated borrowings from idealism.

Thus we can explain the essence of the philosopher at the centre of 'All'uscita' ['At the Gate,' 1916]. This dead man who expresses his own sophistic disillusionment in the mists of the cemetery prefigures the long series of philosophical *raisonneurs* who do not live on the stage, but rather limit themselves to watching others live. They are epic subjects, not dramatic ones; they are the implacable and transgressive commentators who sabotage themselves as they attempt to construct their own mask of respectability, to develop some so-called 'drawing room' coherence, and thereby to ensure for themselves an ontological security. Lamberto Laudisi, Leone Gala, Angelo Baldovino, Luca Fazio – these characters and others like them are endowed with an alienating vertical gaze towards the world. They are the heroes of a dialectic theatre, heads without bodies, words without meaning, empty shells narcissistically gratified by their own lack of *being*. These explosive and dizzying arguers launch 'daring' bombs onto the orchestra (as Gramsci noted during his stint as a reporter), flushing out the contradictions between *Il piacere dell'onestà* [*The Pleasure of Honesty*, 1918] and *Il giuoco delle parti* [*The Rules of the Game*, 1919], between the roles people play on the exterior, and their hidden drives or instincts.

The motif of adultery, with an emphasis on cuckoldry, that was used in various ways in previous bourgeois dramas, such as Giuseppe Giacosa's *Tristi amori* [*Sad Loves*, 1887] and Marco Praga's *La moglie ideale* [*The Ideal Wife*, 1890] is recycled by Pirandello. He adds a grotesque twist, with a form that is more exasperated and nihilistic than the typical works of Italian theatre of the grotesque, since the simulacrum of the philosopher must practice asceticism in its most pure form, leaving aside 'conjugal honour,' adulterous passion, and the bloodstained heritage of the Italian verismo. Problematic and relativistic, Pirandello's protagonist demolishes the institution of matrimony, undermining its very foundations and uncovering the skeletons hidden in closets, perhaps those from past transgressions (see, for instance, *Tutto per bene* [*All for the Best*, 1920]). He simulates derisory contracts, as happens for instance in *Pensaci, Giacomino!* [*Better Think Twice About It!*, 1916], or he resorts to the carnivalesque by portraying marriage with animalistic bunglings, as happens in *L'uomo, la bestia e la virtù* [*Man, Beast, and Virtue*, 1919]. In other cases, he lowers familial orthodoxy to the level of an orgiastic paroxysm typical of tribal celebrations (see *Il signore della nave* [*Our Lord of the Ship*, 1924]). But the *raisonneur* is not content to parody the Philistine formalism of petit-bourgeois prudery. He does not limit himself to frustrating the economic and sexual property of the bunglers and of the supercilious secondary players who are involved in a muddle of vanity; he goes well beyond that. His ferocious quest for the rules of etiquette, which regulate civilized society on and off stage, projects its feverish and apocalyptic

Families of Characters and Families of Actors 69

vocation onto the connecting points of the play, onto the mechanisms that underlie interpersonal communication and ensure consistency in the conflicts.

Through incessant uttering, silence and night are reached. The dialectic theatre owes its irresistible tendency towards metatheatrical solutions to the 'disturbed' presence of its logical reasoner. As early as 1917, in *Il berretto a sonagli* [*Cap and Bells*], we witness some allusive intrusions into the metastage coinciding with the genesis of the character of the philosopher (here, Ciampa, the humble scribe).[2] Thanks to the stratagem of madness imposed on the mistress, Ciampa avoids taking any kind of vengeful or punitive actions that would be seen within the repertory of the familial Grand Guignol. He rises above these, emerging as the lone 'director' of the final solutions, the authentic spokesperson of the author inasmuch as he is conscious of the play in action and the fiction embodied by the 'marionettes'; he is aware of the pulling of the 'strings,' and suggests gestures and cues to the other characters, not only in order to silence the crowd of gossips, but also to bring about the dropping of the curtain. Through the torment that strips him of his dignity, of his status as a respected man, he is capable of resorting to the shrewdness of the *servus malus*, a typical figure of Plautus's tradition, a complicated servant involved in aiding his master in the ancient *atellanae*. In so doing Ciampa can substitute the author's initiatives, and reach a painfully cerebral limbo, such as the one experienced by Serafino Gubbio, the narrator of *Si gira ...*, the underground hero who plays with the nonsense of passions. Jealousy and morbid attachments involve transforming oneself into a marionette moved by plots the self cannot control. One becomes, figuratively speaking, a slave to scripts that are worn-out and dangerous, dangerous to the intellectual freedom of the self. Such a theme became a trademark of Rosso di San Secondo's more didactic and emphatical texts. As Ciampa takes leave of his adversaries and removes himself from the story, thereby relegating the wife (his master's in the metamorphosis of text, and his own in real life!) to an asylum, the clownish sneer on his face may be compared to the gloomy, slothful grimace of the king in *Enrico IV* [*Henry IV*, 1921]; in both these works the solitude of the creator is hinted at with a triumphant good-bye to the every-day; this solitude, however, is veined by a melancholy furor.

Without the body, without the material nature of life as condensed into the heretofore-cancelled presence of the woman, the male hero will be able to venture into lost and intriguing labyrinths of dramaturgy, a dramaturgy which becomes free of codes, of recognizable functioning. The dramaturgical machine jams, while the interruptions and digressions have the advantage over the *fabula*. *Enrico IV* is a discovery of the impossibility of penetrating the mystery of the Other, of breaking down the mysterious wall which everyone constructs in order to defend one's own ineffable inner life. Even earlier, Lamberto Laudisi in *Così è (se vi pare)* [*Right You Are (If You Think So)*, 1917] converses with himself at the mirror as though he were faced with another person. But it is in *Sei personaggi in cerca d'autore* (1921) that autism reaches its disconsolate climax. Here, the line of argument on the theatre annihilates theatre itself; it undermines the possibilities for internal impact. In fact, gestures no longer represent the character from which they originate. The Father's enraged anger attests to this, as he is surprised at the bordello, ignorant of the fact that he is about to copulate with his stepdaughter. Semantic conventions differ among the various interlocutors, each one's words conveying uncommon meanings; sound and meaning do not coincide in the speaker and in the listener. What ensues is, then, not only the impossibility of interpreting others' existential situations, but also a slow movement towards aphasia.

Thus, a scene based on conversation and prudent, diversionary chatter, makes way for a nexus of shouting vs. silence, in which a subjectivity made up of dreamt-up horrors and delirious confessions is shattered among bewitching images. In effect, the narrative plots of the metatheatrical series, from *Così è (se vi pare)* to *Sei personaggi in cerca d'autore*, from *Ciascuno a suo modo* [*Each in His Own Way*, 1924] to the aforementioned *Questa sera si recita a soggetto*, are marked by a woeful, emotional complexity, and by turbid and morbid 'slices of life' in which the institution of the family is ravaged by traumas much more grisly than mere love triangles. The eccentricities of these relationships are pushed to limits of unprecedented, oneiric permissiveness. As an example, we see the strange pair comprised of mother-in-law and son-in-law in the Laudisi drawing room, while the unknown recluse (not unlike the character of Leonora, from the corresponding short story, who will reemerge in *Questa sera si recita a soggetto*) is to be found in the turret. In the morbidity of the relationship and the elimination of certain personal papers swept away by an earthquake (this is paraphrased various times in *Ciascuno a suo modo*) something both dark and awful, not definable within the realm of perspective relativism, is hidden and shown at the same time. In an analogous manner, in

Sei personaggi in cerca d'autore, the explicit incestuous tension touched on in the main scene has even more of an impact when it is coupled with the slaughter of two innocents (the children who are sacrificed in the small garden), an act which we would describe as uncanny, in the Freudian sense, for the event almost seems to expiate the sins of the adults. Meanwhile, the continuous references to 'waking,' to convention and to the falsity of staging, are perhaps the nocturnal 'compromises' used in order to go beyond the taboos of the images.

In the two subsequent installments of Pirandello's metatheatre, *Ciascuno a suo modo* and *Questa sera si recita a soggetto*, we encounter stories that are less disconcerting than those previously discussed. In *Ciascuno a suo modo*, we find a decadent couple who torment each other; this theme of the *amour haineux* [hateful love] adds Anglo-Byzantine and Russian flavours. And, as previously mentioned, in *Questa sera si recita a soggetto* we encounter the recluse in the turret. What is emphasized in these plays is the lack of symmetry of the internal passages. In fact, we notice strident ruptures at all levels: between the figure of the author-father (who is evermore absent) and the characters; between actor and spectator; between annoyed critic and interrupted performance. The play between time and space is shattered and at times dilated to encompass the orchestra and the foyer, with large posters on the entrance walls and the street itself, in an ambiguous Futurist revival that places the accent on death or on the jamming of the dramaturgical machine. Even though Pirandello's writing is able to triumphantly handle the complete destructuring of the staging, the stage itself becomes overwhelmed by new media, or invaded by contaminating elements, with forms of urban spectacles from melodrama to jazz, from religious procession to variety show and cinema. This is due to the fact that the theatre is no longer the central medium in the modern city that exists somewhere in between mass culture and totalitarian regime. The collapse of drama into the chaotic Babel of the metropolis, where the crisis of the self reclaims different, more rapid and nervous techniques in order to free itself, is parallel to the kind of stage we have alluded to here, a stage that renounces its logical and discursive tools, given the driven outburst of the unconscious that can emerge only from unconnected and confused images.[3]

Meanwhile, in the first-person novels, Mattia Pascal, through Serafino Gubbio, has become Vitangelo Moscarda, the Sternian hero of *Uno, nessuno e centomila*. The storyteller has detached himself fully from the return to earth, and has rid himself of the temptations of a gratifying mask. Mattia, for instance, who yearned for a comforting existence, searching for it in unforeseen winnings at the roulette table and love liaisons, is replaced by Vitangelo, who suddenly and unexpectedly breaks his familial ties and leaves behind his relationship despite the fact that it is not a negative one. Vitangelo renounces material goods, and, like Serafino Gubbio and Mattia, lives a series of intermittent and ecstatic epiphanies, outside the shell of the body in which the self may be found, outside the unhappy and tired consciousness of one's own syllogistic categories. To this category of nihilistic pantheism we could easily add Hinkfuss, the deformed salesman of commercialized images and irresistible sensations who sells [his merchandise] to an audience dazzled by surprises and sensuous, sensual findings. The limping Hinkfuss acts, in fact, as a kind of organizing element which governs the flux and cross-overs of self-affirming trances and redeeming reawakenings between the stage and the hall in *Questa sera si recita a soggetto*. Hinkfuss is, in other words, the *deus ex machina* of postmodern theatre who can do nothing but reject the theatrical form.

The only remaining option is to flee the city, to withdraw towards enchanted and fated landscapes, travelling through old, familiar routes, with the joyous self-assurance of the charlatans and street minstrels, in search of unknown audiences. The destiny of fortune/misfortune befalls the eccentric troupe that becomes lost on the mysterious island of *I giganti della montagna* [*The Mountain Giants*]. This work is somewhat testamentary for Pirandello given that it was begun in 1931 and never completed. At this final stage, Pirandello's drama enters the realm of the *mythical,* in its blend of Dionysian and Apollonian themes with frantic oscillation between Gothic darkness and Mediterranean luminosity. In the final phase of Pirandello's short fiction we experience a similar reversal of registers; this phase coincides with the re-presentation (no longer mediated by scientific censorship) of symbolist bric-à-brac, now in a surreal version. From 'Di sera, un geranio' ['One Night, a Geranium,' 1934] to 'Effetti di un sogno interrotto' ['Effects of an Interrupted Dream,' 1936], from 'I piedi sull'erba' ['Feet on Grass,' 1934] to 'Una giornata' ['A Day,' 1936], the perceived indetermination narrated by the page reaches its climax: mirrors, windows, paintings become magic agents of a playful and numinous sarabande in which it is no longer possible to distinguish between who is looking and who is looked at, between the external eye and the scrutinized icon. That which is lived and that which is dreamed, the past and the present, the real and the oneiric, all become indistinguishable, and their respective indicators, confused.

Within the arsenal of apparitions present among the court of miracles of the unhappy but privileged 'Scalognati' (the 'captive' guests in *I giganti della montagna*) we see desire being staged and we witness the surfacing of the deepest recesses of the human psyche, the most shameful aspects of the human soul, spurred on by celestial tunes or inexplicable visual fragments. Private follies, ancient magic, and occultist phenomena are thus imprinted on the internal walls of the mysterious abode, reminding us of Madame Pace (resuscitated from *Sei personaggi*) who is, in a sense, conjured up again with great ardor in the kind of 'foreign' language we witness in *Sogno (ma forse no)* [*I Dream (Perhaps Not)*, 1929].

The work of art in the age of technical reproduction, on the heels of and in competition with the cinema (let us not forget that 1929 is also the year of Pirandello's acceptance of the silent cinema, after he overcame his initial aversion for the medium expressed in *Si Gira* ...), finds its epitaph in this animistic return and along with its humoristic rebirth. This occurs due to Pirandello's focus on the *mythic* trilogy – *I giganti della montagna, La nuova colonia* [*The New Colony*, 1928] and *Lazzaro* [*Lazarus*, 1929] – in which we find mystic shamanism and a pursuit of prodigious and elaborate *coups de théâtre*. The character of the philosopher slowly disappears, and the *raisonneur* of the dialectic brand of theatre becomes silent. Pirandello's dramaturgy no longer attempts to come to terms with the dialectal overindulgences of Angelo Musco, nor does it pursue Ruggero Ruggeri's guttural, falsetto voice; even the faithful actor, Lamberto Picasso, is demoted and fades into the woodwork.

Conversely, what is aimed at is a lyricizing rigidity, an oratory whose goal is to be sublime. The figure of the father-author is definitely absent, condemned to sterility, to a sort of stiffening (as in *Quando si è qualcuno* [*When Someone Is Somebody*], 1933) or to suicide, as happens with the poet in the preface to *I giganti della montagna*. Pirandello's words become *poetic*; they retreat into the ritualistic etymon of the spell. They acquire the ability to evoke and to create reality, allowing, for instance, a young, paralyzed girl to regain her ability to walk in *Lazzaro*, or causing the island of the wicked to disappear in *La nuova colonia* by triggering an expiatory seaquake. These scenes are *meant* to be staged. Gone from Pirandello's work are the ontological fall, the compromise between taboo and desire; these scenes correspond to religious practices that demand rigorous protocols, solemn gestures, and miracle-working pronunciation. And it is now the female actor, not the male, who performs the indispensable task of *minister* in order to achieve thaumaturgical efficacy.

Marta Abba becomes an emblem, our Pirandellian goddess, the 'Nostra Dea,' from the 1925 play by Massimo Bontempelli of the same title, a work that inaugurated the vibrant and tender collaboration between the actress and Pirandello. Pirandello's later feminine roles were created for Abba: Tuda in *Diana e la Tuda* [*Diana and Tuda*, 1927], Marta in *L'amica delle mogli* [*The Wives' Friend*, 1929], Sara in *Lazzaro*, the 'Sconosciuta' (or Unknown Character) in *Come tu mi vuoi* [*As You Desire Me*, 1930], Donata in *Trovarsi* [*To Find Oneself*, 1932], the Russian Veroccia in *Quando si è qualcuno*. The role of Ilse in *I giganti della montagna* was also meant to be played by Abba. Pirandello's writing for Abba and her performances of his roles constituted a phase of coded correspondence between the two, a manneristic code, both public and private, which intertwined the two individuals, revealing an unresolved tension between animality and spirituality, between physiological and esthetic motherhood. To be sure, there had been other actresses whom Pirandello had utilized frequently and on whom he had based characters, but these characters were all constructed on a type of vamp; think, for instance, of Nestoroff in *Si gira ...* or Moreno in *Ciascuno a suo modo* – roles which were based perhaps on the type of fatuous and unstable character sketches found in the early novel *Suo marito* [*Her Husband*, 1911] or in the metatheatrical glimpses of *Sei personaggi*. By the time of Marta Abba, this sketch has been updated as the character's motivations had become more complex. The characteristics of instability, impulsiveness, intolerance towards both bourgeois decorum and male authority, altruism and selflessness, disdainful and quivering sensuality, physical dissatisfaction, anxious inspiration, craving for the 'other,' and disgust towards one's own body, are all creations that converge in Marta Abba, at least as she was culturally mythicized. The characters based on these traits are *divinely* disturbed, and on stage they are able to find an otherwise negated centre, a momentary salvation, precisely because of the fact that their physicality, exhibited yet negated, evokes the phantom of the poet. The stage thus becomes the point of inevitable mediation for a metaphoric pregnancy of an immaculate conception. In the act of fiction, bodies become shadows and shadows become flesh, and the author-character himself, of his own will, melds completely with the author who has become a character, who in turn becomes an offspring of his own creation.

Motherhood is a theme taken up obsessively by Pirandello again and again; it becomes a global theme, a dramaturgical form. The mother/infant duo inspires devotional solidarity, as is seen in the euphoristically catastrophic finale of *La nuova colonia*, or in the initiatory and regressive voyage of *La favola del figlio cambiato* [*The Fable of the Transformed Son*, 1934]. This mother/infant duo is able to overcome the isolation to which the individual is condemned; the 'other' is no longer a repelling wall. For La Spera, the prostitute, in *La nuova colonia* or Sara, the rebellious adulteress in *Lazzaro*, the process of transformation from matter into spirit rises to an astonishing level due to the metamorphosis of the actress-protagonist. This is because a special kind of maternity is needed, a maternity not restricted by the narrow confines of a prosaic and neuroticizing solitude, as in *La vita che ti diedi* [*The Life I Gave You*, 1923] or in *O di uno o di nessuno* [*Either One's or Nobody's*, 1929]. Likewise, an explosive femininity is necessary, a femininity capable of undertaking a winning role or at least a role having poetic connotations – in other words, a role distinct from the suffering, beaten heroines in the earlier dramas, from *La signora Morli, una e due* [*Mrs Morli, One and Two*, 1920] to *Vestire gli ignudi* [*To Clothe the Naked*, 1922]. At this point, all traces of patrilineal heritage are erased, and the pedagogical conflicts between husband and wife for the possession of children are shifted and bestowed imperiously onto the woman.

The cultural referents for the development of such a 'feminist' mythology of the oceanic mother may be a combination of demographic propaganda, Fascist incentives for a theatre designed for the masses, and ideology and iconography of the *strapaese*. And yet this apologia of the *anima* (as opposed to the apologia of the *animus*), this tormented devotion to the 'other' that only a woman and only an actress can incorporate into her being, this inexhaustible, often excessive and rather verbose *profession de foi* which favours the great mother figures, this selfsame peremptory affirmation that a society laughing at this value is destined to perish (see the allusive prophecy in *I giganti della montagna*) – all these preserve their unquestionably provocatory charge, even today, from the point of view of the theatrical performer who takes on a role in any kind of dramatic work.

Translated by Lucia Di Rosa and Manuela Gieri

NOTES

1 For a detailed analysis of the theme of 'character vs. actor' in the dramatic works of Luigi Pirandello, please refer, first and foremost, to the two recent volumes of *Maschere nude*, ed. Alessandro D'Amico (Milan: Mondadori, vol. 1, 1986; vol. 2, 1993), for their vast amount of documentary and philological material. An entertaining contribution by Ferdinando Taviani, removed from D'Amico's work and polemic towards the preceding scholarly works, is published in *La rivista dei libri* (December 1993), 12–14. See also a volume by D'Amico and Alessandro Tinterri, *Pirandello capocomico: la compagnia del teatro d'arte di Roma, 1925–1928* (Palermo: Sellerio, 1987).
2 In relation to Pirandello's dialect plays, see Sarah Zappulla Muscarà, ed., *Tutto il teatro dialettale di Luigi Pirandello*, 2 vols. (Milan: Bompiani, 1993). For a theoretical background, I would suggest my own works, Paolo Puppa, *Dalle parti di Pirandello* (Rome: Bulzoni, 1987), 117–41, and *La parola alta: Sul teatro di Pirandello e D'Annunzio* (Rome: Laterza, 1993), 3–50.
3 A fundamental work is Claudio Vicentini, *Pirandello: Il disagio del teatro* (Venice: Marsilio, 1993). Also useful are: Siro Ferrone, 'I ruoli teatrali secondo Pirandello. *Pensaci, Giacomino!*' Ariel 3 (1986): 100–7; Giuseppina Romano Ronchira, *Pirandello capocomico e regista nelle testimonianze e nella critica* (Bari: Adriatica, 1987); Gigi Livio, *La scena italiana: Materiali per una storia dello spettacolo dell'ottocento e del novecento* (Milan: Mursia, 1989), 148–216; Roberto Alonge, '*Il giuoco delle parti*, atto primo: un atto tabù,' in *Pirandello fra penombre e porte socchiuse: la tradizione scenica del Giuoco delle parti* (Turin: Rosenberg Sellier, 1991), 7–59; and Mirella Schino, 'La crisi metateatrale degli anni venti,' in Luciana Martinelli, ed., *Diffrazioni/Pirandello* (Rome: Japadre, 1993), 137–61.

6

The Making and Unmaking of Language: The Rhetoric of Speech and Silence

MARIA ANTONIETTA GRIGNANI

There are as many truths as there are those who perceive things; naturally, assuming they are searching for the truth. On the other hand, truth is nonsense anyway. For example, even now, I see myself differently than you do, and you see me differently than I see you, and all this mingles, becoming something completely different than that which we perceive, deferred and extravagant, in the moment it occurs. This is true for all those who write; for them it should constitute a new truth.

Thomas Bernhard, *Until the Loss of Hearing and Sight*

First, an explanation of the title is necessary. 'The making and unmaking of language' alludes to a book by Roman Jakobson which studies specular relations between language at its birth in a child and language in the state of dissolution in various forms of aphasia. In our case this phrase serves merely as a convenient metaphor to refer to the themes and rhetoric of our topic. In Pirandello, there is never either stuttering or stream of consciousness, nor are there really any surrealistic free-associations – at the most, prelinguistic expression might play a part.

The Pirandellian subject is full of contradictions and unsoundable depth; he or she is a person who suffers upon being transformed into a mask or multiplied into a thousand different characters. It is a wounded subjectivity that, upon self examination, attaches itself to the rationalization of its own precariousness, fully aware as well of the precariousness of language.[1] When logical paths lead him or her to a dead end or a recognition of his or her humanity before an overwhelming mystery, the subject may wind up breaking the discursive pact that organizes linguistically the instance of communication among the I/you demarcators.[2]

Another preliminary clarification regards the term 'rhetoric.' In *Soggettivismo e oggettivismo nell'arte narrativa* [*Subjectivism and Objectivism in Narrative Art*, 1908] Pirandello takes issue with the last great priests of style, that is, with the ones who excommunicate common language and 'considera la forma come alcunché d'esteriore, di posticcio, e l'immagine come un tropo o un traslato retorico da appiccicare all'acconciatura stilistica quasi un pennacchio o una gemma o uno svolazzo'[3] [considers the form as something exterior, artificial, and the image as a trope or an ornamental metaphor to be stuck to its stylistic hairdo almost like a plume or a gem or a flourish]. In the same year, Pirandello also dedicated an entire chapter of *L'umorismo* (part 1, section 4) to the reproof of any exuberant conception of embellishment, because he identifies rhetoric with imitation and stylistic adornment, according to a derogatory interpretation of the term which was particularly widespread in the last years of the nineteenth and the first years of the twentieth centuries, an interpretation that was justified by the rebellion against ages of dogmatic teaching. In this essay Pirandello states: 'La Retorica, in somma, era come un guardaroba: il guardaroba dell'eloquenza dove i pensieri nudi andavano a vestirsi ... Così i pensieri facevan da manichini alla forma-vestiario.'[4] ['Rhetoric, in short, was like a wardrobe, the wardrobe of eloquence to which naked thoughts went to get dressed ... Thus, thoughts were like mannequins dressed with the apparel of form.'][5]

Pirandello continues by stating that in periods where rhetoric as constituent harmony or 'accordo logicamente ordinato' [logically ordered agreement] dominates, there is no space for humour, given that it 'per il suo intimo, specioso, essenziale processo, inevitabilmente *scompone*, disordina, discorda'[6] ['in its inner and peculiarly essential process inevitably *dismantles*, splits and disrupts'[7]]. A rhetoric understood as a rigid classification of works into stringent literary genres is the enemy of humorists, who have always rebelled against the straight-jacket of traditional literary education, and roamed freely within the judicious bulkheads of genres and rigid registers of writing.

After thirty years of neorhetorical studies spanning from Perelman to the present day,[8] we can now reflect without prejudice on the status of persuasive speech, as well as over the techniques by which one argues in favour of and/or against a given topic of discussion, and over the rhetorical efficacy of the figures of speech. Now that such prejudice has been eliminated, Pirandello appears to be a suitable writer as he defines himself a philosophical author and organizes a highly mobile writing style in which sentiment and reflection coexist in perennial counterpoint. Reflection dismantles sentiment, turning it inside out like a glove, deranging the harmonic organization of images, and inducing the receiver to adhere to the ideas being presented. Pirandello maintains that reflection is like a mirror 'd'acqua diaccia, in cui la fiamma del sentimento non si rimira soltanto, ma si tuffa e si smorza: il friggere dell'acqua è il riso che suscita l'umorista.'[9] ['of icy water, in which the flame of feeling not only looks at itself but also plunges in it and extinguishes itself: the sizzling of the water is the laughter that the humorist evokes.'[10]]. This process produces a cold shower of images not 'associate per similazione o per contiguità' [associated by similarity or contiguity], but rather, by contrast. The result is a thorough overturn of the naturalistic model, a practice intending to surprise the reader, and a commendation of digression as a perpetual flight from the linearity of the story: such a subversive strategy aims at pillorying classical rhetoric through the implementation of a counterrhetoric conceived as the art of unmasking and persuasion.

Alexander Pope's satirical essay *Peri Bathous* comes to mind. In this short essay satirizing the rhetoric of the sublime Pope creates a rhetoric of satire insofar as it is a structurally argumentative metagenre, that is one geared to persuade rather than to move. In chapter 5 of *Peri Bathous*, we find an image of a reversed telescope; in *L'umorismo* Pirandello employs a similar image as an example for the sentiment of the contrary: if a man appears 'small' by looking through a reversed telescope, the awareness of his infinite 'smallness' makes him a giant morally – 'Ma è anche vero che se poi egli si sente grande e un umorista viene a saperlo, gli può capitare come a Gulliver, gigante a Lilliput e balocco tra le mani dei giganti di Brobdingnag'[11] ['But it is also true that if then he feels like a giant and a humorist finds out, Gulliver's fate will await him, a giant in Lilliput and a plaything in the hands of the giants of Brobdingnag'].[12] A reversed rhetoric highlights the estranged perception of the universe by the dialogic provocation that is so profoundly typical in satire.

The defamiliarization of the commonplace and the grotesque contrast of the images are fortes of most Pirandellian narrators. As Renato Barilli has noted, they personally assume investigative responsibility with a constant display of sermocinatory argumentation: the soliloquy of autodiegetic narrators has nothing to do with the confession that relapses into the consciousness of the subject; rather, it is similar to forensic address geared at convincing judge and public line after line.[13]

Theoreticians of persuasive discourse underline the importance of those figures of *presence* that render the object of speech 'real' and topical to the consciousness of the listener: among these, of fundamental importance are the *sermocinatio*, by which the orator introduces another person to speak, and *dialogism*, or fictive dialogue by which one speaks in a question and answer format. Through pseudo-direct speech, a persuasive strategy is activated, one that exploits the aporias of the others' opinions, thus allowing the argument of the main speaker to triumph. Another indispensable practice rests in the figures of *comunione* that create an impression of solidarity with the audience through rhetorical interrogation, apostrophe, and so forth.

The theatricality of the novels with a protagonist-narrator indeed derives from the flattening of the object of narration and by its projection on the actualizing level of a dialogism that absorbs both the time of the narrative and the time of the reader – the latter usually being external in narrative works (it is in theatre that the spectator identifies with chain of events taking place on the stage).[14]

In Pirandello's works, the overcoming of naturalism is therefore brought about by a disturbance of the novel form, which was characterized by the perfectly balanced relationship between diegesis and mimesis within a linear temporal development. The invasion of the Pirandellian *raisonneur* compresses the index of reality of the various temporal domains, and places them at the service of his argumentation. It is thus the triumph of quick repartee enunciation, of theatricalization of one's own speech and of others, that is a speech bearing an ideology to be contested.

Il fu Mattia Pascal [*The Late Mattia Pascal*, 1904] begins by threatening the *memoir* of an extraordinary event and engaging the reader in a close dialogue with the promise of true revelations and overturnings of certainties, in an atmosphere of duplicity characterized by the autobiographer's emotions and by the 'fantastic critic's' humoristic deconstructions that reduce the number of factual details in favour of reflection. The progressive doublings before the mirror and the vertiginous dialogues between the late Mattia Pascal, Adriano Meis, and the writing subject (who is himself deceased according to the General Register Office) permeate a recitative which becomes increasingly puzzling as it acquires a growing awareness of the divorce between words and things. The various statements 'I say,' 'you think,' 'here it is,' and 'excuse me,' the spatial indicators, the emphatic iterations, and the allocutions all conceal the senselessness of experience with the illusion of a speech uttered *in presentia*.

In *Quaderni di Serafino Gubbio operatore* [*Notebooks of Serafino Gubbio, Cameraman*, 1925], Serafino Gubbio takes delight in producing digressions and exempla for humoristic ends, as when he catches the reader ('you ladies and gentlemen') and makes him/her the protagonist of a snipe hunt in order to reverse the anthropocentric point of view:

Retorica, è vero? Eh sì, caro; non vi sdegnate troppo; lo riconosco anch'io: retorica, perché noi, per grazia di Dio, siamo uomini e non beccaccini. Il beccaccino, lui, senza timore di far della retorica, potrebbe sì porre il paragone e chiedere che almeno gli uomini che vanno per piacere a caccia, non chiamino feroci le bestie. (II.3, p. 553)[15]

[Rhetoric, you say? Ah, yes, my friend; do not be too contemptuous; I admit as much, myself; rhetoric, because we, by the grace of God, are men and not snipe. The snipe, for his part, without any fear of being rhetorical, might draw the comparison and demand that at least men who go out shooting for pleasure, should not call the beasts savage. (II.3, p. 56)][16]

Dissatisfied with the constant flight into 'humoristic' digressions, Serafino opens illusory spaces between text and extratext: 'Permettete un momento? Vado a vedere la tigre. Dirò, seguiterò a dire, riprenderò il filo del discorso più tardi, non dubitate. Bisogna che vada, per ora, a vedere la tigre.' (II.4, p. 574) ['Will you please excuse me for a moment? I'm going to see the tiger. I will speak, I will continue speaking, I will bring up the topic of our conversation later, don't doubt it. Right now, I must go and see the tiger.' (4:89)]

The protagonist narrator of *Uno, nessuno e centomila* [*One, No One, and One Hundred Thousand*, 1925–6] stretches the boundaries of his directorial domain and makes up for the chaos into which he has plunged because of the discovery of being for others a plural person, different from the way he perceived himself. He thus proceeds to innumerable reflections and then conclusions on the multiplicity of human beings, on the relativity of consciousness, on the impossibility of being a full subject even for oneself, and on the overwhelming distance between language and concept, constructed and not constructed, and human and not human. All this is enacted in a digressive structure that disintegrates the connections within the story and encourages a series of laboratory experiments in which it is not the tale that is pushed forward by the events, but the word that produces the events.

In the literary context, the narrating hero thus constitutes himself as responsible for the construction, management, and presentation of the text. Furthermore he introduces the reader into this mechanism. As allocutions, 'you, my dear friend,' 'ladies and gentlemen,' and 'my good friends' construct a convenient audience drawn into the dialogism with which Moscarda dismantles the strongest psycho-social convictions in order to devise a subversive, persuasive design, rich with arguments based on notional dissociation: appearance against reality, individual against society, conscience against truth, and so forth.[17]

In order to begin our analysis, we may start with an element apparently external to text, the titles. Within the eight books numbered simply I–VIII, one finds no less than sixty-three titles that radicalize a procedure initiated by *Il fu Mattia Pascal*. The chapter titles (or intertitles in Genette's terminology) by definition function as connectives and have meaning only for an addressee already involved in reading a text; they presuppose at least what precedes them and they prepare for what follows. Such intertitles serve to identify the narrative links and to guide the reading.[18]

The thematic regime of chapter titles is of popular origin, and often serves a ludic and whimsical intent. For example, as Genette reminds us, Rabelais places descriptive intertitles in a completing form, 'Comment ...' ['As ...'], followed by a summary of the topic to follow. Moreover, Cervantes at times alludes, with a humorous wink, to the variable action of reading – 'This will be read by the one who reads,' – or writing – 'This treats things that regard this story and not another.'[19] In *Uno, nessuno e centomila* we find intertitles à la Rabelais, such as 'Com'erano per me Marco di Dio e sua moglie Diamante' ['As Marco di Dio and his wife looked to me'] and more often the announcement of a topic, recalled then to the letter by an enunciation within the chapter. For example, 'Scoperte' [Discoveries, III.2], appears at the end of the chapter in a nominal and exclamative phrase, 'Ah, che scoperta! Mio padre ... la vita di mio padre ...' (790) [Ah, what a discovery! My father ... the life of my father ...] and 'Nuvole e vento' [Clouds and wind, II.9] is repeated in an isolated paragraph.

In a digressive, nomadic, and, in substance, centrifugal book, the cataphoric wink and the resumption certainly carry out the function of provoking and holding attention on the focal point of a single thematic nucleus. However, the fact is that the proliferation of intertitles also responds to a peculiar impulse, to the strangeness of unexpected associations, so that from these focal points, actualized through the stratagem of the resumed title, the anti-novelistic nature of the book is reinforced as its narrative tightness is constantly threatened by the vocation to essay-writing. We must, therefore, reflect upon the relationship between first person narration and titling, and thus address the problem of the identity of the one who enunciates the titles.

Il fu Mattia Pascal, the general title written in the third person, identifies the historical author as the enunciator. Only two intertitles are attributed to the first person, that is, to the narrating subject: 'Cambio treno' [I change trains], VII; 'Io e l'ombra mia' [Me and my shadow], XV). The lack of a proper noun in the inaugurative title *Uno, nessuno e centomila* deprives the author Pirandello of enunciative attribution and fully confers on the narrating subject the right to title, internally, in the first person: 'Mia moglie e il mio naso' [My wife and my nose, I. 1], 'Com'io volevo esser solo' [The way I wanted to be alone, I. 4], 'Parlo con Bibì' [I talk with Bibì, V. 3], 'Seguito a compromettermi' [I go on compromising myself, VI. 3], and so forth. All this establishes the narrating hero in a literary, as well as a narrative, instance precisely 'as author responsible for the constitution of the text, of its management, of its presentation and conscious of his relationship with the public.'[20]

But, may we ask, conscious of what relationship with the public, and of what kind of reader? We are dealing with a volatile enemy brother, sometimes singular, sometimes generically plural, and other times even numerically specified, as in the eighth chapter of Book III: 'Ecco qua, terra, terra. Siete in cinque? Venite con me.' (III.8, p. 801) ['Here we are, firmly on the ground. There are five of you? Come with me.' (III. 8, p .63)]

This is the exasperation of rhetorical figures of presence, *sermocinatio* and *dialogism*, and of communion, in which the orator aims not at obtaining true information from his audience but at persuading them, making them participate in his excursions of reasoning.[21] Also particular to *Uno, nessuno e centomila* is the fact that within this novel one finds actions that disturb the silent communication of the writing-reading trajectory, mixing the time and space of speech with the unknown, future time and space of the addressee. The spatio-temporal interconnection of that which is within the text (the *chronotopos* in Bakhtin's terminology) vacillates in its conventional foundations of narrative and comment on the narrative, due to the violent infringement of the inter- and extra-textual boundaries.[22]

For example, the title 'E il vostro naso?' [And your nose?, I.2] through direct interrogation produces an illusionistic effect of presence, given that the person who is addressed does not correspond to any of the subjects of the dialogic shifts of the chapter, and bounces back and forth between the crooked nose of Moscarda and the dimple in the chin of a fellow citizen within the chronotopos of the city of Richieri, at the time when the first actions of disintegrating madness of the hero unfolded.

At times the spatio-temporal breakdown has an inverted direction, from the inside towards the outside of the text, as in the title 'Con permesso' [May I come in?, II.3], with which Moscarda moves to the house of the faceless antagonist by knocking, he says, 'all'uscio della vostra stanza' (II.3, p 767) ['at the door of your room' (II.3, p. 29)]. He seats himself in the armchair, tabooed by the sweet memory of a deceased mother, and describes the scene with a punctilious series of spatial indicators: 'Queste sono le vostre seggiole. E questo è un tavolino ... Quella è una finestra che dà sul giardino. E là fuori, quei pini, quei cipressi.' (p. 767) ['These are your chairs. And this is a table ... This is a window that opens on to the garden. And there, outside, are those pines, those cypresses.' (II.3, p. 30)]

The scene, evoked with referential recalls pertaining to the context which is familiar to the fictitious interlocutor, doesn't at all involve an increase in the degree of realism; on the contrary, it aims at damaging the relations between the deictic linguistic form and the referent, a fantasmatic object in flight before the corrosive action of time: 'Andate via da codesta casa; ripassate fra tre o quattr'anni a rivederla con un altro animo da questo d'oggi; vedrete che ne sarà più di codesta cara realtà.' (II.3, p. 768) ['Go away from this house; come back again in three or four years and look at it in a spirit different from today's; you will see what is left of your beloved reality.' (II.3, p. 30)]

Having thus captured the tu/voi in the fictive present of his Socratic-humoristic maieutic system, Moscarda also begins capriciously to manipulate the time of his speech: he actually suspends a chapter with a dilatory 'Vi dirò poi come e perché' [I will tell you how and why] (II.5, p. 33) which is picked up immediately in the next title, 'Anzi ve lo dico adesso' [In fact, I'll tell you now] (II.6). Among quick repartees, postponements, and anticipations, the dialogue with the ghost (to whom the narrator pretends to concede the honor of objections promoted to the status of title) proceeds – 'E dunque?' [So?] (I.8); 'Che c'entra la casa?' [What does the house have to do with it?] (II.7) – while the argumentative end is to amplify the counterstatements of the demiurge. The disturbance of the usual convention of distance between narrator and reader removes the latter's right to silent reception; the reader's interpretative activity is not only aggressively forced, it is even shaken by transfers in the illusionistic laboratory of Moscarda, where the subjectivity of others crumbles in the multiple *voi* [*you*] of the guinea pig reader:

E sono contento che or ora, mentre stavate a leggere questo mio libretto col sorriso un po' canzonatorio che fin da principio ha accompagnato la vostra lettura, due visite, una dentro l'altra siano venute improvvisamente a dimostrarvi quant'era sciocco quel vostro sorriso ... Sù, sù, tornate a leggere questo mio libretto, senza più sorridere come avete fatto finora. Credete pure che, se qualche dispiacere ha potuto recarvi l'esperienza or ora fatta, quest'è niente, mio caro, perché voi non siete due soltanto, ma chi sa quanti, senza saperlo, e credendovi sempre uno. (III.10, pp. 804–6)

[And I am pleased that just now, as you were reading this little book of mine with the somewhat mocking smile that has accompanied your reading from the start, two visits, one inside the other, occurred suddenly to show you how foolish that smile of yours was ... Go on, resume reading this little book of mine, but without smiling any more as you've smiled till now. And bear in mind that if the experience just undergone has caused you some displeasure, this is nothing, my dear friend, because you are not only two, but any number, unawares, believing yourself always one. (III.10, pp. 66–7)]

Here, the metatextual index is exceptional (this little book of mine). The subtitle of the magazine edition (later removed) – 'Considerazioni di Vitangelo Moscarda generali sulla vita degli uomini e particolari sulla propria, in otto libri' [Considerations of Vitangelo Moscarda in general on the life of men and in particular on his own, in eight books] – does not concede much space for reflection on the dimension of narrating in writing and does not even open up to interior monologue when a thought related to the narrated time is reconstructed in the act of remembering. For an entire chapter (the seventh of book V) the reflection of Moscarda's most secret *I*, a soliloquy in parentheses, breaks into the reported conversation between Dida, Quantorzo, and Vitangelo; it is, however, announced by 'Ma io intanto dicevo tra me' [But I, meanwhile, was saying to myself], a title that resembles a theatrical stage direction introducing an aside – a falsely self-communicative stance simulated in public.

The tyranny of dialogic events, maneuvered by the locutory triumphalism of Moscarda, dots all levels of the story with exclamative, interjective, onomatopeic, and even intonational vocal traces, generating a perceptive accentuation along the axis of the 'present without past nor future' and the 'recitative that narrates outside duration' that Debenedetti discussed.[23]

The fury of visual evidence that the mask of speech opposes to the eventual regression into interiority manifests itself in the re-viewing and showing, with referential excess, things and sensations of the past outside every attitude towards *reverie*. The mass of signs made present is symmetric with the physical convocation of the model reader constructed by the text, a convocation which is also emphasized so that it collides with and decomposes in the anxiety of meaning and the flight of the real.

The 'pleasure of alienating myself' experienced by Moscarda in the doubly contradictory actions of eviction of and later donation to Marco di Dio is not related with the narrated action, but parcelled in a sequence of auditory and visual elements using verbs in the present tense:

Ho ancora negli orecchi lo scroscio dell'acqua che cade da una grondaja presso il fanale non ancora acceso, davanti alla catapecchia di Marco di Dio ... e vedo lì ferma lungo i muri, per ripararsi dalla pioggia, la gente che assiste allo sfratto ... Solo che, di tanto in tanto, sento il bisogno d'attaccarmi con gli occhi a qualche cosa, e guardo quasi con indolenza smemorata l'architrave della porta di quella catapecchia, per isolarmi un po' in quella vista ... un malinconico architrave; a cui non importa proprio nulla dei rumori della strada. (IV.7, pp. 831–2)

[I can still hear the sound of the water pouring down from a drainpipe near the still-unlit street lamp in front of Marco di Dio's hovel... and I see there, standing along the walls, for shelter from the rain, the people witnessing the eviction ... Only, from time to time, I feel the need to grasp something with my eyes, and with a show of unthinking indolence I look at the architrave of the door of that hovel, to isolate myself a moment with that sight ... a dreary architrave, indifferent to the noises of the street. (IV.7, pp. 92–3)]

It is precisely the actualizations that are clear symptoms of a relaxing of the anthropocentric point of view, parallel to throwing the logocentric point of view into a state of crisis that passes through criticism of the pronoun *I* and of the proper noun; this is a terrifying metaphor for the empty multiplicity to which the social individual is condemned.

Moscarda then interrupts the captious inference with questions about the right to give appearance and voice to others beyond himself – 'Ma con qual diritto ne parlo? Con qual diritto do qui aspetto e voce ad altri fuori di me? Che ne so io? Come posso parlarne?' (III.7, p. 797) ['But what gives me the right to talk about it? What right have I to give an aspect and a voice to others outside myself? What do I know of them? How can I talk about them?' (III.7, p. 59)] – and even to arrange in space and time the human apparitions of his voyage into madness: 'Dico "erano"; ma forse sono ancora in vita. Dove? Qua ancora, forse, che potrei vederli domani. Ma qua, dove? Non ho più mondo per me; nulla posso sapere del loro, dov'essi si fingono d'essere.' (IV.1, p. 807) ['I say "were"; but perhaps they are still alive. Where? Here still, perhaps, and I might see them tomorrow. But here, where? I no longer have a world for myself; I can learn nothing of them, of where they are presumed to be.' (IV.1, p. 69)

The 'horror of locking oneself in a prison of any kind,' the emptiness of an *I* that knows the secret unreality of every situation, and the referential indication of speech also derive from a gaining awareness of linguistic pseudo-communication:

Ma il guajo è che voi, caro, non saprete mai, né io vi potrò mai comunicare come si traduca in me quello che voi mi dite. Non avete parlato turco, no. Abbiamo usato, io e voi la stessa lingua, le stesse parole. Ma che colpa abbiamo, io e voi, se le parole, per sé, sono vuote? (II.4, p. 769)

[But the trouble is that you, my dear friend, will never know, nor will I ever be able to tell you how what you say is translated inside me. You haven't spoken Turkish, no. We used, you and I, the same language, the same words. But what fault is it of ours, yours or mine, if words, in themselves, are empty? (II.4, p. 31)]

The alternative to winking, which is its consequence, will later, in the figurative grotesque and from the point of view of its reception, make theatrical the disheveled expressiveness inaugurated early on with the marionettesque pantomime before the mirror: '(e sbalzavo per ogni nonnulla le sopracciglia fino all'attaccatura dei capelli e spalancavo gli occhi e la bocca, allungando il volto come se un filo interno me lo tirasse.)' (I.5, p. 751) ['(and at every trifle I raised my eyebrows to the roots of my hair and widened my eyes and mouth, lengthening my face as if an inner string were pulling it.)' (I.5, p. 14)] The physiognomic hyperbole represents the unveiling of inexpressible internal lacerations and the self-portrait is strained throughout because being outside, or, better, without oneself, it cannot rest in any form of classical spatial description.

It is known that one of the fixed points of normal persuasive speech is based on the bind of *coexistence* between person and actions and that precisely the idea of person introduces an element of stability: thus it happens in law, where the concepts of *responsibility, merit, guilt*, relative to the person, are bound to the concepts of *rule* and *norm*, relative to the action.[24]

Instead, the Pirandellian thinker, unhinging the bind of *coexistence* between person and actions, cannot appeal to universally accepted principles and is brought, as director of a centrifugal and contestatory self, to continuous attacks on the tranquillity of the reader, compulsorily involved in the epistemic earthquake activated by the dialectic machine.

As Guglielmi observes: '*Uno, nessuno e centomila* is the story of a modification and the discussion of this modification conducted exclusively with the reader who in this way ... comes to be constantly cited.'[25] However, the tendency to multiply the self bounces back like a rubber ball pushed by an unstoppable spring, overwhelming both participants in the discussion. For his part, the *raisonneur*, a prisoner of his own reasoning, exhibits himself in a vertigo of doubles that leave him exhausted, face to face with the solitude of a demarcator of person (the pronoun *I*) by now of no use. Note, for example, the chapter appropriately entitled 'Nel vuoto' ['In the void']:

A toccarmi, a strizzarmi le mani, sì, dicevo 'io'; ma a chi lo dicevo? e per chi? Ero solo. In tutto il mondo, solo. Per me stesso, solo. E nell'attimo del brivido, che ora mi faceva fremere alle radici i capelli, sentivo l'eternità e il gelo di questa infinita solitudine.

A chi dire 'io'? Che valeva dire 'io,' se per gli altri aveva un senso e un valore che non potevano mai essere i miei; e per me, così fuori degli altri, l'assumerne uno diventa subito l'orrore di questo vuoto e di questa solitudine? (VI.2, p. 862)

[Touching myself, wringing my hands, yes, I said 'me'; but to whom was I saying it? And for whom? I was alone. In the whole world, alone. By myself. And in the shudder that now made me tremble to the roots of my hair, I felt the eternity and the chill of this infinite solitude.
To whom would I say 'me'? What did 'me' mean, if for the others it had a meaning and a value that could never be mine; and for me, so outside the others, assuming a meaning, it becomes immediately the horror of this void and this solitude? (VI.2, p. 122)]

'Je est un autre' is true for the Pirandellian subject as it is for Rimbaud: this concept is an artificial relational construct acting as though it possessed an internal *I* destined to remain a mystery, as the philosophical voice of Serafino Gubbio, with authorial authority, explains:

Chi è lui? Ah, se ognuno di noi potesse per un momento staccar da sé quella metafora di se stesso, che inevitabilmente dalle nostre finzioni innumerevoli, coscienti e incoscienti, dalle interpretazioni fittizie dei nostri atti e dei nostri sentimenti siamo indotti a formarci; si accorgerebbe subito che questo *lui è un altro*, un altro che non ha nulla o ben poco da vedere con lui; e che il vero *lui* è quello che grida, dentro, la colpa: l'intimo essere, condannato spesso per tutta intera la vita a restarci ignoto! (V.1, p. 641)

[Who is he? Ah, if each one of us could for an instant tear himself away from that metaphorical ideal which our countless fictions, conscious and unconscious, our fictitious interpretations of our actions and feelings lead us inevitably to form of ourselves; he would at once perceive that this *he is another*, another who has nothing or but very little in common with himself; and that the true *he* is the one that is crying his misdeeds aloud within him; the intimate being, often doomed for the whole of our lives to remain unknown to us! (V.1, p. 193)]

The transgressive but pre-Freudian Moscarda, by now a stranger to 'Mr. Loan Shark' of Richieri and to the proper noun that could be Flik or Flok (like the name of a lost dog) even attempts pantomime as a remedy for the 'empty abstraction of words.' The grimaces before the mirror and the 'winkings' with which he sends prelinguistic messages to the reader produce a disassembling that forces him to withdraw before the limits of language and beyond the plural character that attempted to heal the emptiness of the social situation and the dissipation of meaning: 'Eh! signori, sì , un brutto tiro (scusatemi tutti questi ammiccamenti; ma ho bisogno di ammiccare, d'ammiccare così, perché, non potendo sapere come v'appajo in questo momento, tiro anche, con questi ammiccamenti, a indovinare)' (IV.2, pp. 813–4) [Ah, gentlemen, yes, a nasty trick (excuse me all these coy winks; but I need to hint, to wink like this, because, as I can have no idea how I appear to you at this moment, I try, with these hints, to guess)' IV.2, p. 75].

The pleasure of alienating oneself is yielded then no longer through perceptive actualizations, but in catalogues of sensations or concepts far from verbal action that represent the equivalent of moments of absence. Already, 'the unthinking indolence' with which Moscarda stares at the architrave of the door in the above-cited episode of the eviction of Marco di Dio is a symptom of the fall of a consciousness that dominates the objects, and of the imminent slipping away of the reasoning victim into the vacuum of a time which he cannot master and which is totally foreign to him. Even more revealing is the passage that concludes the re-evocation of the conflict with the father figure:

Mio Padre!
Nel vano, ora, un silenzio esterrefatto, grave di tutte le cose insensate e informi, che stanno nell'inerzia mute e impenetrabili allo spirito.

Fu un attimo, ma l'eternità. Vi sentii dentro tutto lo sgomento delle necessità cieche, delle cose che non si possono mutare: la prigione del tempo; il nascere ora, e non prima e non poi; il nome e il corpo che ci è dato; la catena delle cause; il seme gettato da quell'uomo: mio padre senza volerlo; il mio venire al mondo, da quel seme; involontario frutto di quell'uomo; legato a quel ramo; espresso da quelle radici. (III.3, p. 791)

[My father!
In the emptiness, now, a terrified silence, heavy with all the senseless and shapeless things that lie inert, dumb, impenetrable for the spirit.

It was an instant, but it was eternity. I felt inside all the horror of blind necessities, of things that cannot be changed: the prison of time; being born now, not before and not after; the name and the body that are given us; the chain of causes; the seed sown by that man, my father, without willing it; my coming into the world, from that seed; involuntary fruit of that man; bound to that branch, expressed from those roots. (III.3, p. 54)]

At this point the mask of captious speech, a desperate attempt at rationally testing the disintegration, loosens the coils in which it had attracted the addressee; an antithetic paradigm gradually replaces the active rhetoric, obedient to slowed sentence-making that avoids submitting perceptions to the ordering action of the verb and, at most, concludes with comments set in a dryly nominal syntax:

La finestra; una vecchia seggiola impagliata; un tavolino ancor più vecchio, nudo, nero e coperto di polvere, non c'era altro lì dentro ... I tegoli di quel tetto, il legno verniciato di quelle imposte di finestra, quei vetri per quanto sudici: immobile calma delle cose inanimate. (IV.6, pp. 828–9)

[The window; and old rush-bottom chair; a still older little table, bare, black, and covered with dust: there was nothing else in the room ... The tiles of that roof, the painted wood of those shutters, those panes dirty as they were: the immobile calm of inanimate things. (IV.6, pp. 89–90)]

If time and space are 'traps of life,' if man confers a sense and a value upon nature that it doesn't have in itself and dresses it up with lies, the way to health will consist in the refusal of reasoning and every discursive pact connected with it. Moscarda finds the solution of silence. At the moment of completing one last act of 'alienation' – the least traumatic, the donation of his personal worth to the almshouse – he declares: 'Non volendo più nulla, sapevo di non poter più parlare. E stavo zitto, guardando e ammirando quel vecchio diafano prelato' (VIII.3, p. 899) ['Wanting nothing more, I knew I could no longer speak. And I kept quiet, looking with admiration at that diaphanous old prelate.' VIII.3: 158].

Significantly, the situation is reversed: the protagonist, an investigating judge of a verbal trial of society, in the end becomes the accused in a real trial against the injurer Anna Rosa. Silent, bearded, wearing clogs and the blue smock of a madman, Moscarda translates his inner silence into an ecstatic and receptive rhetoric, governed by an empathetic pulsion, where infinitives – nominal forms of the verb – disintegrate the syntactic dominion of the subject, and propitiate the aleatory nature of 'smemorata lontananza' ['oblivious distance'], and the ontological suspension of 'dolcissima angoscia' (VIII.2, p. 896) ['very sweet anguish,' VIII.2, p. 155] (the oxymoron, a rhetorical figure dear to the mystics, is not by chance):

Ah, perdersi là, distendersi e abbandonarsi, così tra l'erba, al silenzio dei cieli; empirsi l'anima di tutta quella vana azzurrità, facendovi naufragare ogni pensiero, ogni memoria! (VIII.2, p. 896)
Rinascere attimo per attimo. Impedire che il pensiero si metta in me di nuovo a lavorare, e dentro mi rifaccia il vuoto delle vane costruzioni. (VIII.4, p. 902)

[Ah, to be lost there, to stretch out, abandon myself on the grass to the silence of the heavens; to fill my soul with all that empty blueness, letting every thought be shipwrecked there, every memory! (VIII. 2, p. 155)]
[To be reborn moment by moment. To prevent thought from working again inside me, causing inside a reappearance of the void with its futile constructions. (VIII.4, p. 160)]

In this novel, which recapitulates the entire Pirandellian journey, the thematizations of silence follow a persuasive practice of the most exasperated kind.[26] In the process of interpretation, one might wonder if panic identification with the flowing of a nature unconscious of itself is linked somehow to the dramatic turn of history during the 1920s and to Pirandello's own evasion into Utopia – remember that *La nuova colonia* [*The New Colony*] was written between 1926 and 1928. However, as early as 1911, the short story 'Canta l'Epistola' ['Sing the Epistle'] actually involves a receptive philosophy similar in form and substance to that of *Uno, nessuno e centomila*.

It would appear, therefore, that this novel, developed over about fifteen years (from 1909 to 1925), incorporates and radicalizes Pirandello's permanent philosophy, even though the ending displays an optimism that is hardly convincing.

In 'Canta l'Epistola,' in fact, Tommasino Unzio is a subdeacon who has left the seminary because he has lost his faith, and along with his religion he has also lost his trust in the regulating and dominating power of the *I* over reality. He abandons himself, therefore, to a fluid time without memory. For speech that reflects nonsense, and a perception of living that now causes 'tedio angoscioso' [distressing tedium], he substitutes a 'blanda smemorata mestizia' [mild and oblivious melancholy] that accompanies him on his silent walks in the fields. His annihilation as a social being is accompanied by an ablative and empathetic projection towards the immensely small: the mute voice of things that is seized in a growing 'filo d'erba' [blade of grass] stands within the perspective of the reversed telescope alluded to in *L'umorismo*, while the withdrawal below consciousness produces the desiderative or ecstatic infinitives that are repeated, to the letter, in several places in the novel (II.9, VIII.2 and 4):

Non aver più coscienza d'essere, come una pietra, come una pianta; non ricordarsi più neanche del proprio nome; vivere per vivere, senza sapere di vivere, come le bestie, come le piante; senza più affetti, né desiderii, né memorie, né pensieri; senza più nulla che desse senso e valore alla propria vita. Ecco: sdrajato lì su l'erba, con le mani intrecciate dietro la nuca, guardare nel cielo azzurro le bianche nuvole abbarbaglianti, gonfie di sole; udire il vento che faceva nei castagni del bosco come un fragor di mare, e nella voce di quel vento e in quel fragore sentire, come da un'infinita lontananza, la vanità d'ogni cosa e il tedio angoscioso della vita.[27]

[Not being conscious of existing, like a stone, like a plant; not even remembering his own name any more; living to live, without being aware of living, like animals, like plants; without affections, desires, memories, thoughts; without anything that gives meaning to life. Here he is: stretched out on the grass, with his hands clasped behind the back of his neck, watching in the blue sky the dazzling white clouds, swollen with sunlight; hearing the wind roaring like the sea in the chestnut trees of the forest, and hearing in the voice of that wind and in that roaring, as if from an infinite distance, the vanity of everything and the wearisome anguish of life.]

In the two-faced Pirandellian herma, the paradigm of silence is the other face of the coercion to speak. Therefore, like speech, the thematizations of silence are highly varied and of complex motivation. Sometimes silence belongs to ellipsis or reticence – forms of classical rhetoric (found most of all in theatrical dialogues, where the empty reply hides the desire of eluding the solicitations of the interlocutor) – but aphasia is mostly full of tragedy, repressed aggressiveness, or distrust of communication. The linguistic act of degree zero, silencing, is at least as rich and disturbing as the dialectic of speech.

Here are some exemplary samples. One may find mutism or pre-grammatical expression in connection with uncompleted psychological stages or at the margins of a consciousness in the dawning state. The boy Ciaula, able only to imitate crows or emit a rasping protracted moan and, at the most, obey with a 'gna-bonu' [all right], frees himself from this subhuman condition before the miracle of the moon appearing in a placid ocean of silence: his wordless cry spreads 'nella notte ora piena del suo stupore' [in the night now full of his wonder]. There is also the fossilization of the mentally insane woman in *Come tu mi vuoi,* who conserves from an unknowable prehistory only the monotone phrase 'Le-na' repeated in a state of autism that prevents others from reaching her; but that phrase, in the view of the Unknown, saves her from the knowledge of pain: 'Ora – eh, beata in questo tuo riso – sei salva tu – immune' [Now – eh, blessed in this laughter of yours – you are safe – immune].[28]

Silence sometimes is the response to the discovery of a subjectivity that is an abyss of uncontrollable pulsions. In the short story 'Nel gorgo' ['In the Whirl'], Romeo Daddi gives in to the instinct which leads him to betray his wife with her best friend, one knows not how, and then 'come assente da sé' [as if absent from himself], he closes himself in silence, frightening bystanders 'con la fissità acuta, strana' [with the strange, acute fixedness] of his gaze and one single exclamation repeated obsessively: 'Che abisso ... che abisso.' [What an abyss... What an abyss.] The gaze is a privileged instrument Pirandello uses to uncover the innermost *I*. For example, think of the epiphanic gaze that Serafino Gubbio substitutes for the purely reproductive eye of the cinecamera and the inefficiency of words. In the short story 'La maschera dimenticata' ['The Forgotten Mask'], Cirincio, a successful self-made man, is humbled and his mask of respectability disaggregated by the 'occhietti lustri, acuti come due spilli' [bright little eyes, sharp as tacks] of a certain nasty little man who at the electoral meeting 'seguitava a fissarlo, e ora – ecco – allungava il collo verso di lui, con l'indice teso come un'arma presso uno di quegli occhietti diabolici' [kept staring at him, and then – look – he was stretching out his neck towards him, with his index finger rigid like a gun near one of his little diabolic eyes], such that Cirincio 'con gli occhi di quell'ometto si vedeva rientrare in se medesimo con tutte le sue sciagure e la sua miseria' [with the eyes of that little man saw himself come back into himself with all his misfortune and misery]. In 'C'e qualcuno che ride' ['There Is Someone Laughing'], the social setting, reflected like a nightmare in the incommunicability of the masks that inhabit it, is disturbed by the laughter of three improbable characters (the father and the two children), producing anxiety in that it is not interpretable according to conventional understanding:

Serpeggia una voce in mezzo alla riunione:
– C'è qualcuno che ride.
Qua, là, dove la voce arriva, è come se si drizzi una vipera, o un grillo springhi, o sprazzi uno specchio a ferir gli occhi a tradimento.[29]

[There spreads a voice in the midst of the meeting:
– There is someone who is laughing.
Here, there, where the voice reaches, it is as if a viper rises, or a cricket darts, or a mirror sparkles to hurt the eyes treacherously.]

The analogies, the dynamic verbs, and the intense alliterations in groups of hard consonants are an onomatopoeic translation of a threat, represented by something prelinguistic and infracommunicative for a crowd that refuses the uncanny and in turn sends it back to the three unknown individuals with a symmetrical 'enorme sardonica risata' [enormous sardonic laugh].[30]

As I mentioned at the outset, in the essay *L'umorismo*, the Pirandellian dualism between facts and interpretations of facts (interpretations which are as infinite as the faces of reality are innumerable and fleeting) emphasizes most of all the art of controversy, promoted by the humoristic reflection with its play of opposites; by this it shows trust in the dialectic force of thought. However, towards the end of the treatise, the progressive exasperation of relativism, connected to the stratified multiplicity of the psychic and social individual and to the fallaciousness of the communicative circuit, turns against its own verbal means, the aporia insinuates itself in the raving of reason. Through the sophistic deconstruction of the mask, the character who acts as speaker for the author winds up deconstructing even himself. But knowing oneself, says Pirandello, means to be expelled from life: speech, freezing in what he calls the 'sublimato corrosivo della deduzione logica' [corrosive sublimate of logical deduction], makes the fluidity and the mobile equilibrium of the subject absolute in a single form: 'Ciò che noi conosciamo di noi stessi, non è che una parte, forse una piccolissima parte di quello che noi siamo' (p. 158) [What we know about ourselves is only a fraction, perhaps a very small fraction of what we are, p. 135].[31]

Against the pretence of logic reasoning, thus, the experience of 'interior silence' takes shape (chapter V of the second part): a situation of absence from oneself, an emptying out of the values of life, a hallucinatory perception of a reality well outside history, and a human reason conceived as an enormous lacuna in the cohesive principle of the *I* and of intersubjective relationship:

In certi momenti di silenzio interiore, in cui l'anima nostra si spoglia di tutte le finzioni abituali, e gli occhi nostri diventano più acuti e penetranti, noi vediamo noi stessi nella vita, e in se stessa la vita, quasi in una nudità arida, inquietante; ci sentiamo assaltare da una strana impressione, come se, in un baleno, ci si chiarisse una realtà diversa da quella che normalmente percepiamo, una realtà vivente oltre la vista umana, fuori delle forme dell'umana ragione. (p. 152)

[In certain moments of inner silence, in which our soul strips itself of all its habitual fictions and our eyes become sharper and more piercing, we see ourselves in life, and life in itself, as if in a barren and disquieting nakedness; we are seized by a strange impression, as if, in a flash, we could clearly perceive a reality different from the one that we normally perceive, a reality living beyond the reach of human vision, outside the forms of human reason. (p. 138)]

This vertigo produces an internal void, an arresting of time, a discovery of the deception in representation, and an anxiety before the absolute that is translated into key words like 'dismay,' 'astonished silence,' 'astonished wonder,' and 'astonished, oblivious calm.' It is another dimension 'cui l'uomo non può affacciarsi, se non a costo di morire o d'impazzire' (p. 161) [which man can face only at the cost of either death or insanity, p. 138].

The protagonist of the short story 'Da sé' ['On His Own,' 1913] will kill himself, and he moves to a cemetery by the family vault in order to spare his relatives expense and macabre funerary ceremonies. Matteo Sinagra, for three years now a living cadaver, lacks vital impulses due to a 'mysterious breakdown' which took place in the mechanism of his psyche. Since then, with dismay, he perceives the world as 'duro, ottuso, opaco, inerte' [hard, obtuse, opaque, inert], and any act or verbal communication as utterly meaningless: 'Muoversi? E perché? Perché uscire di casa? Inutile ogni atto, ogni passo; inutile anche parlare' [Move? And why? Why leave home? Any act, any step is useless; and equally useless is even to speak]. And precisely because this soon-to-be suicide feels himself removed from socialized life, he can watch with different eyes the 'cose che non sono più per lui, che per lui non hanno più senso' [things that are no longer for him, that for him no longer have meaning], things that exist like pure pulsating matter in a delirium of dispossession and suspension in which sight is clear, but the correspondence between nature and subject is defunct.[32]

The texts in which this ecstatic but horrific suspension is thematized tend towards particular syntactic and stylistic solutions, far from the toil of persuasive logic – texts defined by Terracini as 'linguaggio dell'evasione' [language of evasion] or 'discorso dell'uomo solitario' [discourse of the solitary man].[33] The experience of madness, the halt of vital instincts, and the imminence of death are dominant themes of such texts. In each case, the living creature, alone and, so to speak, naked, emerges from the character, while language makes itself permeable to the passage of sensations by freeing itself from probatory formulae, in a slow, coordinative syntax loaded with nominal phrases.

The 'recovered' protagonist of 'Quand'ero matto' ['When I Was Mad'] recalls his past alienation, a time when he was not at home with himself, and the sensations at the border between a porous subjectivity and a divine vision of an *I* that was an 'albergo aperto a tutti' [hotel open to all]: the style, with frequent use of coordinative conjunctions, imitates the astonished alignment of perceptions:

mi pareva che l'aria tra me e le cose intorno diventasse a mano a mano più intima; e che io vedessi oltre la vista naturale ... E un gran silenzio attonito era dentro di me, ... e andavo un tratto così, estatico e compenetrato in quella divina visione.[34]

[it seemed to me that the air between things around me and myself became more and more intimate; and that I saw beyond natural sight ... And within me there was a grand and astonished silence, ... and I went on for a while like this, ecstatic and permeated by that divine vision.

The loss of the *I* facilitates entry into a dreamy dimension at the threshold between life and death, seen especially in some short stories from Pirandello's final years. In 'Un'idea' ['An idea'] the reader, closely following the nameless protagonist, makes a journey from which speech is almost excluded and in which the silence of an urban and uninhabited nocturnal scene spreads. Active volition is missing, and the succession of impressions is underscored by syntactic inversions and an inclination to nominal forms:

Attraversarla [la piazza] gli pare impossibile; la vita, in cui deve rientrare, irraggiungibilmente remota da essa; e tutta la città, come da secoli disabitata, coi fanali che ancora la vegliano nel chiarore misterioso di quella gelida azzurrità notturna. Impossibile il rumore dei suoi passi in quel silenzio che pare eterno ... Leggero come un'ombra, il suo corpo; e, andando, nessun rumore.[35]

[Crossing [the piazza] seems impossible to him; life, in which he must re-enter, seems unreachably distant from the piazza; and the entire city, as if deserted for centuries, with streetlights still watching over it in the mysterious luminescence of that ice-cold nocturnal blueness. Impossible the sound of his footsteps in that seemingly eternal silence ... Light as a shadow, his body; and, as he moves, no noise.]

The walk takes place in a 'vaporosa evanescenza di sogno' [dream-like misty evanescence], since the dream is a fixed idea (perhaps a temptation to suicide); the present tense of the verb that isolates the faceless protagonist is like a false movement, or a gap in experience, in which a time and a secret outside human dimension accumulate as they are translated into the recurring image of the flowing water.

E resta lì, di nuovo assorto, opacamente, in quella sua singolare attesa. Il tempo s'è fermato e fra le cose rimaste tutt'intorno in uno stupore attonito pare che un segreto formidabile sia nel fatto che in tanta immobilità solo l'acqua del fiume si muova.[36]

[And he remains there, once again absorbed, opaquely, in that peculiar waiting of his. Time has stopped and among the things left all around in an amazed stupor it seems that an incredible secret lies in the fact that in so much immobility only the water of the river moves.]

Terracini comments that there is something irremediably 'distant in these verbs, thanks to which every distinction between past, present, and future dissolves so as to express the emptiness of an immobility where space and time are worthless.'[37]

In its syntactic structure, 'Di sera, un geranio' ['In the Evening, a Geranium'] mimes the last shreds of consciousness of a living creature about to dissolve. The initial counterpoint between imperfect, simple past, and present tenses portrays the twilight passage of perception along stylistic underscorings given by parallelisms and chiastic dispositions: 'S'è liberato nel sonno, non sa come ... Dormiva e non è più nel suo corpo; non può dire che si sia svegliato; e in che cosa ora sia veramente, non sa.'³⁸ [He was released in his sleep, he knows not how ... He was sleeping and now he is no longer a part of his body; he can't say that he has awakened; and what he is now, he doesn't know.]

Immediately afterwards, the loosening of the senses and the consternation of leaving the body comes in a catalogue of spatial indicators without supporting verbs:

là l'udito, dov'è un rumore anche minimo nella notte; qua la vista, dov'è appena un barlume; e le pareti e il soffitto (come di qua pare polveroso) e giú il pavimento col tappeto, e quell'uscio, e lo smemorato spavento di quel letto col piumino verde e le coperte giallognole, sotto le quali s'indovina un corpo che giace inerte.³⁹

[there hearing, where there is even the smallest noise in the night; there sight, where there is barely a glimmer of light; and the walls and the ceiling (which from here appear dusty) and below the floor with the rug, and that door, and the forgotten fear of that bed with a green quilt and yellowish covers, under which one discerns a body that lies motionless.]

The dying man is a thread of thought suspended on the verge of dissolution; his last attempts at rationality yield merely a dry enunciation of objects, a time filled by him with meaning and now frozen in the insignificance of a spatio-temporal solidarity that collapses:

Già, ma ora, senza piú il corpo, è questa pena, ora, è questo sgomento del suo disgregarsi e diffondersi in ogni cosa, a cui, per tenersi, torna ad aderire ma, aderendovi, la paura di nuovo, non d'addormentarsi, ma del suo svanire nella cosa che resta là per sé, senza piú lui: oggetto: orologio sul comodino, quadretto alla parete, lampada rosea sospesa in mezzo alla camera.

Lui è ora quelle cose; non piú com'erano, quando avevano un senso per lui; quelle cose che per se stesse non hanno alcun senso e che ora dunque non sono piú niente per lui.⁴⁰

[True, but now, without a body, it is this affliction, now, it is this consternation of his disintegrating and spreading out over everything, for which, in order to hold on, he goes back to complying, but in complying, the fear arises once again not of falling asleep, but of disappearing into the things in front of him: objects: a watch on the bedside table, a picture on the wall, a rose-coloured lamp suspended in the middle of the room.

He is now those things; no longer as they were, when they made sense to him; those things that make no sense in themselves and thus are now nothing to him.]

The personal pronoun (in this case the third person *he*), against which the author's mouthpieces rage with deconstructive investigations, is here annulled by a biological process deaf to the call of thought: 'Lui è ora quelle cose ... E questo è morire'[41] [He is now those things ... And this is dying]. The narrator accompanies the phantom, already separated from the body, on its flight beyond the walls of the house, and into the garden where the water translates, as usual, the absolute flowing of a non-human time. The narrator proceeds with nominal sequences, with infinitives well outside argumentative dialectic that allude to the non-being of the person (notice the infinitive 'Sparire' [To disappear] isolated in a paragraph by itself),[42] annihilated by an absolute that produces an astonishment symmetrical to the ecstatic pulsion of Moscarda and Tommasino. Here one finds 'vana eternità'[43] [vain eternity], nature made of objects without meaning and value that freezes both subject and language. The desiderative infinitive, with which the creature who *must* re-enter into nothingness takes leave, recalls – but only for a Pirandellian sentiment of the contrary – the empathetic and liberatory desires of the one who had *wanted* to be no longer one hundred thousand but 'nessuno' [no one]: 'Una cosa, consistere ancora in una cosa, che sia pur quasi niente, una pietra. O anche un fiore che duri poco: ecco, questo geranio ...'[44] [A thing, to exist still in a thing, though it be almost nothing, a stone. Or even a flower that lasts a short time: here it is, this geranium ...].

Translated by John Ronan and Manuela Gieri

NOTES

This essay was first published in Italian under the title 'Il farsi e il disfarsi del linguaggio: retorica del discorso e del silenzio' in Maria Antonietta Grignani, *Retoriche pirandelliane* (Naples: Liguori, 1993), 83–106.

1 Wladimir Krysinski, *Il paradigma inquieto: Pirandello e lo spazio comparativo della modernità* (Rome: ERI, 1988); see especially Chapter 2, 'Il discorso pirandelliano,' which contains insightful observations on Pirandellian subjectivity within the framework of modernity.

2 For the correlation of the *I/you* person demarcators reflecting the speech instance, see Emile Benveniste, *Structure des relations de personne dans le verbe* (1946). For the Italian translation, see *Problemi di linguistica generale* (Milan: Il Saggiatore, 1971), 269–81.
3 Luigi Pirandello, *Soggettivismo e oggettivismo nell'arte narrativa*, in Manlio Lo Vecchio Musti, ed., *Saggi, poesie e scritti varii* (Milan: Mondadori, 1960), 183.
4 Pirandello, *L'umorismo* (Milan: Mondadori, 1986), 56.
5 Pirandello, *On Humor*, trans. Antonio Illiano and Daniel P. Testa (Chapel Hill, NC: University of North Carolina Press, 1974), 30–1.
6 Pirandello, *L'umorismo*, 57.
7 Pirandello, *On Humor*, 31.
8 Chaïm Perelman and Lucie Olbrechts-Tyteca, *Trattato dell'argomentazione* (1966; Turin: Einaudi, 1989).
9 Pirandello, *L'umorismo*, 140.
10 Pirandello, *On Humor*, 118.
11 Pirandello, *L'umorismo*, 164–5.
12 Pirandello, *On Humor*, 142. It is perhaps superfluous here to remind ourselves that Pirandello knew and quoted Jonathan Swift. Alexander Pope's satirical essay *Peri Bathous; or, Martinus Scriblerus, his Treatise on the Art of Sinking Poetry* was published in 1727 in a volume of *Miscellanies* by Pope, Jonathan Swift, John Arbuthnot, and John Gay. The passage referred to in *Peri Bathous* can be found in Rosemary Cowler, ed., *The Prose Works of Alexander Pope* (Hamden, CT: Archon Books, 1986) 2:195. The Italian translation by Attilio Brilli is from his volume *Retorica della satira* (Bologna: Il Mulino, 1973). This volume includes a compendious and insightful introduction in which Brilli emphasizes the argumentative and dialogic nature of satire and analyses the characteristics of the reversed rhetoric practised by the members of the Scriblerus Club as a formal network of a distorted perception of the universe.
13 Renato Barilli, 'Il romanzo di Pirandello e il discorso retorico,' in *Il romanzo di Pirandello* (Palermo: Palumbo, 1976).
14 In relation to the problem of temporality, see Vincenzo Lo Cascio, 'Strutture temporali e strategie poetiche in Pirandello,' in Walter Geerts, Franco Musarra, and Serge Vanvolsem, eds., *Luigi Pirandello: poetica e presenza* (Leuven: Leuven University Press; Rome: Bulzoni, 1987), 159–90. For a theoretical discussion of the issue of temporality, see Cesare Segre, *Teatro e romanzo: Due tipi di comunicazione letteraria* (Turin: Einaudi, 1984).
15 Luigi Pirandello, *Quaderni di Serafino Gubbio operatore*, in *Tutti i romanzi*, ed. Giovanni Macchia and Mario Costanzo, 2 vols. (Milan: Mondadori,

1973). Hereafter, the page numbers from this edition will be given in the text.
16 Pirandello, *The Notebooks of Serafino Gubbio or (Shoot!)*, trans. C.K. Scott Moncrieff (Sawtry: Dedalus, 1990). Hereafter, the page numbers from this edition will be given in the text.
17 See Guido Guglielmi, 'Poetiche di romanzo in Pirandello,' in *La prosa italiana del novecento* (Turin: Einaudi, 1986), 102, 'Il momento della ricezione del testo è un momento della sua costituzione' [The reception of the text is a stage in its construction].
18 Gérard Genette, *Seuils* (Paris: Éditions du Seuil, 1987).
19 Genette omits Lawrence Sterne (1731–1760), a well-known model of humorism and digressivity (for Pirandello as well), from his descriptive and typological review. In effect, neither *Tristram Shandy* nor *A Sentimental Journey* contain intertitles. This lacuna has now been filled by Giancarlo Mazzacurati with his 'L'arte del titolo, da Sterne a Pirandello' in *Effetto Sterne* (Pisa: Nistri-Lischi, 1990), 294–332. This noteworthy study, which adds the names of Italians like Dossi and De Marchi to those of Cervantes, Voltaire, and Richter, shows how such Sternism-without-Sterne in the apparatus of internal titling, a sort of 'tradition without archetype,' comes from Frénais's famous French translation, *La vie et les opinions de Tristram Shandy*, which is full of intertitles subsumed by a textual enunciation or addressed to the reader in the form of fragments and allusions interconnected with the pages of the book. Beyond this information, valuable for the study of Pirandello (who surely read French), Mazzacurati documents the humoristic territory of the genre of chapter titles 'in a "warm" authorial line, inclined, that is, to use writing (it is not important whether in the first or third person) as a property of the narrator and of the narrated, of their whims and their subjectivity, free from the pacts of mimetic representation and the contracts of realistic illusion.' (For the original Italian, see p. 316 in Mazzacurati's text.)
20 See Genette, *Seuils*, 297.
21 Perelman and Olbrechts-Tyteca, *Trattato dell'argomentazione*, 181.
22 For the notion of *chronotopos*, see Cesare Segre, 'Cronòtopo' in *Logos Semantikos. Studia linguistica in honorem E. Coseriu* (New York: Gredos-de Gruyter, 1981), 157–64.
23 Giacomo Debenedetti, '"Una giornata" di Pirandello' (1937), in *Saggi critici* (Rome: Nuova Serie, OET, Edizioni del secolo 1945), republished in *Opere*, ed. Cesare Garboli, vol. 2 (Milan: Il Saggiatore, 1971).
24 Perelman and Olbrechts-Tyteca, *Trattato dell'argomentazione*, 310–12.
25 Guglielmi, 'Poetiche di romanzo in Pirandello,' 102.

26 But for the autodiegetic narrators of Pirandellian novels, the resolution to silence always follows the negation of experience and the discovery of temporality as an abyss of consciousness and memory. At the end of the *Quaderni*, Serafino Gubbio falls silent not so much because of the cruel drama that he had to film, but because he has lost his past or his sense of an interior time: 'No, né mondo, né tempo, né nulla; io ero fuori di tutto, assente da me stesso e dalla vita' ['No, neither world, nor time, nor anything else; I was beyond everything, absent from myself and from life'], he confesses after having verified the repugnant metamorphosis of the 'casa dei nonni' ['grandparents' house'] and its inhabitants who had previously lived within him like sweet memories. His *itinerarium mentis in nihil*, too cleverly connected to mystical models by Umberto Artioli (in *L'officina segreta di Pirandello* [Bari: Laterza, 1989]), is this shipwreck of reason and memory.

27 Pirandello, 'Canta l'epistola,' in *Novelle per un anno*, 2 vols. (1957; Milan: Mondadori, 1986) 1:446. More attentive to the divergences than the resemblances between the short story and the novel, Romano Luperini analyses the parable of evolution (in this case, an 'involuted' one) at play in Pirandello's ideology. According to Luperini, Tommasino Unzio is also an aspiring suicide, bored with life and pervaded (in a Leopardian fashion) by a sense of indifference towards nature and by the vanity of everything: Moscarda winds up 'easily' dissolving himself in the 'materiality of a vital flux.' See 'Tematiche del moderno e tramonto dell'Erlebnis in Pirandello romanziere' in Romano Luperini, *L'allegoria del moderno* (Rome: Editori Riuniti, 1990), 254–5.

28 Giovanni Sinicropi, 'L'espressione pregrammaticale in Pirandello,' *Lingua Nostra* 34 (1973): 120–3.

29 Pirandello, 'C'è qualcuno che ride,' in *Novelle per un anno*, 2:824.

30 For an incisive analysis of this short story, see Guglielmi, 'Poetiche di romanzo in Pirandello,' 140–55.

31 On the duplicity of the poetics that emerges from a reading of the essay *On Humor*, see Robert Dombroski, 'Pirandello e la poetica della crisi,' in *Pirandello: poetica e presenza*, 69–79.

32 Pirandello, 'Da sé,' in *Novelle per un anno*, 2:648–54.

33 Benvenuto Terracini, 'Le "Novelle per un anno" di Luigi Pirandello,' in *Analisi stilistica* (Milan: Feltrinelli, 1966), 369–85.

34 Pirandello, 'Quand'ero matto,' in *Novelle per un anno*, 2:163–4.

35 Pirandello, 'Un'idea,' in *Novelle per un anno*, 2:791.

36 Ibid., 795.

37 Terracini, 'Le "Novelle per un anno" di Luigi Pirandello,' 319: 'lontano in questi verbi per i quali vien meno ogni distinzione di passato, presente,

futuro ad esprimere il vuoto di una immobilità, dove spazio e tempo sono privi di valore.'
38 Pirandello, 'Di sera, un geranio,' in *Novelle per un anno*, 2:813.
39 Ibid.
40 Ibid., 814.
41 Ibid.
42 Ibid., 815.
43 Ibid.
44 Ibid.

SECTION 3
MEANINGS

7

Laughter and Political Allegory in Pirandello: A Reading of 'C'è qualcuno che ride'

ROMANO LUPERINI

'C'è qualcuno che ride' ['There Is Someone Laughing'] is part of *Una giornata*, the final section of *Novelle per un anno*. It was first published in the newspaper *Corriere della Sera*, on November 7, 1934.[1] The title is phrasal, as is often the case in Pirandello. It calls to mind a related example, the title of another well-known short story, 'Nell'albergo è morto un tale' ['In the Hotel a Guy Died,' 1929]. In both of these cases a witty line uttered by an anonymous character in the story also serves as its title. Furthermore, both titles suggest the theme of the respective short stories. The titles, therefore, are not only mimetic, but thematic as well. However, whereas in 'Nell'albergo è morto un tale' the witty remark occurs at the end of the narration, thereby recapitulating its meaning, in 'C'è qualcuno che ride' it occurs at the beginning, creating an atmosphere of suspended meaning, expectation, and mystery.

There is another case within Pirandello's repertoire of short stories where the title (similar to 'C'è qualcuno che ride') corresponds to a remark made by a character at the end of the opening sentence of the short story. The novella is 'Tu ridi' ['You Laugh,' 1912]. Here, too, the title highlights the reason for the laughter, and there are also lexical similarities with 'C'è qualcuno che ride' (for instance, the use of the verb *springare* [to kick] to indicate the sudden jump-start that laughter produces). In 'Tu ridi,' however, it is explained immediately that laughter – more precisely, laughter during sleep – is the protagonist of the story and that the sentence is uttered by the wife, who awakens her mate and reprimands him with exactly these words.

In contrast, as it has already been stated, in 'C'è qualcuno che ride' the initial remark is uttered by the anonymous character and remains enigmatic. The narration which follows should resolve the enigma and provide the reader with an answer to the query. In actual fact, the title and the subsequent remark create a double expectation: the characters would like to know who is laughing and why, and the reader adds doubts of his or her own to those of the characters, doubts which call into question the sense of the story and the very meaning of the laughter. According to Lipps (whom Pirandello knew from the time in which he resided in Bonn and whose *Komik und Humour* [1898][2] he quotes in the essay *L'umorismo* [*On Humour*, 1908]) but also according to Freud (who in fact cites *Komik und Humour* both in *Die traumdeutung*[3] [*The Interpretation of Dreams*] and in the *Der Witz und Seine Beziehung zum Unbewussten* [*Jokes and Their Relation to the Unconscious*, 1905]), expectation is one of the conditions of comedy. Thus, laughter is the theme of the short story.

The *incipit* presents a series of verbs in the present indicative and devices (alliteration and other phonic isotopes) that emphasize the poetic function of language. Such use of language that is quite rare in Pirandello, and is, in any case, only verifiable within his creative production beginning with the final pages of *Uno, nessuno e centomila* [*One, No One, and One Hundred Thousand*, 1925–6]. But whereas in the novel the lyrical emphasis is intended to celebrate human existence through a veritable squandering of accessorizing and qualifying adjectives, in 'C'è qualcuno che ride' the poetic function seems to have a heavily semantic emphasis with special attention to phono-symbolic effects:

Serpeggia una voce in mezzo alla riunione:
C'è qualcuno che ride.
Qua, là, dove la voce arriva, è come se si drizzi una vipera,
o un grillo springhi,
o sprazzi uno specchio a ferir gli occhi a tradimento. (p. 689)

[There spreads a voice in the midst of the meeting:
There is someone laughing.
Here, there, where the voice reaches, it is as if a viper rises,
or a cricket darts,
or a mirror sparkles to hurt the eyes treacherously.]

The short *i* of *ride*, so sharp and shrill, is repeated in *arriva*, *drizzi*, *vipera*, *springhi*, and *ferir*. Another dominant sound is achieved by blends of sibilant, labial, and liquid consonants: *SeRPeggia*, *aRRiva*,

Se Si, dRiZZi, viPeRa, gRiLLo, SPRinghi, SPRaZZi, and *SPecchio*. This phono-symbolic effect emphasizes the harshness and stridency of the laughter, as well as its deceitfully dangerous character, akin to a slithering snake. The image of the serpent, introduced in the initial verb, *Serpeggia*, is concretized in *vipera* and in its symbolic associations, including *tradimento*, the concluding word of the paragraph. From the outset, therefore, the narrative voice indicates a vector of meaning that is important to the verisimilitude of the piece, and is insistent in the way it is exhibited. The danger of the laughter is that it represents a rupture of social pact, a disloyal violation, or a betrayal – precisely, a *tradimento*.

The narrative voice is a witness who speaks in the present tense, while the 'recounted' action ('azione raccontata') is still unfolding. We are therefore dealing with a story that has an internal focus. Because events take place as they are being narrated, the narration is open. The subject knows as much as the characters do, and perhaps has more information: 'so che lui è il padre di quei due ragazzi' (p. 63) [I know he is the father of those two kids]), but he does not know how things will end, nor does he arrange a comprehensive explanation of events. The present indicative tense and the inward focus produce two effects. The first is one of suspense – a situation of expectation related to the unfolding events and to the result of these events, a result which remains unforeseeable and open to any solution. The second effect is a search for meaning, given that the narrator does not seem able to grasp the meaning, and is consequently unable to communicate it. The writing strategy used to create the text calls for a reading strategy which collaborates to produce an *in fieri* interpretation, one that is not preconstituted.

The narrating subject is defined exclusively by mental acts that express a reflexive moment of consciousness or a hermeneutic stage in the search for meaning. His presence is alluded to three times in the text: on page 689, 'sorridere di compiacenza sarà lecito, sarà, credo doveroso' [to smile with complacency will be allowed, it will be imperative, I think]; on pages 691–2, 'Il fatto ... che qualcuno ride non dovrebbe far tanta impressione, mi sembra' [The fact ... that someone is laughing should not provoke such an impression, I think]; and on page 693, 'so che lui è il padre' [I know he is the father]. This narrative *I* expresses doubts or makes attempts to sketch out interpretations, but his effort to understand does not lead to a comprehensive explanation:

such an explanation is therefore suspended and left up to the reader. The narrating subject is part of the group of people in attendance at the strange masquerade party, and he shares the increasing uneasiness of this group: at a certain point he goes so far as to use the pronoun *noi* [we] in order to indicate the collective uneasiness that sweeps across the *riunione* [meeting], 'Ma che soffocazione intanto questa commedia con noi stessi' (p. 691) [But meanwhile, how suffocating is this comedy with ourselves]. But unlike the others, the narrating subject maintains a detachment from the events that is essentially intellectual and moral in nature. He seems capable of giving judgments (one of which is implicit in the words *commedia con noi stessi*), hazarding future predictions, and above all, highlighting the incoherence of and the contradiction in the party and its participants, thereby laying bare its inner workings:

Il fatto (se vero) che qualcuno ride non dovrebbe far tanta impressione, mi pare, se tutti sono in quest'animo. Ma altro che impressione! Suscita un fierissimo sdegno, e proprio perché tutti sono in quest'animo; sdegno come per offesa personale, che si possa avere il coraggio di ridere apertamente. L'incubo grava così insopportabile su tutti, appunto perché a nessuno par lecito ridere. Se uno si mette a ridere e gli altri seguono l'esempio, se tutto quest'incubo frana d'improvviso in una risata generale, addio ogni cosa! Bisogna che in tanta incertezza e sospensione di animi si creda e si senta che la riunione di questa sera è molto seria. (pp. 691–2)

[The fact (if true) that someone is laughing should not provoke such an impression, I think, if everyone feels the same. But there is more to it than an impression! It generates a fierce disdain, exactly because everyone feels the same; it is like disdain from a personal offense, that one could have the courage to laugh openly. The nightmare weighs so unbearably on everyone, exactly because no one feels that laughing is permissible. If one starts laughing and the others follow his example, if the whole nightmare suddenly crumbles down into a widespread laughter, that's the end of everything! It is imperative that in such uncertainty and suspension of souls one believes and feels that tonight's meeting is extremely serious.]

With these considerations, the narrator contributes to the interpretation of events, and although he does not explain their complete articulation, he nonetheless illustrates their fundamental logic, a logic to which he will return further on. For now, it is sufficient to observe that the stance of rational observation displayed by the narrator takes on predominantly a form of incomprehension. He does not understand. For instance, he cannot find an explanation for the fact that in a carnivalesque atmosphere someone's laughter should be greeted with disdain, and his starting point is his own incomprehension and failure to interpret what is unfolding before his very eyes. We are therefore dealing with a participating yet alienated witness. The suspension of meaning derives from the fact that, despite being in attendance at the gathering, the narrator is not able to recognize a meaning and legitimacy of the workings of the social group to which he belongs.

In this sense, Pirandello achieves an effect worth noting. By inventing a narrative voice who does not know any more than the other characters know, Pirandello increases suspense and leaves the imagination open; he allows the narrator to manage the defamiliarization of the text, and then gives him a critical function, such as removing doubt and suspending sense and meaning. The handling of defamiliarization through the device of incomprehension is an extraordinary weapon used by authors in order to place human beings in a state of allegory and to unmask the ill conventionality of social relations.[4]

'C'è qualcuno che ride' appears to be divided into three parts, with the points of caesura or rupture marked by blank spaces on the page. The first part, a representation of the objective situation, describes the scene, the atmosphere, and the environment. An entire parenthetic clause is dedicated to the reception hall where the strange ball is held. Within this clause, the primary focus is not, in fact, on the location, but on the participants of the ball. Nevertheless, the description of the reception hall itself links back to a meaning that, although undefined, seems to be suggested with a certain amount of emphasis. The gaze is concentrated upon the high part, that shows itself 'nella tetraggine della sua polverosa antichità' [in the gloom of its dusty antiquity], and in particular on the daub of a seventeenth-century fresco, which is described with phrases such as 'pare allarmata' [it seems alarmed] and 'ha fatto tanto per soffocare e confondere in un nerume di notte perpetua le truculenti frenesie della sua pittura' [it strove to suffocate and blur in the blackness of a perpetual night the truculent frenzies of its painting]. There is a sense of darkness and suffocation, an 'allarme' [alarm], that seems to have something to do with the weight of a dusty tradition, and perhaps with an entire civilization. The fresco itself contributes to this sensation of oppression. The baroque daub is an example of artifice, not of nature: its 'truculenti frenesie' threatened by the 'nerume' are not at all an alternative to the gloom of this 'blackness.' On the next page we learn that in the hall there is only one element that represents spontaneity and nature, in contrast to the artificiality of the furnishings and the situation: 'sulla squallida tavola dei rinfreschi, i fiori non sono finti' (p. 690) [on the squalid table of the refreshments, the flowers are not fake]. On the other hand, the reader is informed that s/he is witnessing a 'finta festa da ballo' (p. 693) [fake ball]. The presence of the same adjective serves to underline an opposition. Artifice and fiction seem to be classified along with dust and death, whereas the flowers and the 'giardini' [gardens] from which they are picked seem to be associated with life.

In addition, there is an ambivalence in the description of the reception hall. On the one hand we have the 'splendore' [splendour] of the four large crystal chandeliers; on the other we have 'tetraggine' [gloom] and 'il nerume di notte perpetua' [the blackness of a perpetual night]. This same duplicity is present in the representation of the participants and of the occasion that has led them to congregate: a party, 'uno dei soliti intrattenimenti cittadini in tempo di carnevale' [one of the usual city entertainments during carnival] and yet also a 'riunione molto seria' [extremely serious meeting]. The masquerade, it could be said, is a product not of carnivalesque gaiety, but rather of an imposition added artificially from the exterior and yet accepted and in large part appropriated and introjected. The couples dance 'per dare alla riunione l'apparenza di una festa da ballo' [to give the meeting the semblance of a ball]; the photographers have probably been 'chiamati apposta' [invited on purpose], and the dancers seem to have been 'estratti di sotterra per l'occasione, giocattoli vivi d'altro tempo, conservati e ora ricaricati artificialmente per dar questo spettacolo' [drawn from underground for the occasion, old-time living toys, preserved and now artificially recharged to give this show]. Once again, artifice and death are juxtaposed: the dancers are described as 'estratti di sotterra,' and the musicians as 'calvi inteschiati' [bold skulled ones]. That which was heralded by the seventeenth-century daub is seen here among the human masqueraders in attendance at the bogus party.

Gradually the expressionistic and grotesque quality (the marionettes, the 'calvi inteschiati,' the atmosphere of progressive hallucination) is submitted to an atmosphere in which the oneiric element is transformed into surrealistic suggestion. The incisive, scathing expressionism that defined Pirandello's artistic maturity does not fall short here; rather it is combined with the surrealism of his old age, thus creating a new synthesis.

The second part of the short story depicts the subjective condition of the participants of the ball. It describes their mood, doubts and fears. They do not know why they have come, but they pretend to each other that they do. Each one is suspicious of the others: reciprocal diffidence dominates, and there is no hint of human solidarity. In short, the group does not show any kind of real unity. Thus, the images of deceit and of the snake return: 'occhiate alle spalle s'allungano oblique che, appena scoperte, si ritraggono come serpi' (p. 690) [gazes to the back lengthen askance so that, as soon as they are caught, they withdraw like snakes]. Every now and then someone is summoned by the leaders who are gathered in a secret room, but it is impossible to understand for what reason and with what outcome. Thus *costernazione* [dismay], *inquietudine* [anxiety], and true *orgasmo* [orgasm] follow one another. In fact, these sentiments constitute the only element of cohesiveness in the group. The tension grows and is diffused like a nightmare (the word *incubo* is repeated three times in rapid succession), that seems intolerable 'perché a nessuno par lecito ridere' [no one feels that laughing is permissible]. Laughter is forbidden not only because it is inopportune and inconvenient, but also because, by contrast, it reveals the cowardly conformity of the participants of the party, who react to the laughter as to 'un'offesa personale' [a personal offense]. In addition, laughter is contagious and for this reason may have a destructive social effect: 'Se uno si mette a ridere e gli altri seguono l'esempio, se tutto quest'incubo frana d'improvviso in una risata generale, addio ogni cosa' (p. 692) [If one starts laughing and the others follow his example, if the whole nightmare suddenly crumbles down into a widespread laughter, that's the end of everything]. The nightmare, therefore, has a function and, one could say, a social utility; it is preferable to the threat which laughter represents. The nightmare serves to guarantee the 'seriousness' of the mask of civility, a seriousness that cannot be put up for discussion without the ruin of all institutions.

But one cannot live for long with the spasmodic tension of the nightmare. The more 'l'incubo grava' [the nightmare weighs] and the 'incertezza' [uncertainty] and the 'sospensione d'animi' [suspension of souls] escalate, the more evident becomes the need for any possible solution that can free the group from the increasing 'orgasm.' The third part of the story is dedicated to action (an element completely lacking in the first two parts) and to its dénouement; it is here that narration reaches its *Spannung*, that is, its peak.

The section opens with a dialogue, that mimics a tangle or interweaving of voices. In the question and answer game, the internal cadences, and the corresponding rhymes, this tangle seems almost to resemble the work of Aldo Palazzeschi:

Chi è? Dov'è? ... Pare che non sia uno solo. Ah sì, più d'uno? Dicono che sono almeno tre. Ma come, di concerto, o ciascuno per sé? Pare di concerto tutt'e tre. Ah sì? Venuti dunque col deliberato proposito di ridere? Pare. (p. 692)

[Who is it? Where is it? ... It seems that there isn't only one. Really? More than one? They say they are at least three. But how? Together or each on his own? It seems they are all together. Really? Thus, they came with the deliberate intention of laughing? So it seems.]

This echoing of Palazzeschi further confirms the aforementioned, highly experimental interweaving of expressionism and surrealism; note also the absence of quotation marks in the dialogue.

The three who laugh are identified. There is the man with the 'faccia beata' [happy face]; it is noted that 'il naso gli ride più della bocca, e gli occhi più della bocca e del naso' [his nose laughs more than his mouth, and his eyes more than his mouth and nose] and that he has two children. The sixteen-year-old 'ragazzona' [big girl] races from room to room hunched over, with her hands over her mouth in an unsuccessful attempt to contain her laughter. (Hers had seemed to be 'un riso da bambina' [a childlike laughter], at least initially). Finally, there is the young girl's brother, 'che ride come un pazzo inseguendola' [who laughs like a madman while running after her]. The girl laughs the most, 'perché è abituata a vivere come una puledra in mezzo a un prato fiorito, una puledra che imbizzarrisca a ogni alito d'aria e salti e corra felice' [because she is accustomed to living like a filly in a meadow full of flowers, a filly that becomes restless at any breath of wind, and jumps and runs happily]. She is altogether unconscious of the meaning of her laughter and its scandal; on the other hand, however, the man and the brother are also 'alieni e lontani d'ogni sospetto' [disinclined and removed from any suspicion]. Only the brother 'di tratto in tratto si ferma sbalordito dall'improntitudine di lei che si ficca da per tutto ... vorrebbe darsi un contegno, ma non ci riesce' [from time to time stops in bewilderment at her effrontery as she plunges herself everywhere ... he would like to strike a dignified bearing, but he cannot]; he bites his lip in order to restrain his hilarity, but in vain.

Even in their essentially consonant behaviour, the two siblings differ in that the sister is much less conscious of the situation in which they find themselves. This distinction is not coincidental; Pirandello uses it intentionally to add something to the story's meaning. The girl has always resided in the country, living 'like a filly in a meadow full of flowers,' and within the system of binary oppositions that governs the story, she belongs to the same order as the flowers (described as 'non ... finti' [not ... fake]) and the gardens (like the meadow, *fiorito*, [full of flowers]) we encountered in the first part of the story. She represents the authenticity and the joyous spontaneity of nature. The brother, instead, 'è agli studi qua in città' [he is studying here in town]. The restraint, albeit partial, that he shows, is a result of his acquaintance with an urban environment. Remember that all we know of the father and daughter is that they reside 'in campagna' [in the country]. This situation outlines, therefore, the city-country opposition that we encounter at the conclusion of *Uno, nessuno e centomila* and that recurs frequently in the theatrical myths and the short stories written by Pirandello in the final decade of his artistic career (1926–36).

When they tire, the three laughing characters finally congregate on a couch. It is at this point that they see coming towards them 'come una nera marea sotto un cielo d'improvviso incavernato, tutta la folla degli invitati, lentamente, lentamente, come melodrammatico passo di tenebrosa congiura' (p. 694) [like a black tide beneath a suddenly engulfed sky, the whole crowd of guests, slowly, slowly, like the melodramatic stride of a dark conspiracy]. The 'blackness of a perpetual night,' first encountered at the beginning in the description of the ceiling of the reception hall, is now used to describe the throng of guests. The nightmare has turned into action. The advance of the throng has an oneiric and hallucinatory cadence, and the scene maintains an expressionistic tone. Yet, soon something artificial, fictitious, theatrical, that might even be described as *buffo* [funny] occurs. At first, the three seated on the couch do not even believe that 'quella buffa manovra' [that funny manoeuvre] is made toward them, but soon they realize that the throng is surrounding them and they huddle together 'atterriti' [terrified], pressing towards the back of the couch.

The scene has the visual strength of a dramatic schematization, and the effectiveness of a skillfully orchestrated theatrical performance. On the one side, there are the three frightened characters, huddled together; on the other, the dark, anonymous crowd advancing in a threatening manner, headed by the 'tre maggiorenti' [three notables] (the leaders who had been meeting in the secret room), who stand apart from the others. The spaces are delineated in an exact manner, and the distinctions between the three groups are clear. The opposition of the three 'maggiorenti' and the three family members who had been laughing is typical of a mirror construction.

I tre maggiorenti, quelli che, proprio per loro e non per altro, s'erano riuniti a consulto in una sala segreta, proprio per la voce che serpeggiava del loro riso inammissibile a cui han deliberato di dare una punizione solenne e memorabile, ecco, sono entrati dalla porta di mezzo e sono avanti a tutti, coi cappucci del domino abbassati fin sul mento e burlescamente ammanettati con tre tovaglioli, come rei da punire che vengono a implorare da loro pietà. Appena sono davanti al divano, una enorme sardonica risata di tutta la folla degli invitati scoppia fracassante e rimbomba orribile più volte nella sala. (pp. 694–5)

[The three notables, those who had conferred in a secret room, simply because of them and nothing else, that is, because of the spreading rumor of their inadmissible laughter to which they resolved to give a solemn and memorable punishment, there, they entered from the middle door. Now they stand in front of everybody, with their domino's caps lowered to the chin, handcuffed with three napkins in a burlesque fashion, as if they were guilty ones to be punished and came to beg for mercy. As soon as they face the couch, a gigantic and sardonic laughter breaks out from the entire crowd of guests, and repeatedly resounds in a horrifying manner in the hall.]

The scene staged by the three notables underlines, through an ironic reversal, the reality of power relationships. By presenting themselves handcuffed like criminals who are about to be punished and are asking for mercy, the leaders are drawing on the hierarchy of the social order and of established power; through an overturning of values, the imminent threat to the three naïve countryfolk is made clear. The laughter of the family, an act which had been, unbeknownst to them, a judgment of an entire society, itself becomes implicitly judged and neutralized. With the recognition of the three leaders as judges whose mercy must be sought, the treachery represented by the family's naïve and unwitting laughter becomes void of meaning. He who is parodied is led to sense his own ridicule, is 'obbligato a negarsi nella sua immediatezza' [forced to deny himself in his own immediacy], he is obliged to recognize the power of culture and civilization, of its duplicity and masking, and of its most coherent weapon, irony.[5] Civilization, in order to impose itself, assumes all the forms of ceremony and ritual. The implicit comparison and the obvious discrepancy between the unfolding 'play' and reality (the handcuffed notables are, in reality, the absolute holders of power, including the power to have the members of the small family arrested) provoke the sardonic laughter of the throng. This laughter not only expresses a sense of superiority and an intention of aggression, but also serves to re-establish the unity of the group. The nightmare dissolves through the identification of the 'diversi' [different ones], chosen as sacrificial lambs to be offered up in order to obtain social reunification.

If one thinks of the year of composition of the short story, 1934, and of the events occurring in Germany at this time, the story may also take on an implicit political interpretation. However, as much as the text might authorize this layer of meaning, the story itself is too enigmatic and complex; therefore, such a reading is not wholly satisfactory.

Turning expressionism into surrealism, the narrated parable reveals itself as an allegorical apologue, a fable recounted to express 'something else.' However, in the case of this story as often happens in the twentieth century, the allegory runs the risk of remaining enigmatically void of meaning. A key that leads back to a pre-established code found in traditional allegory is obviously lacking. Nonetheless, the reader is driven by the very mechanism of the story to decipher its hidden meaning. The allegorical suspension of meanings, as pursued by the narrating voice through the figure of incomprehension, does not reach an explicit reintegration of meaning in the end, and yet it demands a hermeneutic effort from the reader. It is therefore impossible to escape an attempt at interpretation.

Two modes, or rather, two typologies of laughter face one another in the short story. On the one hand, the naïve and unwitting laughter of the family represents natural spontaneity; as a description, on might use Freud's statement regarding the laughter of children – 'a laughter born out of pure pleasure.'[6] On the other hand, the sardonic and conscious laugher of the throng reveals a sense of superiority. According to Freud's theory,[7] the 'comic difference' emerges from the 'confrontation' which involves a conservation of emotional energy (which here puts an end to a nightmare). According to this theory, laughter reveals a preconscious link with all that is associated with childhood; the confrontation occurs through a linking back to the phase of infancy, to which the adult is able to look back with satisfied superiority.

One may also confirm Pirandello's interest in exploring various types of laughter during the latter part of his career by examining another apologue from *Una giornata*: 'La prova' ['The trial']. The two types of laughter we encountered in 'C'è qualcuno che ride' are present here, as well. At first the novice monks (who are the story's protagonists) laugh 'inconsapevolmente' [unconsciously] when they read fear in the face of the other; in so doing they are saved from the bears. Later, as the two animals are retreating, they laugh 'sguajatamente' [boisterously] because their 'naturale goffaggine' [natural clumsiness] appears ridiculous to them; at that point they truly risk their lives by irritating the bears. In 'C'è qualcuno che ride' the two modes of laughter are attributed to two distinct groups, the family and the throng of guests, and this division creates a dramatic effect of contradiction. In 'La prova,' the two types of laughter are produced in succession by the same characters. And whereas 'La prova' portrays a successful rite of initiation, 'C'è qualcuno che ride' is more 'una parodia dei miti di iniziazione'[8] [a parody of rites of initiation]. 'La prova' is a fable which celebrates a nature-god; 'C'è qualcuno che ride' stages a conflict. As we shall see, these are the two paths taken by Pirandello in his latest works. Although the first edition of *Der Witz und Seine Beziehung zum Unbewussten* dates back to 1905 (the definitive edition was not published until 1921), and although Lipps was a source for both Freud's and Pirandello's work (so that Lipps may have served as a go-between), we are unable to establish if Freud's essay on jokes had been read by the author of 'C'è qualcuno che ride.' It is more likely that Pirandello had in mind Henri Bergson's *Le rire* [*On Laughter*], which was published in 1900 and was translated into Italian by Laterza in 1916.[9]

In *Le rire*, Bergson's thesis is that laughter is an instrument of social control. Society makes use of laughter to defend itself, using it to penalize asocial behaviour, since, as stated by Bergson,

Il faut que chacun de ses (de la societé) membres reste attentif à ce qui l'environne, se modèle sur l'entourage, évite enfin de s'enfermer dans son caractère ainsi que dans une tour d'ivoire. Et c'est pourquoi elle fait planer sur chacun, sinon la menace d'une correction, du moins la perspective d'une humiliation qui, pour être légère, n'en est pas moins redoutée. Telle doit être la fonction du rire. Toujours un peu humiliant pour celui qui en est l'object, le rire est véritablement une espèce de brimade sociale.[10]

[Therefore society holds suspended over each individual member, if not the threat of correction, at all events the prospect of a snubbing, which, although it is slight, is none the less dreaded. Such must be the function of laughter. Always rather humiliating for the one against whom it is directed, laughter is, really and truly, a kind of social ragging.][11]

In Pirandello's short story a 'punizione solenne e memorabile' [solemn and memorable punishment] is devised by the three leaders. Yet, the controlling function of laughter reveals itself as conclusive as the social contract is fragile. The crowd of guests appears divided, nagged by doubts and insecurities, and lacking any solidarity. The short story, therefore, bears witness to a moment of affliction and crisis. Precisely because the situation is the way it is, the masqueraders sense that the 'commedia' [comedy] in which they must perform is 'soffocante' [suffocating]. Heavy also, is the burden of their masking, or rather the burden of the forms and institutions that rigidify social life. The laughter of the three characters is extremely dangerous precisely because it could provoke the uncovering of latent contradictions and reveal the void and the absurdity of the social contract. This explains the secret meeting of the leaders and their decision 'to give a solemn and memorable punishment' to the three who laugh. It also explains the unification, through laughter, of a community that risks disintegration on account of a lack of social identification. The 'sardonica risata' [sardonic laugh], by ridiculing a naïve, natural kind of laughter, restores the seriousness of the party, and this re-establishes both the power of the masqueraders, and the primacy of civilization over nature.

The spontaneous laughter of the family represents, as we have seen, the joyous instinctiveness of the natural world. The young girl lives like a filly, just as Vitangelo Moscarda lives (or wishes to live) at the conclusion of *Uno, nessuno e centomila* like an animal or a plant or a stone. Nature is a state which exists in opposition to civilization. This concept is analogous to one that sustains the conclusion to Michelstaedter's *La persuasione e la rettorica*.[12] Freud also, in his *Das Unbehagen in der Kultur* (*Civilization and Its Discontents*, 1929), written a short time earlier, had illustrated the price, necessary as it may be, in his opinion, that civilization had to pay in choosing to impose itself on a series of instincts that are anarchic in nature. Freud states that 'Der Kulturmensch hat für ein Stück Glückmöglichkeit ein Stück Sicherheit eingetausch'[13] ['Civilized man exchanged a portion of his possibilities of happiness for a portion of security'[14]]; Michelstaedter could have used the same words that, in any case, touch repeatedly upon this very concept.

The short story is not lacking in clues – some of them linguistic in nature – that seem to indicate that what is being depicted is Fascist society. Leonardo Sciascia has emphasized the Fascist term *adunata* [assembly] that appears in the short story (p. 690) in order to define the gathering, and has read the short story as a 'satire' or a sign of 'intolerance' to the regime.[15] This intention cannot be ignored. However, this short story is contemporary to *I giganti della montagna* [*The Mountain Giants*], in which similar allusions are not lacking. It is not difficult to see the giants, who ignore art and dedicate themselves only to commerce and war, as representatives of the regime.

Nonetheless, here Pirandello's target is much larger than a single nation's Fascist phase. It is not coincidental that several stories in *Una giornata* take place in the United States and have the intention of representing the most advanced (and most monstrous) aspects of Western civilization. The author wishes to disclose the means by which society represses natural instincts. This society, rotten and void of any values, is able to unite its members and to exclude the 'other,' the one who is 'different' and thus threatens society itself merely with its presence. 'C'è qualcuno che ride' should undoubtedly be read as a political allegory, but its polemical objective cannot be reduced to merely a satire of an assembly of hierarchs.

'C'è qualcuno che ride' exemplifies one of the directions taken by Pirandello in his overcoming of the poetics of humour, a direction he had already initiated with the conclusion of his novel *Uno, nessuno e centomila*. In the short story we never experience humoristic laughter, and here lies the difference between this story and 'Tu ridi.' In the latter story the protagonist, after discovering the reason for his laughter in his sleep, smiles about it with bitter and pitiful consciousness; thus we have both spontaneous and unwitting laughter produced by a dream, and humoristic laughter, that springs from reflection and compassion. This is not the case in 'C'è qualcuno che ride.' The family's laughter is not humoristic, in that it remains untainted by consciousness; nor is the crowd's, because among them there is the 'avvertimento del contrario' [perception of the opposite], but not the 'sentimento del contrario' [feeling of the opposite]. If spontaneity is lacking in the crowd's laughter, then so, too, is the reflection that induces a sense of pity and of moving bitterness. The narrative voice does not pick up even a hint of reason for the development of either the perception or the feeling of the opposite within the family. In fact, the narrative voice limits itself to the observation that the carnivalesque soirée would have adequately legitimized the laughter of the three presumed disturbers. In the end, from the point of view of the reader, it cannot be said that the narrative voice is able to laugh humoristically, either at the family's laughter or at the punishment that the leaders inflict on them. Humour does not exist here because the primary condition for it – the suppression, even partial, of the elements that create 'a painful emotion.' – is missing.[16] Here 'la liberazione delle emozioni penose' [the release of painful emotions] never occurs, not even in the form of distraction or digression, as often happens in Pirandello (for example, the diversion caused by Mattia Pascal's cross-eyed look in the scuffle with the widow Pescatore). Conversely, the author of 'C'è qualcuno che ride' focuses on the most disturbing and perturbing aspects of the event, and accentuates the hallucinatory tones. The entire story not only seems to be constructed from oneiric material, but also proceeds uninterruptedly with the suffocating rhythm of a nightmare. The reader finds no relief, even at the end. The expectation that had sustained his or her attention is not satisfied by the discovery of the identities of the parties responsible for the disturbance. In fact, the search for the meaning of the disturbance continues, as does the search for the meaning of the apologue.

Thus, we are dealing with neither a comic nor a humoristic narration. Rather, 'C'è qualcuno che ride' is a story with sinister and perturbing tones, a tale dealing with laughter and its social function within any type of 'advanced' civilization. The object of the story, despite the narrative pretext of an assembly of Fascist hierarchs, is the functioning of power itself; better still, it is the relationship between power and civilization, and the necessarily repressive character of any civilization. Pirandello's anarchic nature resurfaces here; it is a petit-bourgeois subversiveness of the generation which had established itself in the first two decades of the twentieth century.

Therefore the text is, only in this sense, a political allegory, an allegory which is propelled forward by a discourse on laughter presented in its two principal values: as a possible anarchic subversion, and as an element of social stabilization and conversion. The opposition between nature and civilization is articulated in the opposition between instinctive, naïve laughter on the one hand, and aggressive, conscious laughter on the other. Through the latter, power is able to give back identity and unity, at least temporarily, to an uncertain and disoriented society, thereby blocking and repressing its consciousness of the artificial, intrinsically inauthentic, fake character of the social pact. This society is also reunited through the identification of those who are 'different,' who are offered up as sacrificial lambs – an act which allows society itself to forget the void on which the entire system rests. The mechanism through which society unifies and excludes its outcasts is the primary theme of 'C'è qualcuno che ride.' It is through this mechanism, within Pirandello's ideology, that death triumphs over life.

In his later works Pirandello seems to be clinging to a Utopia, that of nature. It is unlike the nature portrayed negatively in Leopardi and referred to by Pirandello himself in the introduction to *Il fu Mattia Pascal* [*The Late Mattia Pascal*, 1904]. Beginning with *Uno, nessuno e centomila*, nature had been transformed into a positive ontology. This leeway to Utopia may determine the mystical yieldings of the first two theatrical myths, but may also be overturned to serve as a criticism of civilization and of society. Surrealism can be used as a sort of permit for evasion or consolation, but can also be joined with an expressionistic accusation. These were the two paths open to Pirandello during the latter part of his artistic creation: the first is that depicted in *La nuova colonia* [*The New Colony*, 1928], in *Lazzaro* [*Lazarus*, 1929], or in the short story 'La prova' ['The Proof']; the second path is that taken in *I giganti della montagna* and in 'C'è qualcuno che ride.' Pirandello either celebrates the nature of existence lyrically and symbolically, or he dramatizes a conflict allegorically. This latter mode is utilized in the tale of Ilse and Cotrone, in which the combined forces of nature and art must succumb to the social brutality as represented by the giants and their servants. It is also employed in the recounting of the terrifying flight of the innocent family of the short story when they are faced with the parodied ritual dramatized by the powers that be. The 'polverosa antichità' [dusty antiquity] of civilization, with the weight of its masks and death, its ossified tradition, its meaningless institutions, and its culture made up of sadistic ritual and artificiality, has irremediably gained the upper hand.

In this regression to nature, anarchism might potentially be associated with a genuinely reactionary attitude of refusal of the social. In addition, a characteristic frequently found in high bourgeois art, which still exists in our century, is the ability to speak in the name of a Utopia, and in so doing gain a critical perspective which is alternative in nature.

Translated by Lucia Di Rosa and Manuela Gieri

NOTES

This essay was first published in Italian under the title 'Riso e allegoria politica in Pirandello: Lettura di "C'è qualcuno che ride,"' *Rivista di studi pirandelliani* 11 (December 1993): 17–27.

1 This short story is included in the Italian edition of *Novelle per un anno*, ed. Mario Maurizio Costanzo (Milan: Mondadori, 1990), vol. 3, tome 1: 689–95. The page numbers cited in my text refer to this edition. All quotations from Pirandello's texts have been translated by Manuela Gieri.
2 The essay is published in Theodor Lipps, *Aesthetik: Psychologie des Schonen und der Kunst* (1898; Leipzig: Verlag von Leopold Voss, 1923), vol. 1: 585–96.
3 Sigmund Freud, *Die Traumdeutung* (Leipzig: F. Deuticke, 1900).
4 Mikhail Bakhtin, 'Forms of Time and of the Chronotope in the Novel,' in *The Dialogic Imagination* (Austin: University of Texas Press, 1981), 162.
5 See Guido Guglielmi, *La prosa italiana del novecento. Umorismo metafisica grottesco* (Turin: Einaudi, 1986), 150–1.
6 Sigmund Freud, *Jokes and Their Relation to the Unconscious*, ed. and trans. James Strachey (New York: Norton, 1960), 228–35.
7 Ibid.
8 Guglielmi, *La prosa italiana*, 151.
9 Henri Bergson's essay first appeared in English in 1911, as *Laughter, an Essay on the Meaning of the Comic*, trans. Cloudsley Brereton and Fred Rothwell (London: Macmillan, 1911).
10 Henri Bergson, *Le rire: Essai sur la signification du comique* (Paris: Presses Universitaires de France, 1967), 103.

11 Bergson, *Laughter, an Essay on the Meaning of the Comic*, 135.
12 Carlo Michelstaedter, *La persuasione e la rettorica* (Milan: Marzorati, 1972).
13 Sigmund Freud, *Das Unbehagen in der Kultur* in *Gesammelte Werke* (London: Imago, 1948), 14:474.
14 Freud, *Civilization and Its Discontents*, trans. James Strachey (New York: W.W. Norton, 1961), 62.
15 Leonardo Sciascia, *Pirandello e la Sicilia* (Rome: Salvatore Sciascia, 1983), 80–2.
16 Freud, *Jokes and Their Relation to the Unconscious*, 228–35.

8

Pirandellian Nakedness

ROBERT DOMBROSKI

At the turn of the century, the experience of the machine and new modes of production heightened a self-awareness of individual crisis and displacement throughout Western culture. We are often reminded that the modernization of European society was very much the product of positive science which left very little, if anything at all, to chance or spiritual agency. From this premise developed the wave of anti-modern modernism that in Italy found its crest in two writers so very different from one another that they are seldom mentioned in the same breath: Luigi Pirandello and Gabriele D'Annunzio. Yet their writing shares at least one important characteristic: it revives older, even archaic, forms of life and consciousness. The difference between them consists largely in the way they undertake their respective projects of restoration and renovation.

I have brought D'Annunzio and Pirandello into conjunction with the expressed purpose of citing the most extreme contrast to the theme I propose to discuss. D'Annunzio's protagonists are always literally and figuratively overdressed, clad in layer upon layer, residue upon residue, fold upon fold of sacred, archaic, and religious materials. They survive in the modern world by virtue of their belonging to the past and tradition. The world they inhabit is transformed, in a baroque manner, through infinite abundance; enormous façades hide their fear of dispossession. These characters belong to a kind of 'secular scripture,' replete with spiritualistic activity designed to encode an unimaginable new social order.

Pirandello's characters have shunned all illusory emblems of accommodation. They are born onto the stage in much the same way as Pirandello himself claims he saw the light of day: naked, having fallen like a firefly under a solitary pine tree. The passage from 'Informazioni sul mio involontario soggiorno sulla terra'[1] ['Information on My Involuntary Sojourn on Earth'] is well known and needs no further mention. But the situation of nakedness and of self discovery (for which nakedness is a metaphor) is, I think, deserving of more concern, because it constitutes an important variation on a theme as old as modernity itself, namely that of 'unaccommodated man,' to borrow a phrase from Marshall Berman's classic *All That Is Solid Melts into Air*.[2]

The list of Pirandellian propositions devoted to the fate of humanity in the modern world is long. The concept these propositions embrace is their very narrative or drama; the subjects they embody are that endless monologue on alienation and loss of identity that even those readers least familiar with Pirandello's works have come to know by heart. It may be summarized in the desolate portrait of his age painted by Pirandello in 1893, a portrait that forms the basis of all of his subsequent literary and dramatic production.[3]

Pirandello asks what has happened to our world. His answer is that the world has become incommensurably small, a top spinning aimlessly in space. Man has been unseated as king and plunged into the mud of existence. His fear of annihilation makes him delirious and his delirium causes him to ascend, with his mind, to every corner of creation; but there he finds no God in waiting, only horrific emptiness. Man is lost in an immense labyrinth, surrounded by the impenetrable mystery of life. Like that top spinning aimlessly in the dark, he has no stable position from which he can know and make judgements.[4]

Modern tragedy for Pirandello begins at this moment of dispossession when King Lear, broom in hand (the reference is Pirandello's own), leaves his castle, having lost everything that others can take away. But this is Pirandello's Lear, not Shakespeare's. His nakedness begs to be redeemed, epistemologically and aesthetically; he is much too afraid to face off squarely against the Other, too afraid to 'feel what wretches feel.' Pirandello's Lear is Henry IV, deprived of life itself, thrown out of doors, and stripped naked of his dignity, a solitary and poor abandoned child. Unlike Shakespeare's Lear, Pirandello's naked king cannot become a more humane, authentic king by experiencing the suffering and dispossession that others experience; nor can he discover new truths that accompany his nakedness. Pirandello's ruler has experienced a disaster that holds no remedy; he cannot rise from his fall, except in the guise of a madman. Pirandello's king must do exactly what Henry IV has done: he must construct a mythic self (the Emperor) in order to mask the reality of who he really is.

Pirandello concludes the essay 'Arte e coscienza d'oggi' ['Art and Conscience of Today'] with the following:

A me la coscienza moderna dà l'immagine d'un sogno angoscioso attraversato da rapide larve or tristi or minacciose, d'una battaglia notturna, d'una mischia disperata, in cui si agitino per un momento e subito scompaiano, per riapparire delle altre, mille bandiere, in cui le parti avversarie si sian confuse e mischiate, e ognuno lotti per sé, per la sua difesa, contro all'amico e contro il nemico.[5]

To me modern consciousness is like a disturbing dream riddled with fleeting images of a nocturnal battle at times desolate, at times frightening, a desperate struggle in which thousands of banners are waved for a moment and quickly disappear to make room for others: a battle in which the adversaries mingle in confusion, each fighting to defend himself against friends and foes alike.

The event of this dream is the advent of modernity: perpetual disintegration and renewal, struggle and contradiction, ambiguity and anguish. The world has been shattered into a multitude of fragments, incommensurable private languages.[6]

Out of this experience evolves the conceptualization of such extraordinary plays as *Enrico IV* [*Henry IV*, 1921] and *Sei personaggi in cerca d'autore* [*Six Characters in Search of an Author*, 1921]. Some concrete historical situation, such as the rise of technology and the expansion of the market to include and determine cultural production, has dissolved all the pleasing illusions of life and has destabilized the economic base of artistic careers. For the Pirandellian subject this causes a fall into the nothingness of psychic fragmentation and its complementary text of perpetual experience and lived time, as represented by Pirandello's characters through the attendant conditions of their nakedness. The subject I would like to address in this essay is just what is achieved by the embodiment of a modern consciousness in the persona of a mad king. To do so, it will be necessary to approach the question of nakedness from a different perspective and, thus, to propose the existence of a sub-text or allegorical register, a kind of 'political unconscious'[7] at the base of the aesthetic ideology of *Henry IV*. My purpose is to expose an objective possibility from which the text draws its power and thus attempt to replace a subject that has been blotted out.

I shall begin by citing another very different account of nakedness that appears in Marx's *Communist Manifesto*:

> The bourgeoisie, historically, has played a most revolutionary part ... has put an end to all feudal, patriarchal, idyllic relations. It has pitilessly torn asunder the motley feudal ties that bound man to his 'natural superiors,' and has left remaining no other bond between men than naked self-interest ... It has drowned the most heavenly ecstasies of religious fervor, of chivalrous enthusiasm, of philistine sentimentalism, in the icy water of egotistical calculation. The bourgeoisie has stripped of its halo every occupation hitherto honored and looked up to with reverent awe ... has torn away from the family its sentimental veil.[8]

Marx believed that the bourgeois revolutions had liberated, and thus transformed, the world by stripping it of its illusions, and in doing so had left in plain view, 'naked,' the realities of power and exploitation. The cruelty of the oppressors and the misery of the victims were exposed like open wounds. But Marx's main point, reiterated throughout the *Manifesto*, was that the bourgeoisie in uncovering the myths of natural superiority had given humankind new hopes and desires.[9]

Italy's own bourgeois revolution was late in coming, but when it did it too exposed dreadful realities, particularly of a wretched and downtrodden southern population. In Pirandello's Sicily, among the island's many festering wounds, the working conditions in the sulphur mines no doubt stood out as the most infamous. Vincenzo Consolo has written perhaps the most stirring account we have of the mines and the life of the *zolfatari*:

> È certo che lo zolfataro, vivendo una vita da sottosuolo, una vita all'estremo limite della sopportazione, al limite del rischio, facendo un lavoro (a cottimo) dove l'illusorio salario, taglieggiato dall'anticipo del gabellotto, dal *truck system*, dal *soccorso* e dal sostentamento del caruso, dalle spese per gli attrezzi di lavoro, dipende solo dalle sue braccia, dalla quantità di zolfo che riesce ad estrarre, lo zolfataro ha dovuto per forza far saltare gli schemi conosciuti (quelli contadini) del vivere. Egli non è più paziente, rassegnato, parsimonioso, non immagina più la vita come un lento fluire in cui l'unica speranza è riposta in una vita migliore per i figli. [Egli vive] nella fatica senza rimedio, ai margini, negli abissi, nella precarietà, nella costante visione della morte ... Vita a nudo ... quella dello zolfataro, vita prosciugata come il corpo dalla fatica e dal caldo

... vita sull'estremo crinale da cui si può precipitare verso la disperazione, l'annientamento, la follia.[10]

[It is certain that the sulphur miner lives a life beneath the earth at the limits of risk and of what can be physically tolerated. He works for an illusory wage, based on what he mines, less contributions to the *gabellotto*, the truck system, emergencies, the care of his *caruso*, his work tools. Depending only on the strength of his arms and the quantity of sulphur he is capable of extracting from the earth, the miner must necessarily break with the traditional life customs of the peasantry; he is no longer patient, resigned, parsimonious; he no longer imagines life as a fluid movement of time in which his only hope rests in the prospects for a better life for his children. [He lives] a life of suffering which has no end, on the margins, in the abysses ... a naked life ... as dry and hot as his exhausted body; a life on the brink of extreme desperation, annihilation and madness.]

Unlike Verga, Consolo remarks, Pirandello is a *uomo di zolfo* [man of sulphur], the most *sulfureo* [sulphureous] of Italian writers, and he reminds us that Pirandello was born 'in quel Caos a ridosso dello scalo di Porto Empedocle' [in that chaos behind the harbour of Porto Empedocle], a major repository and port for the exportation of sulphur from the nearby mines. Consolo also recalls that Pirandello's father, a sulphur merchant, leased a mine, and that the young Luigi worked for a short time in the warehouses, and so was acquainted with the mines and with the lives of the workers. A checklist of references to the mines and the *zolfatari* would include 'Ciàula scopre la luna' ['Ciàula Discovers the Moon,' 1912] and 'Il fumo' ['The Smoke,' 1922]. These *novelle* describe the inhuman experiences of the miners, but they also contain impulses which invest their respective narrative systems, transforming ostensively social narratives into a new mythic or existential vision. The hard reality of the concrete social situation is displaced in these texts, and ultimately discredited, while the attention of the reader is directed toward an authenticity existing above and beyond the mines. In the case of 'Ciàula scopre la Luna,' we are made to focus on the valorization of an authentic personal temporality – the journey toward light, knowledge, and expression – in opposition to the inauthentic time of the work space. In 'Il fumo,' what could be regarded as environmental concerns on Pirandello's part may be best understood as a desire to preserve the archaic life and world of the peasant farmer. In other words, in both these stories while Pirandello unveils and denounces the devastating effects of sulphur mining on people and land, his purpose in doing so is not to bring attention to the social question, described by Consolo in the passage cited above, but rather to contain that social question within the boundaries of myth.

Sulphur is also – as Consolo remarks – a dominant theme of Pirandello's one and only historical novel, *I vecchi e i giovani* [*The Old and the Young*, 1913], which culminates in the revolt of the mine workers and, at their hands, the deaths of Aurelio Costa and his mistress. But here too in this vast fresco of the political and social problems that beset Italy at the turn of the century, Pirandello proposes a logic of content that substitutes, for the rational knowledge of political relationships and conditions associated with the problem of unification, the mystique and promise of another more vital existence, as embodied in the protagonist Lando Laurentano.

For Pirandello, writing in the aftermath of the unification of Italy, the naked reality of the disinherited popular masses marked not only exploitation, cruelty, and misery, but also a potential for revolution (a revolution initiated by the sulphur workers which grew into the Sicilian fasces). Politically, Pirandello may be regarded as a conservative, committed to the preservation of the privileges enjoyed by his class. At the same time, his work contains strong populist and anti-capitalist impulses. As a threatened middle-class subject, Pirandello senses the practical dangers of socialism, yet he draws on its sense of vital bonding to discredit and, ultimately, to subvert the various middle-class ideologies responsible for the breakdown of liberal subjectivity. The inner logic of his position is based on the fundamental contradiction of dismantling the epistemological base on which the bourgeois subject constructs his identity, while at the same time searching for a means to reconstitute that subjectivity in more absolute terms. Hence the nakedness which liberal ideals and positive reasoning have exposed, and which could spark, as Marx hoped, a completely new 'unalienated' relationship to the world, must be re-dressed, rendered invulnerable to reason and historical contingency.

The status of the individual subject in Pirandello is wholly relational. Its crisis is demonstrated by its persistence and overbearing centrality as the subject of attention. That is to say, in contrast to verismo or other varieties of realism (where the consciousness of conflict is embodied in a particular character-type that constitutes one among many elements of narration or drama) or in contrast to the post-modern dissolution or absence of a controlling point of view,

Pirandello's fragmented selves are given centre stage. This is so even in *Così è (se vi pare)* [*It Is So (If You Think So)*, 1917], where the subject of the drama is an absent presence, withdrawn from the stage until the last scene, contained, as she is, by irrational reason, and fancied as a continuous source of different meanings. In *Sei personaggi in cerca d'autore*, the problem of individual subjectivity is elided with the problem of the subject of representation. The illusions of self-representation are banished from the scene (the theatre exposed as theatre); the naked subjectivity of the realist subject in crisis finds its objective correlative in the naked subjectivity of the Six Characters who walk on to the stage from the back of the theatre (or descend on the scene from above, as having fallen), to proclaim their right as characters to wear their masks as they choose. The situation is indicative of a genuine revolution in drama; in the end, the revolution is contained within the structures it has overturned, but it also succeeds in endowing what had deteriorated into a nightmare of multiple points of view with an aesthetic consistency, both formal and thematic, a consistency which consists in the Characters' ability to perpetually re-create themselves. Their identities do not evolve from genetic or social predispositions, nor are they conditioned by historical factuality; rather these identities are aesthetic constructs: they are social masks covering an existential nakedness that are themselves signs of their own nakedness. They are *maschere nude* [naked masks], insofar as they, like human existence, are stripped of every substance, every social and historical point of reference. The stripping bare is, however, not an attempt to get at some genuine and timeless essence, but rather to posit as humankind's irremediable condition its opposite: inauthenticity, inessentiality.

What character in drama is more inauthentic and inessential than Henry IV? A king without a kingdom? A madman imprisoned in the fortress of his fantasy? Another, more authoritative spokesman for Pirandello's desolate vision of human existence? Certainly all of these. No doubt, Pirandello's ambition in writing this play was to dramatize the condition of nakedness described above, a condition which, as we have seen, translates into the question of modernity. How it translates or, rather, how it allegorizes that question is another matter.

Enrico IV can be most usefully read as an allegory of capitalist economic development, an allegory that captures in a unique way the psychic disorientation and derangement and the great emancipation that result from being released from the feudal confines of a precapitalist past.

The play's reference to Henry's fall from horseback during a pageant is significant in this regard; the pageant, like Henry's new existence, was another game of roles and hierarchies, organized and realized as a means of distraction, a psychological hiatus, from life in an expanded and fragmented world. Henry's fall is at once a fall from pretence (literally from the condition that precipitated his exile) and a fall that is symptomatic of the experience of modernity: a 'thrownness' (*Geworfenheit*), in the Heideggerian sense, into being-there that refers to the momentous transformation of individual subjectivity occurring under the impact of the capitalist market place; a fall into profound disorientation and insecurity that only madness can systematize:

Gli uomini del mille e novecento si abbaruffano ... s'arrabattono in un'ansia senza requie di sapere come si determineranno i loro casi, di vedere come si stabiliranno i fatti che li tengono in tanta ambascia e in tanta agitazione.[11]

[Men of the 20th century fight and struggle in ceaseless anxiety to know where their faiths and fortunes will bring them and to see how the things that hold them in such anguish and agitation will end.]

Pirandello, in other words, joins the ranks of those many writers and thinkers for whom modernity was a prison of conformity, or as Perry Anderson puts it, 'a spiritual wilderness of populations bleached of any organic community or vital autonomy.'[12] The players in Henry's fatal masquerade are the living proof of such conformity, as they all must conform to the new context that Henry has opened for them, dressing and speaking in accord with the world of the Emperor's castle. It is not by chance that Pirandello depicts these characters (Matilde, Frida, Carlo, Belcredi, and Doctor Genoni) in all their mediocrity as representatives of the modern world. Nor is it an accident that at the play's thematic core the passion of love, unabated by twenty years of reclusion, violently surfaces at the end of act 4. For into a world in which social identities and hierarchies have been uprooted humankind carries old drives and pulsations, the old libidinal self, as it were. The great, tragic emperor has been stripped bare of, among other things, the time of passion; emotional time has been replaced by the time clock which brutally ticks away his years.

But while Henry IV can be considered by his own admission a victim, he has found a way of avenging his tragic fate – he becomes an actor in a play that he himself has written, one in which he plays the part of a mad king. His fall from horseback into the madness of modernity activates a tremendous emancipation; he becomes literally bigger than life and capable of acting beyond all moral boundaries within a realm of absolute possibility. In the temporal perspective of his madness, history becomes totally subjectified and made to be experienced as theatre. The play-acting of the carnival (the pre-text) is transformed into the reality of the play; the player in the clothes of the emperor becomes the emperor-player. The erasure of real history – we learn of the hero's past only what is essential to provide the events with a sense of verisimilitude – makes it impossible for us to probe the social or psychological dimensions of Henry's predicament. Only the past of madness can be restored.

From this 'historical past' emerge the representatives of a lost collectivity, real persons who are forced to become characters in Henry's play. They symbolize the fragments of the world that Henry's madness transcends. Theirs is an attempt to reconstruct that world by means of a return to order, which means defeating the derangement that their own lifeworld has generated. Henry, we know, can be either mad or perfectly sane; it makes no difference whatsoever, given the achieved purity of his being.

The reasons Henry gives for his condition are all founded in his capacity for self-deception. He remembers how he used to elude the gaze of the Other, but in so doing plunge himself into the wholly private sphere of illusion where no stable identity could be found. Being forced to present always another image of self, he could never become real. His person, instead, is symbolic and, therefore, equivocal. By accepting his naked mask and becoming a Holy Roman Emperor, he has accepted the fate of living out his nothingness in a mythical presence: that of the Emperor, as an idea or institution, a bodyless self that exists everywhere and in no particular place.

It is not hard to understand why the character of Henry IV elicits in us contrasting feelings and why his equivocal and ambiguous persona can be regarded as a powerful voice of modern consciousness. The destabilizing potential of this character, and the transgressive nature of his existence are properties of the objective universe of commodity forms. He in many ways embodies the logic of the commodity: at once 'radical and conservative,' 'iconoclastic and incorporated,'[13] his existence is deliberately contradictory; he can become whatever he wants; his activity is determined by the fluctuations in the objective context; his identity, as with all of Pirandello's characters, is the identity of the Other.

But what makes this character such a powerful expression of human alienation is the simple fact that he is a king: that is, he is symbolic of a world still dominated by agrarian and aristocratic ruling classes.[14] Between this ancient regime and the modern world of capitalist economy there is obviously an enormous gap, one virtually present in the figuration of the Emperor, but this gap is bridged by the Emperor's alleged madness – the madness of being an Emperor in a world where the market is the organizing principle of culture and society. Hence, Henry's madness, which is emblematic of the spirit of the modern age, becomes a means of domination, indeed, of dictating. The game played out in *Enrico IV* is, in fact, a fantasy of domination. Henry represents the state that has become an omnipotent father who presents to the others not his fragmented existence, not his vulnerability, but rather an almost divine power. We are confronted not by the ontological insecurity of existential death and cultural despair characteristic of Pirandello's experience of modernity, but instead with a totalitarian microcosm, explicitly voiced by the hero: 'Eccomi qua: potete credere sul serio che Enrico IV sia ancora vivo? Eppure, ecco, parlo e comando a voi vivi. Vi voglio così!'[15] [Here I am: can you really believe that Henry IV is still alive? Yet, here I am, I speak and give you my commands. This is how I want you!].

Admittedly, my argument so far builds into a glaring paradox. How can the play's allegorical register contain two thoroughly opposing impulses? How can Henry IV be at once a figure for the emancipation of the individual self from the new bourgeois conformity that results from society's break with its pre-capitalist past and also an avenging victim of this emancipatory fall into madness? A simpler way of putting the question is: how can the hero be radical and iconoclastic and at the same time endeavour to restructure his life and world according to roles and hierarchies?

To explain the paradox we must consider the persona of Henry IV (and of the Pirandellian character in general) as the object-product of an economy at the beginning of its industrial course in which the still predominant artisanal organization of labour is confronted by the emergence of the new technologies associated with the second industrial revolution.[16] (For the playwright Pirandello, the cinema meant nothing less than the mechanization of art.) At the same time, the development of capitalism brought with it the fear of social revolution; the downfall of the old order, particularly in Italy, in no way ensured the welding of bourgeois democracy into a strong capitalist economic system. At the end of the First World War, the ancient regime was represented by a feeble monarchy, while socialism and liberalism appeared to walk hand in hand.[17] Pirandello's king is the allegorical embodiment of such a condition. First of all, he is a symbol of the ancient regime; his figure is emblematic of the universalizing claims of that order, but in a manner consistent with the precarious nature of Italy's own royal house – Henry IV can only govern within the confines of his castle. Second, Henry's exile is a return to a world before the advent of modern technologies, but one that offers no secure refuge. Third, Henry is fearful of being dispossessed; he has already lost his youth and his love, but now he stands to lose the liberty that his madness affords him. The ambiguity of his position, which he must preserve at any cost, is his only strength. The space his madness opens is left empty, undetermined by any one specific meaning, as the play concludes in the uncertainty as to whether his vengeful act is or is not the act of a madman. The breakdown of liberal reason and of positivist claims to knowledge offers no structured alternative. But the impulses that rule in *Henry IV* are not those of contingency, or of the limitless duration of illusion; they are not nihilistic in any current sense of the term. Henry does step off the stage to become a one in the many. He persists in believing in the transcendental identity of the subject, a unity that he can recompose only by means of domination, by persevering in the myth of self until his madness becomes the others' reality. Put differently, Henry's madness is an impulse toward a universality of pure being; his persona is the symbolic legitimation of such an imagined universality.

Henry's nakedness then is portrayed as the nakedness of humankind. The real nakedness of the sulphur mine workers that Pirandello knew first hand and the naked vulnerability of his class-bound social body fearful of revolution are incorporated into the divine body of the Emperor. This dislocation erases all references to history; we have passed on to another book, to another order of experience. What is this experience? For Pirandello it is madness: not madness in the proper clinical sense of the term, but rather metaphorically, the madness of convulsive disorder – a madness that has to be treated, aesthetically transformed into its own opposite, given plenitude, dilated in time, and dispersed indeterminately. What is distinctive about Henry IV is that he is not distinct, but that he is everything and thus no 'body.'

The nakedness of real historical referents has been , in other words, re-dressed.

In conclusion, I should like to return to the reference made at the outset to Shakespeare's King Lear. Here are Pirandello's own words:

Che è divenuto l'uomo? Che è divenuto questo microcosmo, questo re dell'universo? Ahi povero re! Non vi vedete saltar dinanzi Re Lear armato d'una scopa in tutta la sua tragica comicità? Di che farnetica egli? C'era una volta un superbo castello, un castello meraviglioso edificato su una rossa nube, una nube che parea di fiamma. Quel castello era la sua reggia, e il vento se la portò via. Tramontò il sole, e la nube si cangiò: divenne livida e poi man mano nera; finalmente si sciolse in acqua e quelle gocce parvero lagrime.[18]

[What has become of man? What has become of this microcosm, this king of the universe? Oh you wretched king! Don't you see King Lear spring up before you armed with a broom in all of his tragic comicality? What is he raving about? There was once a proud castle, a marvellous castle built on a red cloud, a cloud that looked like a flame. That castle was his palace, and the wind blew it away. The sun set, and the cloud changed: it became livid and then black; finally it turned into water and those drops resembled tears.]

For Pirandello, Lear is a tragic-comic figure, a raving fool, left naked in the cold, bereft of his power and grandeur. In Pirandello's view, Lear is tragic because he has suffered an irremediable loss, comic because he still thinks he is king. That Pirandello has distorted the meaning Shakespeare has given to Lear is less important than the cancelling of the tragic dimension that such a reading involves. The epistemological manoeuvre consists in hypostasizing the loss into *the* condition of modern existence and thus erasing Lear's enormous gain: not madness like Henry's (Lear is mad only in the sense that as a king he walks with mere mortals), but rather his consciousness of the suffering of others. Hence, for Pirandello, the liberating force of Lear's nakedness becomes an existential prison that knows no escape save that made possible by its transcendence in humour.

The technique of distancing through humour, we all know, is the principal characteristic of Pirandello's aesthetics. It allows readers or audience to suspend knowledge indefinitely in paradox. Who is the veiled woman of *Così è (se vi pare)*? Did the boy shoot himself at the end of *Sei personaggi*? Is Henry mad or is he just playing at madness?

While there are no answers to these questions, the posing of them diverts attention from the human nakedness from which they derive and which, as epistemological masks, they cover.

NOTES

1 Luigi Pirandello, 'Informazioni sul mio involontario soggiorno sulla terra' in *Saggi, poesie scritti varii*, ed. Manlio Lo Vecchio-Musti (Milan: Mondadori, 1960), 1101–9.
2 Marshall Berman, *All That Is Solid Melts into Air* (New York: Penguin Books, 1982). This work studies the relationship of modernity and revolution. For Berman, 'To be modern is to find ourselves in an environment that promises us adventure, power, joy, growth, transformation of ourselves and the world – and at the same time threatens to destroy everything we have, everything we know, everything we are. Modern environments and experiences cut across all boundaries of geography and ethnicity, of class and nationality, of religion and ideology; in this sense modernity can be said to unite all mankind. But it is a paradoxical unity, a unity of disunity; it pours us all into a maelstrom of perpetual disintegration and renewal, of struggle and contradiction, of ambiguity and anguish. To be modern is to be part of a universe in which, as Marx said, "All that is solid melts into air."' The present essay draws heavily on Berman's description of modernity and modernism as a historical experience.
3 Pirandello, 'Arte e coscienza d'oggi,' in *Saggi, poesie scritti varii*, 865–80. See, in particular, 871.
4 Ibid., 871–2.
5 Ibid., 880.
6 On the meaning of modernity, see also David Harvey, *The Condition of Postmodernity* (London: Basil Blackwell, 1989): 10–38.
7 Frederic Jameson, *The Political Unconscious* (Ithaca, NY: Cornell University Press, 1981).
8 Karl Marx and Frederick Engels, *The Communist Manifesto* (New York: Washington Square Press, 1969): 61–2.
9 See Berman, *All That is Solid*, 109.
10 Vincenzo Consolo, introduction to '*Nnfernu veru: uomini e immagini dei paesi dello zolfo*, ed. Aurelio Grimaldi (Rome: Edizioni Lavoro, 1985), 17.
11 Pirandello, *Enrico IV*, in *Maschere nude*, ed. Manlio Lo Vecchio-Musti (1958; Milan: Mondadori, 1978), 1:355.

12 Perry Anderson, 'Modernity and Revolution,' in *Marxism and the Interpretation of Culture*, ed. Cary Nelson and Lawrence Grossberg (Urbana and Chicago: University of Illinois Press, 1988), 319.
13 Terry Eagleton, *Ideology of the Aesthetic* (London: Basil Blackwell, 1990), 370.
14 See Anderson, 'Modernity and Revolution,' 324–5.
15 Pirandello, *Enrico IV*, in *Maschere nude*, 1:350.
16 Anderson, 'Modernity and Revolution,' 324.
17 Ibid., 325.
18 Pirandello, 'Arte e coscienza d'oggi,' 870.

9

Eros and Solitude in Pirandello's Short Stories

CORRADO DONATI

The problem of eros in Pirandello's work can be correctly investigated only if placed within the wider conception of the world which stands at the very foundation of his poetics and deals with life drives, in the general sense as they are defined by psychoanalysis:

Grande categoria di pulsioni che Freud contrappone, nella sua ultima teoria, alle pulsioni di morte. Esse tendono a instaurare unità sempre più grandi e a mantenere la coesione. Le pulsioni di vita, che sono designate anche col termine di Eros, ricoprono non solo le pulsioni sessuali propriamente dette, ma anche le pulsioni di autoconservazione.[1]

[Life drives are a large category that, in his latest theory, Freud juxtaposes to death drives. They tend to institute ever larger units and to maintain cohesion. Life drives, also designated by the term 'Eros,' include not only sexual drives, but also self-conservative drives.]

In this essay I shall limit my analysis to the relationship between affectivity and sexuality, using Pirandello's short stories as a privileged field of investigation because of the richness of the cases they present – these variety and wealth are thoroughly reflected in the author's novels and dramatic works.

My field of study leads me to work in that specific area in which life and sexual drives touch and interact, activating and/or negating themselves in opposite death drives. It is imperative to clarify this point here in order to avoid the error of reducing the theme of eros in Pirandello entirely to sexuality. Such specification, widely foreseen by psychoanalytic theory, will allow me to account for the narcissistic investments activated in the field of affectivity and sexuality that provoke behaviour far more complex than it seems at first reading.

In general terms, the problem falls within the boundaries of the relationship between social collectivity and individual subject, a relationship that always displays an oppositional nature in the Pirandellian character. Society has a series of strictly codified and widely binding norms that regulate individual behaviour and intersubjective exchange. From the point of view of the author, these norms are the connective tissue of society in a situation of crisis in which subjectivity no longer manages to identify with common values. Life thus unfolds in the forced respect of a play of appearances – 'masks' or 'forms' – which are mostly responsible for the alienation of an individual; the seriousness of this alienation is often measured by the degree of humoristic awareness. In any case, all Pirandellian heroes come out defeated from this conflictual relationship with the world, both those who suffer the contradiction between life and form, and those who *la agiscono* [act it out], as Barilli rightly observed,[2] with a rebellious gesture or a planned and lucid subversion of behaviour.

Falseness and fiction are unavoidable laws of our being-in-the-world, since, as one reads in Pirandello's essay *L'umorismo* [*On Humour*, 1908], the 'simulation' and 'dissimulation' that we exert in our relationship with others make us accustomed to pretending even with ourselves, so that we build a false identity. We do this with the noble intention of conforming such an identity to what psychoanalysis defines as the 'Ideal I'; Pirandello identifies as a stratification of behavioural schemes drawn from the external world or even inherited by race and mixed with powerful illusions which aid us in living.

This situation is reproduced, or rather, finds exemplary reflection, in the domestic microcosm. The family is a prison that becomes more and more oppressive as the laws that regulate this pivotal institution of society become stricter and stricter, since society itself imposes on the family unavoidable principles such as fidelity, respect, honour (including murder which takes its name from lost honour), dignity, and procreation.

It is mainly in this primary trap that, in the Pirandellian context, the wounded subjectivity of the character tries to redeem its alienation, to exit from the ties of conventions and appearances in order to realize itself in freedom. At certain times rebellion takes on sensational proportions that go beyond the boundaries of the family; at other times rebellion is disguised in small *escamotages*, furtive and surreptitious behaviour aimed at singling out small spaces for life in the suffocating context of daily existence. The defeat of the individual, inherent in the very structure of the world, recomposes the veil of respectable appearances momentarily torn apart by the revolt of the character. For this individual, the only choices are to reintegrate into the pre-existing order, to be emarginated from it forever in a condition which brings no harm (madness), or to enact a narcissistic defense through estrangement – a desperate, often self-inflicting logic (itself a form of madness, as Henry IV proves) – or through the *filosofia del lontano* [philosophy of farness].

In order to highlight the field in which eros brings all its subversive strength into play, I have simplified the view of a variety of cases not always reducible to a single typology by schematizing them.[3] In the situation described above, which stands as a common background to the stories of the characters, it is quite clear that eros taken as a category of the life drives cannot but represent a reference to an individual's longing for authenticity, a surfacing of a primordial need for freedom of desire, even and especially when such a desire belongs to the unconscious or instinctual self. As such, the surfacing of eros involves the disconnecting and destabilizing of a normative system that, by definition, is averse to eros itself. Here, we are beyond the Freudian 'discontent of civilization,' for in Pirandello it is not the super ego and the censorship it exerts over the subject that is at stake. What is brought into play is the claim that the authenticity of human beings and of life in its entirety is a necessary premise to civilization and history,[4] as they stand in a mythical and now unreachable time, and are enclosed in the darkest part of the unfathomable abyss of consciousness.[5] However, Pirandello experiences an incurable contradiction: one cannot do without civilization and history, and one cannot ignore the fact that conscience 'is no self-sufficient absolute' but is 'the others in ourselves.' Thus, on the one hand, in Pirandello and in a large segment of contemporary literature, eros represents a call for origins, for the myth of a whole and pure man; on the other hand, eros is always a discourse addressed to others and dealing with justice – the laws of man's desire – and with a possible world. It is relevant to underline this aspect, and thus avoid the interpretation of 'Pirandellism' as total negativity and absolute pessimism. This is certainly an inherent component of Pirandello's work, but one that may lead to a misinterpretation of the complexity of his message and, thus, of the issue here at hand. Critical historicism has taught that

Pirandello's man is first of all a twentieth-century man, and that the society within which he finds himself struggling between anguish and alienation is our bourgeois society. Thus, his needs, desires, impulses as well as his own eros are conditioned by a well-defined social *milieu*.

In 'Scialle nero' ['Black Shawl,' 1922] the female protagonist, Eleonora, sacrificed her own existence for her little brother and one of his friends, who had also become an orphan in his earliest youth. Now that both boys have a life of their own, Eleonora feels the weight of her own solitude:

Quei due o tre che un tempo l'avevano chiesta in matrimonio, avevano ormai moglie e figlioli. Prima, non se n'era mai curata; ora, a ripensarci, ne provava dispetto; provava invidia di tante sue amiche che erano riuscite a procurarsi uno stato.

Lei sola era rimasta così ...

Ma forse era in tempo ancora: chi sa? Doveva proprio chiudersi così la sua vita sempre attiva? in quel vuoto? doveva spegnersi così quella fiamma vigile del suo spirito appassionato? in quell'ombra?[6]

[Those two or three men who, at one point, had asked her in matrimony, had now wife and children. She had never cared about this before; now, thinking about it, she felt vexed by it; she felt envy for many of her friends who had found a social state.

She was the only woman in such a condition ...

Yet, perhaps there was still time left: who knows? Was her constantly active life to close in such a manner? in that void? was the alert flame of her passionate spirit to die out in such a way? in that shadow?][7]

The call of eros urges her to abandon herself to a love relationship with a much younger man, but an incipient pregnancy forces her to unveil her state. Thus, the repressive mechanisms of society are activated: the others' indignation and condemnation and a repairing marriage have the power to transform the impulse to affection into guilt and even into horror for the physical contact with the young husband. As he, urged by a powerful impulse, approaches her quivering with desire, Eleonora chooses suicide by letting herself fall from a precipice.

Placed in the opening section of *Novelle per un anno*, Eleonora's story is an exemplary case of how society manages to exercise an oppressive control over an individual's urges; eros is transformed into a negative condition for the subject to the point where the subject is pushed beyond narcissistic defenses and the very instinct of self-preservation.

This occurs even when sexuality is experienced with ignorance as a mystery over which the 'mana' of the collectivity projects a sense of guilt and horror. Such is the case of 'Pubertà' ['Puberty,' 1926], where a girl, as she perceives the unequivocal symptoms of her 'ripening' as a woman, reacts to the first erotic disturbances by throwing herself from the window.[8]

At times the narrative situation is more complex, as in the story of 'Zia Michelina' ['Aunt Michelina,' 1914], the young and attractive bride of a well-off old man. Marruca, a childless widower, adopts his beloved nephew, and then marries Michelina in the hope of giving his nephew the maternal affection he lacked. After Marruca's death, the feelings the nephew nourished for his young aunt turn into an authentic, passionate love. Because of economic concerns connected with Marruca's estate, the boy's true father tries to exploit the love story. In the end, troubled by the torpid interplay of conformism and slander developing around her personal life, Michelina agrees to marry her nephew, merely 'pro forma,' in order to demonstrate her total indifference. However, this event leads her to misinterpret the young man's true feelings for her, and to presume that he is faking as well. Once the nephew-husband forces her to meet her marital sexual duties, she commits suicide, still unaware of his authentic passion.

Whenever a victory of eros over social proprieties and conventions seems possible, a tragic event sanctions the prevailing of incomprehension over an individual's authenticity. Here, the young man, faced with the misunderstanding caused by the distortion of his real intentions, instead of resorting to the sincere feelings that fill his soul, is subjected to social conditioning and brutally claims his rights as husband.

In Pirandello's works there are several male characters whose physical impotence is the correlative of a violent and oppressive behaviour towards women. Men who are *affocati* [flared up], *stravolti* [upset], *scontraffatti* [twisted] manifest their eros only and merely as beastly sexuality exercised by right – a thoroughly macho right – over women, thus shattering their desire for a relationship built on affection and tenderness.

The case of 'Un cavallo nella luna' ['A Horse on the Moon,' 1925] seems emblematic. At a wedding party, the bride, 'una vera bambina ancora, vispa, fresca, aliena' [a true child still, lively, fresh, unaware] is next to her husband, a 'giovanotto grasso ... dal volto infocato' [fat young chap ... with a burning face] who, prey to an erotic frenzy, 'diventava di punto in punto più pavonazzo, quasi nero'[9] [was turning more and more purple, almost black]. The woman, still pervaded by the emotion of the event and the farewell to relatives as the banquet comes to an end, proposes a walk in the country to her husband, and in so doing tries to alleviate the state of excitement she reads on his face. As it often happens in Pirandello, the writing symbolically underlines the diverse moods of the two characters. Thus, to the young bride the country is filled with gay cries of 'calandre' [wood-larks], auspicious cock-crows, and refreshing breezes; to her husband, it is charged with 'un alido denso, ... grassi tepori, ... fragranze pungenti'[10] [a dense breath of wind, ... heavy warmths, ... stinging fragrances]. The romantic stroll turns into tragedy when Ida, taken by compassion for a dying horse abandoned to itself, rushes for help and, upon coming back, finds her husband having the death-rattle, killed by his own sexual furour.

Often violence dirties the purest feelings of delicate female presences with fragile and unripe bodies. Frequently the woman-victim has a name which includes the sema *luce* [light] and *leggerezza* [lightness], to underline the contrast between female candour and male violence. Only on occasion, however, are Pirandellian heroines equal to men; one example is Carlotta in 'Acqua amara' ['Bitter Water,' 1922] who, at first a tender lover, once married becomes her husband's most ferocious persecutor.

In the complexity of its drives, eros manifests for both man and woman an authentic desire that involves an intersubjective dialectic based on the unconditional recognition of the other. According to Pirandello, such an event occurs only outside any institutionalized relationship. The play of roles between husband and wife inevitably transforms a sentimental relationship into a battle for control.

This mostly happens when the object of desire, absent or lost, continues to dominate the subject from its institutional superiority. In 'L'uomo solo' ['The Lonely Man,' 1922], four friends, one of whom is divorced, bitterly contemplate their own solitude while sitting, as usual, at a bar table, and spying upon the 'fremito di vita' [throb of life] that propagates from the female bodies at strolling time:

Non staccavano gli occhi da una che per attaccarli subito a un'altra, e la seguivano con lo sguardo, studiandone ogni mossa o fissandone qualche tratto, il seno, i fianchi, la gola, le rosee braccia trasparenti dai merletti delle maniche:

storditi, inebriati da tutto quel brulichìo, da tutto quel fremito di vita, da tanta varietà d'aspetti e di colori e d'espressioni, e tenuti in un'ansia angosciosa di confusi sentimenti e pensieri e rimpianti e desiderii ...

Sentivano tutti e quattro, ciascuno a suo modo, il bisogno cocente della donna, di quel bene che nella vita può dar solo la donna, che tante di quelle donne già davano col loro amore, con la loro presenza, con le loro cure, e forse senz'esserne ricompensate a dovere dagli uomini ingrati.[11]

[They never detached their eyes from one but to attach them immediately to another woman; they would then follow her with their gaze, examining each move or staring at some traits, the breast, the hips, the throat, the pinky arms showing from the lace of the sleeves: dazed, intoxicated by all that swarm, by all that throb of life, by such a variety of appearances and colors and expressions, and held in an anguished anxiety made of confused feelings and thoughts and regrets and desires ...

All four of them, each in his own way, felt the acute need of a woman, of the good that in life only a woman can give, that so many women already gave with their love, presence, attentions, and perhaps without proper recognition from ungrateful men.]

When the friends find a solution to their problems by approaching women easier to meet, Groa, the divorced one, freezes in a refusal: 'Impossibile! Impossibile! Tu non puoi comprendere ... Il pudore! La santità della casa!'[12] [Impossible! Impossible! You cannot understand ... The decency! The sanctity of the home!] Evidently the idealized object of desire is no longer the absent woman, but the wife, with all the symbolic emblems that society attaches to her. The two components of Groa's behaviour are renunciation and narcissistic defense. In his conflict with eros, the death drives win and force him to suicide. This is the supreme assertion of the unicity of the object of desire and, at the same time, the integrity of the *I* .

One finds an analogous case in 'L'uscita del vedovo' [The Exit of the Widower,' 1922], where the call to life, after mourning, is embodied in a 'woman of pleasure,' already possessed by the protagonist before marriage. Here too, the image of the wife, who sadly overpowered him in life, is sacralized in the respect for family duties and nullifies his drives.

The so-called *condizione negativa* [negative condition] of eros in Pirandello's works is characterized by the clash of life drives and negative social and human contexts. Such contexts, by exercising a powerful repressive action, play on the ambiguous nature of the pleasure principle, and thus often convert the unsuccessful drive discharge into self-destructive behaviour.

Within a psychological perspective, one must also linger on one of the more complex short stories, one extremely dear to Pirandello, 'Pena di vivere così' ['Grief of Living in Such a Way,' 1920].[13] Mrs Lèuca, whose husband has abandoned her for a vulgar woman who attracted him in the trap of the senses, has been living for years in complete solitude. Dedicated to charitable institutions, and closed into a rational dimension of her own from which feelings are virtually excluded, she has become almost oblivious to the world around her. For her even charity is more an exercise of will than a way of participating in life. At a certain point, urged by the parish priest and a lawyer, Mrs Lèuca agrees to meet her husband occasionally in order to satisfy a need for moral support he manifests in his state of prostration. These meetings, together with her husband's confessions, provoke an anxiety which is however compensated by her satisfaction of being able to overcome a wife's wounded pride. All this she does in the name of Christian piety and charity.

Once her husband's lover is dead, Mrs Lèuca, who never had children and feels the weight of a missed maternity, agrees to give a home to the three girls born from his adulterous relationship. With them, she takes back her husband as well, on condition that he will not demand a regular married life. The new state of things upsets her orderly and rational existence; she begins to neglect the charitable organizations to devote herself to the anomalous family that has brought a breath of life into her home. It is evident that Mrs Lèuca secretly wishes a total plenitude in her female function, but she refrains from it out of dignity and distrust. She feels both attraction and uncontrollable horror toward any physical contact with her husband. He abides by the set rules, and respects them until he elopes once again with the niece of one of her friends. Mrs Lèuca is then left alone with the young girls and her grief of living. Such grief is the signal of a painful fracture between desire and reality, but also of an awareness of her incomplete life that lacks the fulfilment of those drives of eros, repressed or negated, that would allow her to acquire plenitude.

Pirandello's writing is not limited to a description of Mrs Lèuca's psychological states, using indirect speech in such a thorough manner that it denounces the identification between narrator and character. Often his narrative language resorts to rhetorical images that create the protagonist's emotions in a metaphorical fashion on the page. For instance, the opening description of the story – 'silenzio di specchio, odore di cera ai pavimenti, fresca lindura di tendine di mussola alle finestre'[14] [silence of glass, smell of waxed floors, fresh cleanness of muslin curtains at the windows] – is already the description of an interior universe in which order and ataraxy conceal a repressed anguish. Such an idea is reinforced by a dense presence of objects that complete the psychological panorama: the 'pendola grande' [big pendulum-clock] with its 'tic e tac lento e staccato' [slow and detached tick-tock], the 'oggettini di vetro e d'argento' [little objects in glass and silver], the 'gocciole di candelabri dorati sulla mensola' [drops of gilt candelabra on the console], the 'bicchierini della rosoliera sul tavolino da tè' [little glasses around the bottle of rosolio on the tea table]. All these objects correspond to the image of Mrs Lèuca as 'alta e dritta, e così fresca, così bianca e così rosea'[15] [tall and straight, and so fresh, so white and so rosy] – drawn with the excessive use of adjectives typical of Pirandellian characterizations.

As a matter of fact, the narration immediately focuses on the central issue: the relation between this non-life, closed in sterile perfection, and true life, which is felt as,

Una vergogna da non potersi nemmeno confessare: una miseria da compatire così, stringendo le spalle e socchiudendo gli occhi, o spingendo sù sù il mento come fosse anche un ben duro e amaro boccone da ingozzare.[16]

[A shame that one cannot even confess: a misery to endure in this way, shrugging one's shoulders and half-closing the eyes, or pushing the chin up high as if it were also a tough and bitter pill to swallow.]

There seems to be a precise choice in favour of the values of a spirituality strictly connected to the exercise of a reason that repudiates feelings as if they were the product of a compromise with the materiality and ugliness of the world. Frequently, in fact, life and eros bear the connotation of something that dirties and muddies, and they stand in evident opposition to the cleanness of the house and soul of Mrs Lèuca. However, if we consider the select environment to which she is proud to belong, we perceive equally negative signals. Miss Trekke, a member of the benevolent society '(è) lunga di gambe, corta di vita e con la schiena ad arco' [has long legs, is short-waisted and has an arched back], she has a 'bianca bocca sdentata' [white and toothless mouth] and two eyes 'come due chiari laghi che tra la desolazione s'ostinino a riflettere i cieli innocenti e sorridenti della sua giovinezza'[17] [like two clear lakes that in the general desolation insist on reflecting the innocent and smiling skies of her youth]. As always in Pirandello, body disproportions and malformations are symptoms of an intimate condition, especially an affectation which is out of key with the context of the story but in key with the person. Thus, in Miss Trekke, 'la sua bontà, che pure è vera, assume spesso apparenze d'ipocrisia' [her goodness is true and yet often has the appearance of hypocrisy].

It is not possible to institute a radical opposition between the positive world of spiritual values and the negative one of corrupted physical values. This is even more so since there are numerous stylistic references to a conflict between these two worlds, a conflict that is latent in the soul of Mrs Lèuca. Far too many are the denials that populate her interior discourse every time there is a suspicion of yielding to desire; far too obsessive are the references to the horror of the flesh, insisted upon as much as those to her lucid conscience, estranged from the world of feelings. Ultimately, far too ostentatious is her aversion towards the turpitudes that the husband confesses to having performed with the other woman. Pirandello plays on those confessions with psychological ability, by exaggerating the ardour with which the husband flagellates himself in front of Mrs Lèuca and feigns a repentance for base actions that he obviously does not view as such, and by showing the woman as excessively upset – a symptom of a conflict between moral reproach and the unconfessed desire of her libido.

As Freud taught us, it often happens that a subject asserts by negating. The indirect confession of a repressed eros surfaces here and there with the exercising of her will to 'vincere l'orrore del suo stesso corpo, della sua stessa carne, per tutto ciò che nell'intimità si passa, anche senza volerlo, e che nessuno vuol confessare nemmeno a se stesso'[18] [overcome the horror of her own body, of her own flesh, because of all that one must face in one's intimacy, even without wanting it, and nobody confesses even to oneself].

On the other hand, when she was living with her husband, her body did not give in merely because of marital duties, but:

anche per sé, anche sapendo bene che non poteva valer per esso la scusa di quel dovere di fronte alla sua coscienza che, subito dopo, si risvegliava disgustata, perché già da un pezzo, non pur l'amore, ma ogni stima le era caduta per quell'uomo.[19]

[for herself as well, even though knowing that the justification of that duty could not count for it in the face of her conscience since, immediately after, she would awake in disgust, because she had long lost not only love but also respect for that man.]

It is not a case of true sexual phobia but one of refusal of the fracture between emotional life and sexuality, a fracture that occurs when there is a lack of total recognition of the other, a recognition that should be the vital foundation of eros in a couple. One could say that in psychoanalysis, the case of Mrs Lèuca is a trauma connected to the misrecognition of her desire as a woman even before her desire as a wife. The wound without compensation, together with the blocked discharge of a complex aggressive instinct born out of it, have strengthened the narcissistic barriers and awakened the self-destructive instinct that is connected to them.

That very 'silence of glass,' a silence of a reflected image void of autonomous life, is the symptom of a *Hilflosigkeit*, a state of psychic impotence connected to anguish.[20] In Mrs Lèuca, the repressed eros induces a fear of facing the trial again, and reproducing the conditions of the trauma she had to suffer, and at the same time, urges her to desire it; here lies the reason of her ambiguous psychological condition. The reiterated awaiting, mixed with repulsion, that her husband, once at home again, might demand from her the sexual act, turns into disappointment at the second abandonment:

E' sicura di potere ancora affermare a se stessa, non ostante lo sdegno di cui è piena per la sua carne miserabile, che se una di quelle sere il marito, nel silenzio della casa, la avesse ghermita, non avrebbe ceduto, lo avrebbe respinto, opponendosi anche alla lusinga della sua coscienza, la quale tentava d'indurla a considerare che, respingendolo, avrebbe dato lei a quell'uomo il pretesto di ricadere nell'orribile vita di prima ... Sì; ma è ugualmente sicura la signora Lèuca che, se questo fosse avvenuto, il supplizio per lei sarebbe stato molto meno crudele di quello che ha sofferto, non essendo avvenuto.

Perché a poco a poco l'orrore del corpo di lui, in tutte quelle immagini indelebili che le si erano destate durante la confessione delle sue turpitudini, era divenuto orrore del suo stesso corpo; il quale, ogni sera, davanti allo specchio, appena ella si richiudeva in camera (e senza più girar la chiave nella serratura!) le domandava, se davvero esso fosse ormai così poco desiderabile, da non esser più nemmeno guardato di sfuggita da un uomo come quello, che s'era contentato fino a poco fa d'una donnaccia volgare.[21]

[She knows that she is still able to assert herself notwithstanding the disdain she is filled with because of her miserable flesh; so much so, she knows that, if one night her husband, in the silence of the home, had snatched her, she wouldn't have given in, she would have rejected him, opposing even the enticement of her conscience, which induced her to think that by rejecting him she would give him a reason to fall back into his earlier horrible life ... Yes; but she, Mrs Lèuca, is equally certain that, if this had happened, the supplice for her would have been far less cruel than that she had to suffer for it not having happened.

Little by little the horror for his body, in all those ineffaceable images born in her during the confession of his turpitudes, had become horror for her own body. Every night, in front of the mirror, as soon as she would close herself in her room (not even locking the door!), her body would ask her if it was truly so undesirable that even a man like that, who up to that point had been content with a vulgar loose woman, wouldn't even want to catch a glimpse of it.]

The passage exemplarily demonstrates the play between desire and denial in Mrs Lèuca. The refusal of sexuality occurs only insofar as the return of repression again proposes the theme of the wound, and the idea of the sexual act as violence that reduces the woman to an object of possession (to be 'snatched'). The fact is that for Mrs Lèuca, as for all the various Luciettas and Lucillas of Pirandello's universe, eros involves an investment that is contemporarily lustful in general and affective in particular. Life and sexual drives, as stated above, touch one another wherever life, in the fullness of its becoming (outside the play of fictive forms), equals authenticity of the self. In the erotic relationship this authenticity is, for Pirandello, the inescapable form of the other's desire.

This schizophrenia of the female protagonist ultimately reflects the schizophrenia of the outside world, with the charitable ladies and petit bourgeois niceness that serve as an excuse for backbiting and suspicion, and with the play of roles between husband, wife, and lover. The husband is also schizophrenic as he, conditioned by that society and his machismo, separates love and sex, dignity and turpitude, sense of family and desire for pleasure, wife and woman.

This analysis is further reinforced by all those short stories in which a kind of 'positive version' of eros (with all the limits that the term 'positive' imposes when one speaks about Pirandello) is thematized. In Pirandello's work, eros can manifest itself only in the remote parenthesis of a dream or in a spatio-temporal dimension removed from a social context. The narrative exemplification in 'La realtà del sogno' [The Reality of Dream,' 1914] is comparable to the best analytic literature by Freud. Pirandello's decision to use nameless characters symbolizes his exclusive interest in the psychological analysis of the case. The protagonist is a woman whose femininity has been repressed in youth by a father who was 'più geloso di una tigre' [more jealous than a tiger] and who prevented her from having any relationship – even if only cognitive – with any other man, including her fiancé, till the day of their wedding.

Here we face a classical oedipal situation experienced by a woman with a high degree of awareness. After the marriage, this situation translates into the wife's acute disdain for her husband as one who continues her father's authoritarianism and yet is also guilty of moments of weakness that increase her anger. Thus she is forced to ascertain that her companion 'non capiva niente, proprio non capiva niente di quanto avveniva in lei!'[22] [did not understand anything, truly did not understand anything of what was happening in her!].

The result is that the woman suffers from an almost total inability to face social relationships with other men, even the most intimate friends of the family, to the point where she rushes to lock herself in a room when visitors arrive. It is evident that her contempt for her husband derives from his unawareness of her desire for him to have the role of father-lover. That is precisely the role that she identifies as the correct social function of the father, one which finally explicates itself through the acknowlegment of her own femininity, and thus abolishes the censorship of her childhood years. On the contrary, the real heart of the matter lies in the husband's inability to take on this role. His banal attempts to convince his wife that her hiding from others is merely due to a kind of fixation translate into superficial praise of her intelligence and liveliness, and silly acknowledgments of a feminine impudence.

Avrebbe dovuto metterlo almeno in apprensione il fatto che ella non protestava contro quella sua cento volte asserita 'fissazione', e accoglieva quelle lodi sul suo parlar franco e disinvolto e finanche ardito, con evidente compiacimento.[23]

[He should have been alerted by the fact that she did not protest against her one hundred times stated 'fixation,' and welcomed those praises of her open and easy and even daring way of speaking with overt satisfaction.]

Only the closest friend of the family, whose company the woman accepts at times, understands that underneath this behaviour there lies a repressed sexuality which demands the chance to manifest itself freely.

Pirandello displays great interpretative acuity by expressing the 'request' the woman poses to her husband precisely through an act of negation. Her refusal to accept male presence by declaring embarrassment with blushing and an inability to speak is nothing but a request addressed to her husband through symbolic and bodily order. Indeed she asks him to be the first to recognize her female identity, and, most of all, the part of her pulsional life that defines and characterizes her as a woman. With an increased psychological probing, Pirandello notes how sexuality, misrecognized by the husband, changes into aggressiveness at any occasion of crisis, so that she feels 'la tentazione di graffiarlo, di schiaffeggiarlo, di morderlo' [tempted to scratch him, to slap him, to bite him]. Such a feeling is a way to give vent to libidinal energies cumulated but never employed in the erotic-affective investment to which they were destined. In fact, when the friend instills in her the doubt that her decency is 'la vendetta dell'insincerità' [the vengeance of insincerity], the mask for a strong sexuality she has unconsciously repressed, her first reaction is an excess of aggressiveness towards her husband. Since he does not seem to understand the meaning of these metaphoric messages, desire resorts to dream to find its own fulfilment.

Even the narration of the oneiric event itself, in which the woman has an erotic rendezvous with the family friend, corresponds to perfect psychoanalytic patterns: the previous dialogue with him, by unveiling indirectly the unconscious reasons of her neurosis, causes a transfer that charges the manifest content of her dream with precise characteristics: 'Cominciò come una sfida, quel sogno, come una prova a cui quell'uomo odiosissimo la sfidasse, in séguito alla discussione avuta con lei tre sere avanti.'[24] [It started as a challenge, that dream, as a trial to which that hateful man challenged her, as a consequence of the argument they had had three nights before.]

The concept of challenge symbolizes that stage of psychological analysis in which the analyst approaches an understanding of the unconscious motivations that determine a pathological state in the subject, who then activates his/her defenses by masking his/her own interior truth and even by trying to distract and deviate the interpretative work. It is meaningful here that the hatefulness of the challenge is thrown entirely on the family friend, who embodies the woman's *alter ego* that is removed by the censorship of the superego. Once the censorship is avoided, the hatefulness turns into an erotic and affective impulse, exactly like the case in which a patient tries to 'seduce' an analyst.

Once the dream has ended, or rather is interrupted by an anguished awakening, the unconscious causes of her complex appear clearly to the woman:

Ecco: ella lo aveva tradito in sogno; tradito, e non ne aveva rimorso, no, ma rabbia per sé, d'essere stata vinta, e rancore contro di lui, anche perché in sei anni di matrimonio non aveva saputo mai, mai farle provare quel che aveva or ora provato in sogno, con un altro.[25]

[Here it is: she had betrayed him in a dream; betrayed, and she did not feel remorse, no, but anger towards herself for having been defeated, and rancor towards him, even because in six years of marriage he had never been able, never to make her feel what she had just now felt in a dream with another man.]

But if we go beyond the literal meaning of the dream, and think about its possible latent content, we notice first of all that the adultery is accepted as if it had really happened not to fulfill a desire, but to 'punish' her husband. It is thus evident that in the dream the character of the friend with its hatefulness represents, because of a phenomenon of displacement, the hatefulness of the husband who challenges the wife with his own erotic abilities to manifest her own sensuality and satisfy it. This is indeed the real desire of the woman, and yet it has not taken place in reality. Thus the oneiric action acts as a hallucinatory compensation, and in the wake is turned into a punitive action towards the true offender.

The woman does not immediately narrate the dream to her husband, since she knows that he would not be shaken by a merely oneiric fantasy. On the contrary she awaits the next visit of the friend to stage a hysterical crisis in which, almost raping him under her husband's amazed eyes, she gives a real body to her dream fantasies. In so doing she reveals a desire which has acquired pathological dimensions.

Being unconsciously safe from an adulterous desire which the superego was obviously censoring and, thus, attributing that desire to an irresponsible dream, the woman can finally recount it in detail to her stupefied husband, as if she really experienced it. Through the aggressiveness of the punishment she inflicts on him, she obtains the goal of making her own desire explicit, thus avoiding the sense of guilt she would have felt in freeing and clearly expressing her own sensual nature.

In 'La realtà del sogno' Pirandello displays an almost perfect knowledge of unconscious psychic mechanisms, and the language of hysteria which comes to express the profound reality of the human soul whenever such a reality is rejected by others. Yet, most of all, he highlights the nature of the specular relationship between the self and the other, and identifies eros as the sphere of human life in which this relationship is explicated in its radical evidence.

Another short story in which eros manifests itself in a dimension removed from the social context is the tale 'Rondone e Rondinella' ['Swift and Swallow,' 1913]. Here the poetic nicknames designate a couple of unknown and anonymous foreigners who every year during summer return to their love nest in an out-of-the-way mountain village. It is an adulterous love, outside conventional schemes, that finds its vital space in the isolation, anonymity, and cyclic rhythm with which it renews itself and comes to life outside the normal flowing of time. In this context, even the traditional rapport of strength and violence between a man and a woman is annulled:

Ma tra le braccia di quell'omone, che nella villetta lassù l'attendeva impaziente, con un fremito di belva intenerita, ella, così piccola e gracile, correva ogni anno a gettarsi felice, senza nessuna paura, non che di spezzarsi, ma neppur di farsi male un pochino. Sapeva tutta la dolcezza di quella forza, tutta la leggerezza sicura e tenace di quell'impeto, e s'abbandonava a lui perdutamente.[26]

[But in the arms of that big man who awaited her impatiently in the little villa up there, with a thrill similar to that of a softened wild beast, every year she, so tiny and delicate, threw herself happily and with no fear of breaking or even hurting herself a little. She knew all the sweetness of that strength, all the firm and tenacious lightness of that impetus, and she would give herself up to him hopelessly.]

In this case the bond of eros is so intense and total as to challenge death itself. One year Rondinella comes back without Rondone to die in their nest, suggesting that he is dead. She is accompanied by her husband who is identified by the 'legality' springing from his bearing:

Non poteva essere che il marito, colui! La legalità, pareva, fatta persona. E, *legalità*, pareva dicesse ogni sguardo degli occhi ovati dietro gli occhiali; *legalità*, ogni atto, ogni gesto; *legalità*, *legalità*, ogni passo ...[27]

[He could be nobody else but her husband, that guy! Legality, it seemed, turned into a person. And, *legality* seemed to be expressed by every gaze of the oval eyes behind the glasses; *legality*, by every act, every gesture; *legality*, *legality*, by every step ...]

Rondinella's death is a 'je t'accuse' to this legality which kills eros:

Ridete forte di quest'uomo composto e rispettabile, che sa parlare così esatto e compito! Egli mi fa morire, con la sua rispettabilità, con la sua quadrata esattezza scrupolosa![28]

[Laugh hard at this dignified and respectable man, who can speak with precision and politeness! He makes me die with his respectability, with his rigid and scrupulous exactitude!]

To conclude our brief review of the theme of eros and solitude in Pirandello's short stories, one must examine the most intense and poetic tale 'Il viaggio' ['The Journey,' 1928]. It is the story of a woman who goes on the first and last journey of her life in the vain hope that some doctor can cure her from an apparently incurable disease. During the journey, accompanied by her brother-in-law, she discovers the emotional and sensual fullness of an authentic love relationship.

The short story is built on a dense texture of symbolic references. Adriana's living conditions are similar to a situation of spiritual death, a situation which finds a physical correspondent in the real death impending over her. It is not by chance that the incurable disease affects her lungs, the site of that *flatus vitae* which has been extinguished in her for a long time. In this sense, the journey, proposed by her brother-in-law and prolonged from Palermo, which was to be the supposed last stop, to Naples, and then to Venice, is no longer 'quell'ultimo e straordinario svago, come un tenue compenso alla crudeltà della sorte' [that last and extraordinary diversion, like a feeble reward for the cruelty of fate] but becomes a journey of initiation to another life. Adriana clearly feels the symbolic value of this act:

Poteva ella confessargli l'oscuro presentimento che la angosciava alla vista di quel mare, che cioè, se fosse partita, se si fosse staccata dalle sponde dell'isola che già le parevano tanto lontane dal suo paesello e così nuove; in cui già tanta agitazione, e così strana, aveva provato; se con lui si fosse avventurata ancor più lontano, con lui sperduta nella tremenda, misteriosa lontananza di quel mare, non sarebbe più ritornata alla sua casa, non avrebbe più rivalicato quelle acque, se non fosse morta?[29]

[Could she confess to him the obscure foreboding that anguished her at the sight of that sea, the fact that, if she had departed, if she had detached herself from the shores of that island which already appeared so distant from her village and so new; a feeling that had already provoked in her a great and strange excitement; if, with him, she had ventured even further away, with him lost in the terrible and mysterious farness of that sea, she would have not come back to her home, she would have no longer traversed those waters, if she did not die?]

To plough the waters is a rite of initiation of the spirit which inevitably precludes the possibility to return to the previous state. In Adriana the very perception of reality changes. In Palermo the water of the Hercules fountain had seemed to her 'vitrea' [vitreous] and the 'alito fresco [che] veniva da quell'acqua' [fresh breath coming from that water] had opened her mind to a 'lucida, sconfinata coscienza di tutto' [lucid, unlimited consciousness of everything],[30] an experience which would compensate her for a poor existence with a moment of eternity. But in Pirandello this 'unlimited consciousness' (see also 'Di sera, un geranio' ['One Evening, a Geranium,' 1934]) is already a surrender to the vanity of existence.

Once on the sea, the 'lugubre maschera di fuoco' [gloomy mask of fire] of the rising moon changes, 'man mano schiarendosi, restringendosi precisa nel suo niveo fulgore che allargò il mare in un argenteo palpito senza fine' [slowly clearing, growing smaller in its snow-white brilliance that made the sea grow larger with a silver infinite throb]. This throb is the sign of the awakening of eros as it evokes its close links to Thanatos: dismay and anguish of a 'delirio che la rapiva e la traeva irresistibilmente a nascondere, esausta, la faccia nel petto di lui'[31] [delirium that ravished and urged her to hide, exhausted, her face in his chest].

The love that is coming to life between the two has the strength of a pulsional charge equal to the death drive that accompanies her – it is a 'fire,' a:

delirio, una frenesia, a cui diedero una violenta lena instancabile la brama di ricompensarsi di quei pochi giorni sotto la condanna mortale di lei, di tutti quegli anni perduti, di soffocato ardore e di nascosta febbre; il bisogno di accecarsi, di perdersi, di non vedersi quali finora l'uno per l'altra erano stati per tanti anni, nelle composte apparenze oneste, laggiù, nella cittaduzza dai rigidi costumi, per cui quel loro amore, le loro nozze domani sarebbero apparse come un inaudito sacrilegio.[32]

[delirium, a frenzy, to which the yearning to reward themselves for those few days lived under the siege of her mortal sentence, for all those lost years of repressed ardour and hidden fever gave an indefatigable and violent energy; the need to become blind, to lose oneself, not to see each other the way they had been for one another for so many years, in the dignified and honest appearances, down there, in the small town with rigid customs, according to which that love of theirs, their wedding tomorrow would have seemed an incredible sacrilege.]

This strength is subversive: it destroys the 'dignified and honest appearances' which entrap true life within rigid social customs; it denies institutionalizing and denies life itself as a return to continuity in the play of false proprieties.

Adriana's suicide in Venice, the city of waters that the literary tradition has linked to the symbolic union of life and death, does not seem so much a yielding to the disease that condemns her but a tragic choice for freedom, the fulfilment of a destiny in the unrepeatable, final instant of the plenitude of living.

The Pirandellian eros is a transgressive strength that is only possible in the atemporal space which encloses a person between the death in life and the surrender to the boundless evanescence of nothingness. This instant, in which there is no place for the cruel play of appearances, is the eternal instant in which life finds its agreement with the becoming that generates life. In this instant life discovers the authenticity of being; it burns and is consumed in the fire of a subjective truth.

In Pirandello the place of eros is thus, in general, the place of his most severe critique of a society that no longer recognizes the value of rejoicing, and hides its own failure behind the irrevocable condemnation of any form of pleasure.

Translated by Manuela Gieri

NOTES

This essay was first published in a longer Italian version under the title 'Eros e solitudine nelle novelle di Pirandello' in Corrado Donati, *Il sogno e la ragione: Saggi pirandelliani* (Naples: Edizioni Scientifiche Italiane, 1993), 51–80.

1 J. Laplanche, and J.-B. Pontalis, *Enciclopedia della psicanalisi* (Bari: Laterza, 1973) 2:473.
2 Renato Barilli, *La barriera del naturalismo* (Milan: Mursia, 1964), 55.
3 For an in-depth analysis of 'transgression,' an analysis developed with an anthropological perspective and aimed at defining a typology of human behaviour in Pirandello, see the useful work by A.P. Mundula, *Pirandello e le violazioni del proibito* (Rome: Lucarini, 1986).
4 On this matter see Arcangelo Leone De Castris, *Storia di Pirandello* (Bari: Laterza, 1962); see also the more recent study by Umberto Artioli, *L'officina segreta di Pirandello* (Bari: Laterza, 1989), which offers a new and in many respects surprising interpretation of Pirandello as 'guardian of archetypes.'
5 The issue of consciousness of the Pirandellian man, seen in the perspective of modernity and in its psychoanalytic and philosophical implications, is a fundamental theme of the 'paradigmatic' vision of Pirandello that Wladimir Krysinski discusses in his volume, *Il paradigma inquieto: Pirandello e lo spazio comparativo della modernità* (Naples: Edizioni Scientifiche Italiane, 1988).
6 Luigi Pirandello, 'Scialle nero,' in *Novelle per un anno* (Milan: Mondadori, 1985), 1:13.

7 English translations of the selected passages from Pirandello's short stories were done by the translator.
8 An analogous case, extensively analysed by Lugnani within the wider theme of childhood, can be found in 'La veste lunga' ['The Long Gown']. See Lucio Lugnani, *L'infanzia felice* (Naples: Liguori, 1986), and especially the chapter bearing the same title as the volume.
9 Pirandello, 'Un cavallo nella luna,' in *Novelle per un anno*, 2:682.
10 Ibid., 684.
11 Pirandello, 'L'uomo solo,' in *Novelle per un anno*, 1/1:639–40.
12 Ibid., 647.
13 This short story is the object of a long analysis in a volume by Gioanola, who discusses it for an entire chapter dedicated to the 'impossible sexuality' in Pirandello. Gioanola's lucid and rigorous Freudian reading leads the critic to talk, in general, about the schizophrenic personality of Pirandellian characters, and, in relation to the theme at hand, about a true sexual phobia that masks their latent homosexuality. As usual, Freudian analysis involves, I believe, a certain degree of determinism, mostly linked to the fact that the subject is considered to be a self-sufficient psychic entity, and little or no relevance is given to the exchange between the *I* and external reality. While examining the story of Mrs Lèuca (a name that contains the sememe 'light'), I would like to demonstrate the problematic and complex nature of this relationship, one which requires a much more articulate evaluation. See Elio Gioanola, *Pirandello la follia* (Genoa: Il Melangolo, 1983), and in particular the chapter 'Pena di vivere così: la sessualità impossibile.'
14 Pirandello, 'Pena di vivere così,' in *Novelle per un anno*, 2:205.
15 Ibid., 205–6.
16 Ibid., 206.
17 Ibid., 206–7.
18 Ibid., 208.
19 Ibid., 222.
20 On the concept of *Hilflosigkeit* in Freud, see Laplanche-Pontalis, especially the considerations on the 'State of impotence,' 227–9. See also the important observations made by Green, 85–6.
21 Pirandello, 'Pene di vivere così,' 259–60.
22 Pirandello, 'La realtà del sogno,' in *Novelle per un anno*, 3:480.
23 Ibid., 483.
24 Ibid., 486.
25 Ibid., 487.
26 Pirandello, 'Rondone e Rondinella,' in *Novelle per un anno*, 2:670.

27 Ibid., 673.
28 Ibid., 674.
29 Pirandello, 'Il viaggio,' in *Novelle per un anno,* 3:226.
30 Ibid., 224.
31 Ibid., 227.
32 Ibid., 228.

SECTION 4
INNOVATIONS

10

Enacting the Dissolution of the Self: Woman as One, No One, and One Hundred Thousand

DANIELA BINI

Mattia Pascal, Lamberto Laudisi, Leone Gala, Serafino Gubbio, Enrico IV, and Vitangelo Moscarda are perhaps the best known of Pirandello's *raisonneurs*, the humorist protagonists of his works. The ideal space for this type of character is the novel – the genre suited for reflection, monologue, and philosophical analysis. Three of the characters mentioned above are the sole protagonists of Pirandello's most famous novels, where page after page is devoted to their endless philosophical monologues that replace actions. The traditional dichotomy of life/thought or action/reflection, a central topos of twentieth-century literature, is taken to its extreme by Pirandello. Pascal, Gubbio, and Moscarda reflect and do not act. Laudisi, Gala, and Enrico IV also reflect and do not act, but they are characters of plays, and theatre is, as Pirandello said, the art form closest to life. Theatre is action and movement; little or no place can be given to reflection. Leone Gala, Lamberto Laudisi, and even more Enrico IV, in fact, are outsiders, spectators, non-participants in the life that goes on beside them. Their detachment from life enables them to observe and judge. Pirandello's male philosophers claim their intellectual superiority over the rest of humanity – male and female – which is too involved in the chaos of existence to be able to analyse and understand it.

Reason is the exclusive attribute of the male, as western philosophy has taught us since the times of Plato and Aristotle. Nature and instinct are the female sphere. This dichotomy of spirit as male versus matter as female, male mind versus female matter, has come down to the present through the writings of philosophers like Schopenhauer, Nietzsche, and Weininger. Woman, however, has had her exclusive domain too, totally inaccessible to men: procreation. Her being – nature, matter, earth – has its fulfilment in motherhood. Karen Horney traced this dichotomy back to its origin, arguing that man's exclusive appropriation of the realm of reason, and the exclusion of woman from it, was caused by his womb's envy.[1] Excluded by nature from procreation, man made himself the sole proprietor of reason, legitimizing his claim by a similar natural law. Being the possessor of reason, hence the creator of systems of values and ideals by which to think and judge, man devalued the realm of nature, woman's territory, as the realm of change and 'becoming' (in the Parmenidean sense of the word), of matter and deterioration. He made for himself the fictitious and abstract realm of thought, of immutable and absolute ideas, that he named the world of truths, from which woman was excluded. As Hannah Arendt ironically put it, in this tradition 'whatever is not given to the senses ... is more real, more truthful, more meaningful than what appears.'[2] From Plato and Aristotle through Christianity, the world of the senses has been constantly demeaned, the body debased and its needs and feelings repressed, with the absurd and dangerous consequence that only the non-existent 'being,' a man-made invention, has maintained absolute value and power. Philosophy, as Cixous and Clément rightly saw, was then 'constructed on the premise of woman's abasement.'[3]

This cultural tradition, exasperated by Christianity, became pathological in Sicilian culture. In the essay 'Pirandello e la Sicilia' Leonardo Sciascia elaborated the formula *stilnovismo patologico* to explain the complex and ambiguous Sicilian view of woman.[4] The assimilation of a primitive religion with its cult of the Mother earth – a symbol of life and fertility – into the Christian tradition, where the spirit is exalted and the flesh is condemned, and where the central figure becomes the Virgin Mary, can help to explain in part the Sicilian male's ambivalence toward women. In speaking of Pirandello, therefore, we should never forget his background; we should keep in mind not only the advanced philosophical thought he encountered as a student in Bonn, but also the puritanical, stifling environment of Girgenti, his birthplace. The powerful influence of the latter, in fact, is clearly visible, though seldom commented upon, in Pirandello's acceptance of a family-arranged marriage. How could a man with such a revolutionary intellect, capable of shattering to fragments solid 'truths' and immovable pillars of century-old beliefs, how could such a mind accept the wife his father had chosen for him? A wife, moreover, raised by an overly possessive, authoritarian, puritanical father, one who locked his daughters in the house, forbidding them even to look out the windows? What intellectual companionship, or even conversation, could he expect from a wife whose education had been entrusted to nuns? Could he not foresee the shocking effect the letters he wrote to his young fiancée from Rome would have on her naïve mind?[5] Attempting to answer these questions would take us away from the aim of this study, which is to show how Pirandello the artist, with a typical humorist twist, leaves behind the traditional Sicilian male Pirandello, and places woman in a privileged space.[6]

The central position of the male *raisonneur*, holder of the *logos*, subject and creator of discourse, and the subordinate place of woman, deprived of any autonomy, object and creature of the male subject, have been underlined by critics. The recent study by Maggie Gunsberg reads some of Pirandello's plays as the realization of 'the traditional binary allocation of cultural creativity to the masculine, and biological procreation to the feminine domain.'[7] This is certainly a legitimate interpretation. Yet Pirandello cannot be reduced to such a reading alone. His plays cannot be inscribed in a fixed form, for example, that of a patriarchal code, which, though undoubtedly present, hardly exhausts their implications. We should not forget what Hinkfuss says in *Questa sera si recita a soggetto* [*Tonight We Improvise*, 1930]: 'La vita deve obbedire a due necessità che per essere opposte tra loro non le consentono né di consistere durevolmente né di muoversi sempre ... E la vita bisogna che consista e si muova.' [Life must obey two principles that, for being in opposition to each other, do not consent either to persist forever or to move constantly ... And life must persist and move].[8] This paradoxical principle rules human life. It cannot be forgotten even in our interpretative processes which belong clearly to the realm of form, thus consistence. When Gunsberg states that motherhood is incompatible with sexuality, as is femininity with intellectual activities, she is right and she is certainly not the first one to say so.[9] Yet she should not stop here. Pirandello, in fact, is aware that such antitheses are the product of a patriarchal society which fears woman's power. The abasement of woman's intellect and sexuality is a clear sign that society fears the threat she poses. Far from immune to fear, Pirandello is clearly aware of it. And he becomes aware of something more significant still. With all their analytical tools and profound reasoning what do his male *raisonneurs* accomplish? Where do their logical discoveries take them? At the end of his strange adventure, Mattia Pascal is able to 'live' only as the late Mattia Pascal; at the closing of the curtain, Lamberto Laudisi remains with sarcastic laughter before the mystery of every being's identity (and not only of female identity as Gunsberg claims)[10]; after the success of his very clever plan, Leone Gala faces the most desolate, silent void. Vitangelo Moscarda renounces life altogether, chooses silence, abandons the city and society, and hopes for the dissolution of the self in nature. What do these *raisonneurs* accomplish? What do they finally understand through the use and abuse of reason? That life is a 'flusso incandescente'; that it is chaos; that there is neither order nor logic in it. In his sad attempt to rationalize chaos, to find reasons where there are none, man stops and dissects life, thus killing it. Man's privileged, rational place is thus undermined by its tragic paradox: reason tries to make sense out of a life that has none. The much praised logic is 'una macchinetta infernale' [a hellish little machine] Pirandello had written in *L'umorismo* [*On Humour*, 1908]. It is a pump that filters feelings and emotions, cools them down, and reduces them to dry carcasses, to concepts and ideas. But at this point, life has disappeared.

Women are excluded from philosophical monologues. But why? Do we really believe that Pirandello thought that women were incapable of them? that women had little or no reason? that they belonged only to the realm of nature, drastically separate from the realm of the spirit? Could Pirandello ever believe human nature to be so simple that human beings could be catalogued so naïvely, and their identity reduced to rigid categories? But then, why is the philosophical monologue so completely foreign to Pirandello's female characters? Is the *logos* really inaccessible to them? Could it not be, instead, that woman for Pirandello, precisely because she has been excluded for centuries from the production of *logos*, has remained truer to life than man, and can therefore see more clearly the risks and limitations of the logocentric discourse? Could it not be that woman, aware of such limitations and risks, consciously renounces *logos* and turns to other forms of communication? Could the humility, insecurity, and modesty of so many female characters be founded precisely in their greater sensitivity to the limits of communication, to the impossibility of absolute knowledge, and to life as chaos? What good is the rigorous pursuit of a logical discourse that in the end will be self-defeating? What good does Cosmo Laurentano's philosophy do but blow dust off the numerous volumes of human stupidity? Is the *raisonneur* not a pathetic figure if he takes his audience to the abyss of the absurd? Is it not more honest then to speak modestly, or even to keep silent, and to listen to other voices and sounds, as inarticulate as they might be? Sounds that, though devoid of logic (or maybe because of it), lend themselves to other types of interpretation and may yield different meanings and values?

In order to answer these questions I would like to read some of Pirandello's female characters in the light of a philosophical trend that centres on the concept of the crisis of reason – to use a term employed by the Italian philosopher Aldo Gargani.[11] Within it I place various theoretical discourses, such as Vattimo's 'pensiero debole' [weak thought], Carlo Sini's combination of Peirce's unending semiosis and Heidegger's hermeneutical cycle, and feminist thought. In view of the fact that my analysis focuses on female characters, feminist discourse is naturally best suited for it. It is, in fact a theoretical approach that, as Rosella Prezzo writes, 'permette al filosofo di uscire dalla "solitudine della ragione essenzialmente una"',[12] [allows the philosopher to come out from the solitude of reason]. If the self, the individual is language (as Charles Sanders Peirce maintained) and the spoken word is also the speaking word (as Merleau-Ponty stated) if language is gesture, if it is body, then the linguistic horizon must expand, receiving within itself a variety of signs. It must renounce 'la violenza dell'astrazione e del *logos*'[13] [the violence of abstraction and *logos*].

In the last twenty years the work of feminist scholars has reinterpreted biological and neurophysiological studies that underline the different cerebral organization in the two sexes. The functionality of the female brain is bihemispherical, but in the male brain, the two hemispheres form two independent neurological systems. This difference has generally been used to support the hypothesis of the inferiority of the female sex, although it actually points to a higher plasticity of the female brain, which functions simultaneously on various levels.[14] Such a difference, the feminists claim, is precisely what woman must value as capable of producing communication on various levels. This type of communication is possible only in so far as it denies fossilization into the male *logos*. French feminists, for example, counter the logically constructed male discourse with the importance of linguistic gaps, white spaces, and the tonality of the voice. Such elements tear the artificial logic of male discourse, letting material impulses come through.[15] What I would like to argue in the following pages is Pirandello's awareness of woman's higher ability not only to live life, but paradoxically to understand it, if we give to the word understanding a spectrum of connotations that go beyond the strictly logical ones. Women understand more precisely because they proceed in their experiences with an open perception, calling into play a variety of faculties, contaminating reason with emotions, concepts with feelings. What feminist thought says about the nature of the feminine must be rescued also for the masculine. It is not man's mind and identity that are simpler, more logical, and more orderly than the female. Males have for centuries hidden, repressed, and denied the 'beast' that hides in all of us, as Pirandello calls it. Man has pretended to be made in a more logical form than women. What Rosella Prezzo says about the inquiry into the feminine, should in fact be extended to the exploration of all human beings. Such exploration will not take us to the safe shores of philosophical systems. It will take us to 'un intrico maggiore di quello che il paesaggio filosofico pretende di offrire e di essere, a un paesaggio più "vero" solo perché più complesso, più complicato e co-implicato' [a thicker maze than the one to which the philosophical landscape would take us; yet a truer one precisely because of its complexity]. To open oneself up to the question of the feminine means to acknowledge that philosophical language is constructing itself also 'grazie a quel significante intrinsecamente ambiguo, fatto di molti predicati contraddittori' [thanks to that intrinsically ambiguous signifier made up of many contradictory predicates].[16]

In giving voice to women, Pirandello accomplishes the goal of his male characters: the defeat of logical discourse, the unveiling of the fallacy of words. If, in fact, the male *raisonneurs* denounce the trap of language and logic in which human beings are inescapably caught, the female characters, especially in the plays, enact the deconstruction of logic and of language by relying on different elements for communication, such as silence, touch, facial expressions, and tonality of voice. It is with the use of this different language that woman will enact the dissolution of the self and honestly accept the heavy burden of being at the same time none and one hundred thousand. As emblematic of our analysis we could take the character of Signora Ponza, the personification of 'truth' – that polyhedric, multifaceted, chameleonic truth of which woman is the embodiment. In the few and lapidary final words of *Così è (se vi pare)* [*It Is So (If You Think So)*, 1917] there is implicit a complex discourse, one that cannot be verbalized, on the necessity of tolerance and respect, even when rational understanding is lacking. There is an appeal to that sphere of emotional impulses, of the unsaid and inexpressible; there is an appeal to those empty spaces which must be respected for what they are, spaces that cannot be violated by being filled with external meanings.[17]

It is in the theatre that women become absolute protagonists, where action must take the place of reflection, where life renews form and movement defeats fossilization. And it was Marta Abba's entrance into Pirandello's life that galvanized the writer's ideas and gave birth to plays centered on female characters. The following analysis, however, will concentrate on the pivotal section of Pirandello's dramatic works, that of the first two plays of the trilogy of the theatre-within-the theatre. The aim is to examine the transitional phase – from male to female protagonist plays – and to show that even before Marta Abba's appearance, Pirandello had already made woman the generating force of his theatre. In the plays that represent the confusion and coincidence of life and theatre (that is, the plays that assess the superiority of theatre over life, of artistic characters over human beings) woman, as the being truer to life, as the challenger of the *logos*, has a central role. The female character who remains the sole protagonist of all Pirandello's plays will, at the end of his life, through the influence of Marta Abba, coincide with the figure of the actress. Character and woman will thus be one and the same, and Marta Abba will realize in herself, on the stage, the coincidence of art and life, Pirandello's supreme ideal. If the *raisonneur* Moscarda discovered that we are one hundred thousand, wearing an infinite number of masks that we and the others construct of ourselves, if our innermost self, whose existence we do feel strongly, can never be known and expressed except through the medium of our artificial constructions, then the actress Donata Genzi in *Trovarsi* [*To Find Oneself*, 1932], who consciously chooses to live on stage forever the various roles of life, is certainly the truest and most honest being that Pirandello created.

The open challenge to the male *logos*, the Derridian parricide, is performed on stage by the Stepdaughter, and rightly so, in the first play of the trilogy. *Sei personaggi in cerca d'autore* [*Six Characters in Search of an Author*, 1921] should therefore be considered the turning point to all successive dramatic creations. In her essay 'Modes of Narration in *Sei personaggi*' Mary Ann Witt centred the Father-Stepdaughter, male-female relation in the play on the couple's diegetic and mimetic codes.[18] The father, possessor of the *logos*, narrates, explains, reasons. The Stepdaughter, who is *mimesis*, represents, acts out. The contrast, which Witt examines on a literary and theatrical level, underscores on the existential level the dichotomy of reason/life. Pirandello, in an enlightening page of his *Foglietti* (precisely, the page that precedes his discourse on the mystery of fantasy's creation that, for him, coincides with the mystery of life itself), writes:

L'immaginazione ci mostra la corrispondenza incessante della natura e del pensiero, il movimento perpetuo dall'uno all'altro, e pare che risolva, senza che noi ce ne accorgiamo, il problema insolubile dei rapporti dello spirito e del corpo. Lo spirito si fa corpo, il corpo si fa spirito. L'immagine ... materia nella origine, spirito nella sua vita interiore, unisce il mondo e il pensiero.

[Imagination shows us the unending correspondence of nature and thought, the perpetual movement from one to the other, and seems to resolve the insoluble problem of the spirit/body relation without us realizing it. Spirit becomes body, body becomes spirit. The image ... that is matter in its origin and spirit in its inner life, combines together world and thought].

Shortly after he concludes: 'L'immaginazione continua la fecondità della natura, combina gli elementi in forme originali, e l'opera sua è spontanea come ogni azione vitale' [Imagination continues the fertility of nature, combines elements in original forms; its activity is as spontaneous as any other vital action].[19] If the image represents the communication code of the feminine, imagination is thus woman's peculiar faculty. If thought finds its conduit through logical discourse, imagination finds its life in the representation, in the scene. In *Sei personaggi* these antagonistic terms are embodied in the Stepdaughter and the Father.[20]

The Stepdaughter enacts the progressive deconstruction of the paternal text, performing, little by little, a true parricide. That she is Stepdaughter and not a daughter of the Father is the first signal. That the Father coincides with the author and with the authority of the *logos* is clear when the Stepdaughter appears to be happy that the author for whom the characters are searching cannot be found. 'Tanto meglio, tanto meglio ... Potremmo essere noi la loro commedia nuova' [Better this way ... so we could be your new comedy].[21] The Stepdaughter refuses the paternal *logos* and poses herself as creator of images, author of the representation. Her rebellion, as Witt convincingly points out, is obvious in her refusal of any role, but, one could add, is evident also in her struggle against the Father to keep the Mother on her side. Furthermore it is she who takes over the Mother's script, in order to correct it. Symbol of illegitimacy, she forces the Mother, who is searching for excuses to justify her adulterous life, to admit that in such a life – outside legitimacy – she, the Mother, had been happy. Thus the Stepdaughter tries to drag The Mother into the refusal of authority – in her case, of the husband-owner, the male author. 'So che con mio padre, finché visse, tu fosti sempre in pace e contenta. Negalo, se puoi!'(63) [I know for fact that as long as my father lived you were happy and at peace with him. Contradict me, if you can!]. After this scene the duel between the possessor of the *logos* and the representative of life reaches its climax. Sentences and images are juxtaposed. 'Frasi! Frasi! Come se non fosse il conforto di tutti, davanti a un fatto che non si spiega, davanti a un male che ci consuma, trovare una parola che non dice nulla, e in cui ci si acqueta!' (64) [Phrases! Phrases! As if they were not anyone's consolation, before a fact that cannot be explained, before an evil that eats us up, to find a word that says nothing, but that calms us!] It is the Father of the *logos* who reveals his weakness, thus admitting his own defeat. The 'frasi' do not explain; they console, illude. Is it not then more courageous and honest to represent without words the tragedy of life, or to throw those words like stones one after the other without any hypocritical attempt to impose upon them a form or a meaning? 'La camera ... qua la vetrina dei mantelli; là il divano-letto; la specchiera; un paravento ... quel tavolino di mogano con la busta cilestrina delle cento lire' (65) [The room ... here the shop-window with the cloaks; there, the sleeping sofa; the mirror; a screen; and before the window, that little mahogany table with the pale blue envelope and inside the one hundred lire.] The language of the Stepdaughter shows a great use of parataxis, a syntactical device that places elements one next to the other without pretension of systematizing them or making sense out of them. By contrast, the philosophical language of the Father is characterized by syntactical connections that point to the coherent construction of his discourse and to its logical meaning. But 'Qui non si narra! qui non si narra!' (65) [There is no place for narrative here!], she insists. It is at this point that the Father must confess his defeat, since, as he himself admits soon after, 'è tutto qui il male, nelle parole!' (65) [words are the cause of all evil], those words to which each of us attributes our own value and meaning and that can hold you forever in a mask in which you cannot recognize yourself. He who constantly underlines the evil of words cannot but continue to rely heavily on them. It is precisely this paradox represented by the Father, that explains the

Stepdaughter's ferocious sarcasm. Away with words! Let's then live the scene on stage. Away with narrative! Let's create drama!

From the start the Father appears as the true author of the drama, whose script he seems to control. He had married a simple, humble woman precisely because she was simple and humble. In fact, he states that he loved those feminine virtues. Still by his decision, the son was sent to be raised in the country away from his mother, who had no say in this decision and who, according to her husband's judgment, was too weak to raise him herself. It is still he who, when he realized that there was understanding and affection between his wife and his secretary, fired the man and encouraged his wife to leave with him. Even when the two were away, he continued to control their lives. He is husband, father, owner, creator of the life of the others. The logical and dialogical ability of this character is so overpowering that he takes over his audience, and with the strength of his arguments makes us deviate our attention from the real drama of the play: the ancestral struggle between man and woman, between the father of the *logos* and the object of it. This is where the greatness of the drama lies – in the power of the male *logos* that takes possession and control of the audience. The Stepdaughter, as antagonist, therefore, has a very difficult task because she starts from a position of weakness and lack of recognition. The Father and the Capocomico, another auctorial and authoritative figure, try to shut her up. She does not appear as an appealing character; she is too provocative, aggressive, sarcastic, and worse of all, too impudent. Yet she slowly succeeds in undermining the power of the Father by disseminating throughout the play the elements of the feminine dissension. These elements progressively rupture the logical plot of the father-author and lead her to her final liberation. In the end, in fact, she alone succeeds in tearing herself away from the creation of the Father by physically leaving the scenic space.

It is after the Father's first long philosophical monologue that the Stepdaughter openly assumes the role of the challenger. She begins by appropriating an offensive feminine stereotype created by man, which the Father had used to justify the weakness of his flesh. 'La donna, infatti,' he had said previously, using the same words as in the story 'La trappola' ['The trap,' 1912], 'com'è? Ci guarda, aizzosa, invitante. La afferri! Appena stretta, chiude subito gli occhi. È il segno della sua dedizione. Il segno con cui dice all'uomo: "Accecati, io son cieca!"' (71) [How is woman, in fact? She looks at us provoking, inviting; you grab her. As soon as you have her in your hold, she closes her eyes.

It is the sign of her total submission – the sign with which she says to the man: 'Blind yourself, as I myself am blind!']. The Stepdaughter openly rebels against this offensive statement that sees woman first as a demonic temptress who entraps the unfortunate man, then as an object of consumption and finally as a wild beast that once caught by the hunter abandons herself to his ownership. 'E quando non li chiude più? Quando non sente più il bisogno di nascondere a se stessa, chiudendo gli occhi, il rosso della sua vergogna,' – another cowardly weapon used to keep her under control with the myth of purity – 'e invece vede, con occhi ormai aridi e impassibili, quello dell'uomo, che pure senz'amore s'è accecato?' (71) [And when she no longer closes them? And when she no longer feels the need to hide her shame to herself, and instead, sees with eyes by now dry and impassive, the shame of the man who without love blinded himself?]

Woman has finally opened her eyes, eyes that man has desired and forced to be shut for centuries, and she uses them now to unmask the hypocrisy, the power politics, the 'schifo di tutte codeste complicazioni intellettuali, di tutta codesta filosofia che scopre la bestia e poi la vuol salvare' (71) [disgust of all these intellectual complications, of all this philosophy that at first reveals the beast and then wants to save it]. What pours out of this invective is indignation about and the resentment against all this philosophy by which woman has been held on a leash and forbidden to open her eyes. The rationalization of life performed by man, the attempt to find reasons and causes, puts out the vital flame within him. It is in the name of this vital flame that the Stepdaughter fights her battle, in order to usurp the power from the *logos*. In fact, after her own father's death, she re-enters her stepfather's house (together with her mother, little brother, and sister) as *padrona* openly challenging the Father on his territory. His attempts to take the word away from her and shut her up fail, and she brings her battle to a larger ground, turning her weapons even against the author and the Capocomico. The latter, in fact, after having followed with serious interest the advice of the Father in the organization of the scene to be acted, resents the Stepdaughter's attempts to do the same. 'Oh guarda! Ma insomma, dirige lei o dirigo io?' (89) [Well, look! Are you directing or am I?] And for daring so much she cannot but be labelled as 'male-ducata' and 'presuntuosa' (95) [ill-mannered and presumptuous] by the male Capocomico. With a typical male-dominant speech, he tries to intimidate the Stepdaughter by forcing her into the stereotypes of female behaviour. 'Bisogna che lei si contenga, signorina. E creda, nel suo stesso interesse; perché può anche fare una cattiva impressione, glielo avverto, tutta codesta furia dilaniatrice, codesto disgusto esasperato' (98) [Young lady, you must control yourself. And believe me, in your own interest, I warn you, because all this destructive fury, all this exasperated contempt can really make a bad impression]. Aggressive behaviour is not proper for a woman.

Alone in her struggle, the Stepdaughter is well aware of the male plots that try to deny her the drama, to silence her voice. 'Quello che è possibile sulla scena ve lo siete combinato insieme tutti e due, di là, grazie! Lo capisco bene!' (97) [You two have decided back there, what is suitable for the stage, thanks a lot! I understand]. But, she states, 'Non ci sto! non ci sto!' [I will not give in!]. From now on she does the directing: she tells the Mother to scream at the right moment; in act 2, she gives instructions to the Capocomico, who continues to rebel against such abuses of power; and finally she takes into her hands the lives of all the other characters. She shows affection and tenderness only for the Little Girl, the innocent victim of a logic of power that sacrifices her to the legitimacy of the male Son. It is not by chance, in fact, that the Stepdaughter insists on the representation of yet another feminine sacrifice, which must, therefore, take place on stage, under the eyes of all.

The challenge of the Stepdaughter reaches its climax in the last act, in the scene where the father of fathers, the author himself, who gave life to the six characters, is called into question. It is once more the Father who begins the narration of their visits to their author in order to convince him to give their life a scenic space. His narration is interrupted and taken up by the Stepdaughter, who thus takes possession of the word of the Father, that same word with which all the characters, but she in particular, would tempt their author in his study. 'Che scene, che andavamo a proporgli! – Io, io lo tentavo più di tutti!' (106) [Which scenes we would propose to him! And I, I tempted him more than all the others!] The challenge between Stepdaughter and Father becomes the challenge between daughter and author. Might not the author's refusal to give them life have been prompted by the hubris of the daughter? It is the Father, as personification of authority, who suggests this hypothesis. 'Ma forse è stato per causa tua: appunto per codeste tue troppe insistenze, per le troppe incontinenze!' (106) [But maybe it was because of you, for these too many demands of yours, for your intemperance!] Is Pirandello trying to confess that the father-author denies life to the character who challenges his authority and tries to usurp his place? 'Ma che! Se egli stesso m'ha voluta così!' (106) [But what are you talking about! If he himself wanted me to be like this!]. The father of the *logos* is fully aware of his limitations and clearly sees the impasse in which he is caught. Escaping it will be possible only through humour and the provoking laughter of his creature.

Laughter is language, it is signifying gesture, in the sense given to it by Merleau-Ponty, just as are silence, scream, and cry. They are expressions of a feminine language that, as Luciana Martinelli writes, shatters the orderly and rational male discourse.[22] Man, who throughout the centuries has become used to building stable truths and points of reference, can no longer function when this ably constructed ground begins to shake under his feet. Feminine discourse precisely performs this task, in order to vindicate the language of sexual difference that woman had been denied for centuries by man who has held exclusive power over language.

The second play of the trilogy, *Ciascuno a suo modo* [*Each in His Own Way*, 1924], begins with a brief discussion by two men – a young and an old one – about the need to know more facts in order to build stronger opinions. As they are speaking, two Young Ladies enter and their conversation, significantly placed just after that of the two men, presents itself from the start as a counter-discourse on the linguistic as well as on the philosophical level. The two men, who are looking for the truth about the mysterious Delia Morello, construct their sentences with subordinate clauses logically woven together. Their discussion has the characteristics of a philosophical dialogue, where each speaker is careful not to be caught making contradictory statements. The women (La Prima and L'Altra), instead, construct their discourse by parataxis, and from the beginning they disclaim any certain knowledge. As they enter the stage we realize they have been talking about a man, probably the lover of La Prima, who has left. L'Altra must have met him and has probably expressed her impression of him to her friend who now becomes very excited. 'Ma non è niente più che una mia impressione, bada!' [But it is nothing more than an impression of mine, beware!] cautions L'Altra, 'Mi parve così'[23] [It seemed so to me], repeating that it was just the impression he made on her, and that the other should not, therefore, take it as the objective truth.

In her recalling the last adieu to her lover, La Prima reproaches herself for not having followed her heart and the true communication that without words took place between them. 'Non dovevo lasciarlo partire. Ah, il cuore me lo diceva! Gli tenni la mano fino alla porta. Era già lontano d'un passo fuori della porta e ancora gli tenevo la mano. Ci eravamo baciati, lasciati, ed esse no, le nostre mani non si volevano staccare. Rientrando, caddi come rotta dal pianto.' (128) [I should not have let him go. Ah, my heart was telling me not to! I held his hand until the last minute. He was already out of the door and I was still holding his hand. We had kissed, we had left each other, and our hands, no, they did not want to separate. Going back in, I fell, overwhelmed by sobs.] It is the language of the body that speaks here, for the message is untranslatable through verbal language. It could even be argued that the separation of the two lovers was reached by logical arguments that, as it clearly appears here, had falsified, even violated their true feelings. It is still La Prima who reaches this conclusion when she comments on her lover's silence with such revealing words: 'Eh, perché lui lo sa! Lo sa quanto male ci facciamo per questo maledetto bisogno di parlare.' (129) [Because he knows; he knows how much we hurt each other with this darned need of talking.]

Why did these two lovers break off? What brought about the end of their relationship? Certainly it was not the end of their love; probably it was the mutable nature of the woman, her lack of a fixed identity, the impossibility, therefore, to be the solid possession of her man. 'E come sono? Non lo so più! Ti giuro che non lo so più! Tutto mobile, labile, senza peso ... Che angoscia! E continuamente mi nascondo la faccia, davanti a me stessa, tanto mi vergogno a vedermi cambiare!' (129) [And how am I? I no longer know it! I swear, I do not know it any more! Everything is unstable, weightless ... What anxiety! And I am constantly covering up my face, before myself, feeling shameful for seeing myself change so!] Although at first sight this outpouring could be taken as the confession of woman's flighty nature, thus confirming the phrase that someone unknown had uttered shortly before. – 'Le donne, come i sogni, non sono mai come tu le vorresti,' (129) [Women, like dreams, are never as you would want them.] – it should be taken, instead, together with this phrase, as the foreshadowing of the existential drama that will take place shortly: a drama of identity, not only of woman's identity, as feminist criticism generally sees it, but of anyone's identity. La Prima feels shame about her fleeting self only because she has been defined and judged by men's hypocritical moralism and artificial rules of coherence and consistence. In order to control and know women, man must inscribe them in a limited space and force them to remain there forever. But true life cannot stand such constrictions; it constantly moves, changes without any order or criterion. Woman is courageous enough not only to admit it theoretically, as the male characters do, but also to live by this principle. Delia Morello possesses this courage of admitting and living her own fleeting essence.

True daughter of Signora Ponza, Delia Morello has galvanized around herself the curiosity of an entire city. It is Diego, the *raisonneur* of the play, who tells us at the start: 'Ma lo sa lei, signora mia, che da una ventina di giorni non si fa altro che discutere di Delia Morello? Se ne dicon di cotte e di crude, in tutti i ritrovi, salotti, caffè, redazioni di giornali.' (132) [But do you know, my dear lady, that the whole town has been talking about Delia Morello for the last three weeks? She is the object of everyone's conversation, everywhere, at clubs, cafés, even in the newspapers.] We are, therefore, warned right away against the cruelty of people's curiosity, their gossiping, judging, interpreting other people's lives. The more mysterious the other is, the less comfortable they feel, and the stronger the urge is to trap the other into a net of meanings. 'È un' attrice ... È una pazza' [She is an actress ... She is a madwoman].[24] But Diego tries to explain: 'È di quelle donne fatte a caso, sempre fuori di sé, fuggiasche.' (134) [She is one of those women made by chance, constantly beside themselves, always fleeting from something.] He immediately lets the audience know that Delia is certainly not the traditional *femme fatale*, conscious and proud of her feminine power. She is a victim of her nature, or better, she has always followed her nature, refusing to conform herself to the fixed roles others wished to impose on her; and 'se male ha fatto agli altri quella disgraziata, il più gran male l'ha fatto sempre a se stessa.' (134) [if she has hurt anyone, the greatest hurt she has done to herself.] The same *raisonneur* who criticizes the town's curiosity, placing himself in the privileged position of tolerance and respect, is subtly delivering his knowledge and superior judgment about the absurdity and violence of judging.

At the arrival of Doro, the defender of Delia Morello against Francesco Savio in the discussion of the previous night, we witness the first *coup de scène*. Doro is once more outraged at the cruel and abusive talk that everybody is now engaged in concerning his discussion with Francesco Savio. People must invent explanations to justify actions they do not understand. If Doro has defended Delia Morello, whom everybody, and Francesco Savio in particular, is accusing, then he must be madly in love with her. His mother is beside herself, worrying about her poor son captured in the trap of this dangerous sorceress, and anxiously awaits a reassuring word from him. But words are not reassuring, Doro warns, they are powerful and dangerous tools. Explaining his behaviour of the night before – because we always need and demand explanations – he says his words were not uttered as a defence of Delia Morello – the first, unjustified interpretation made of his intervention – but to combat an opinion expressed by Francesco Savio that seemed wrong to him. The real objectives of Doro's fight are the violence and the dictatorial nature of people's beliefs, and he also warns, just as Diego had done before, against the danger of words. Doro realizes, in fact, that in his discussion, he might have said 'un cumulo di sciocchezze! Quello che ho detto non lo so! Una parola tira l'altra!' (136) [a pile of nonsense! I don't know what I said. A word drags out the other.] He is irritated, not for having being misunderstood, as his mother suggests, but 'per le esagerazioni a cui mi sono lasciato andare vedendo bestialmente incornato su certe false argomentazioni Francesco Savio, il quale poi – sì – aveva ragione lui, sostanzialmente,' (136) [for the exaggerations I let come out of my mouth, only out of spite, when I saw Francesco Savio so stubbornly fixed in some false arguments – and he was right, after all.] Words are dangerous because they can take over the speaker's intentions and lead him astray. Corrupted by the power of the *logos*, man cannot restrain himself from intervening in the fight against 'false argomentazioni' [false arguments] even when they have nothing to do with reality. Two proud men are battling on the male ground of logic for an abstract victory that has lost sight of the true issue.

The readers and the audience of the play know Delia Morello only through what they have heard up to now, and the opinions expressed have been contradictory. She has been present only as an absence, literally as well as figuratively. Her appearance on stage brings about the second *coup de scène*, another humorist twist. Delia arrives at the Palegari's residence to thank Doro; but not, as everyone immediately assumes, for his defence of her. 'No! credete per la difesa che avete fatto di me? Che volete che m'importi di difese, di offese! – Mi dilanio da me – La mia gratitudine è per quello che avete pensato, sentito; e non perché l'abbiate gridato in faccia agli altri!' (144) [What could I care about defences or offences. I tear myself to pieces all the time. My gratitude is for what you thought and felt, and not because you shouted it in others' faces!] The first characteristic that strikes us in this

Enacting the Dissolution of the Self 179

emotional speech is Delia's total indifference to people's opinions, an indifference that places her in a wholly different sphere from anyone else. She appears immediately as the strongest of the characters. She is grateful to Doro because she has recognized herself in his words. Is Doro then right in his opinions? 'Giusto o ingiusto – non m'importa!,' she comments, 'È che mi sono riconosciuta, capite, "riconosciuta" in tutto quello che avete detto di me, appena me l'hanno riferito.' (144) [Right or wrong, it does not matter to me. What matters is that I have recognized myself, do you understand? I have recognized myself in everything you said of me, as soon as I heard it.] The acknowledgment of Doro's insight into Delia's nature – undoubtedly a dramatic coup – overshadows, in my opinion, the core of her comment which consists in the words 'Giusto o ingiusto – non m'importa!' Right and wrong are two abstractions, two concepts, words which have little to do with ever-changing reality. Delia is aware of the absurdity of those labels and is not concerned with the rightness of Doro's comment. What she knows and is concerned with is that she has recognized herself in those comments.

At this point it is extremely easy for us, as readers, to follow the commonplace of man's definition of woman.[25] Doro understands Delia better than she does, and reveals her innermost self to her. Yet, if we read this part together with what follows, that is, the overturning of the argument, we can say that this is not Pirandello's objective. Moreover and more importantly, we can see that man's presumed capacity for knowing more and understanding better than woman is a farce. That knowledge and understanding have little to do with what is happening is clear from Delia's following remark: 'Amico mio, vivo da stamattina di codesta vostra divinazione ... Tanto che mi domando come abbiate potuto fare ad averla, voi che mi conoscete così poco, in fondo; e mentr'io mi dibatto, soffro – non so – come di là da me stessa! come se quella che io sono, debba andare sempre inseguendo, per trattenerla, per domandarle che cosa voglia, perché soffra, per placarla, per darle pace!' (145) [My friend, since this morning I have been living of this inspiration of yours ... And I ask myself how you could have had it, since, after all, you know me so little; while I struggle, suffer – I don't know – as though I were beside myself! As though I were constantly groping to find out who I am, to hold on to a self and understand what it wants, why it suffers.] Delia's words are not the admission of Doro's, and by extension of man's, rational superiority – after all we have learned from him that he had said 'un cumulo di sciocchezze

... esagerazioni' [a bunch of foolishness ... exaggerations]. They are simply the recognition of her own fleeting nature and, by extension, of human nature as such and of the casual and precarious quality of our insights.

The long dialogue between Doro and Delia that follows is ably constructed to take readers and audience right to a logical end, an end that will suddenly be turned upon itself by another humorist's twist. Delia enacts the deconstruction of the male *logos* in an extremely subtle manner. She first accepts the male interpretation of her actions and even shows him her gratitude for being capable of throwing his Apollinean light onto her sentimental *ingorgo*, thus playing the card of her adversary. As Doro explains to Delia the motives behind her actions, and the audience follows step by step the almost maieutic procedure that brings forth Delia's self revelation, his power suddenly receives a mighty blow and crumbles mercilessly to the ground. Precisely at the moment when Doro is tasting his victory, commenting sarcastically on his opponent's opinions, Delia, as a perfect humorist, suddenly sees the possibility of their truth. She, writes Pirandello, '(resterà per un lungo tratto in silenzio, fissa a guardare innanzi a sé ... infine dirà aprendo desolatamente le braccia): E chi sa, amico mio, ch'io non l'abbia fatto veramente per questo?'(150) [(she will remain silent for a while, staring immobile at a point in the distance... Finally, opening her arms in desolation, she will say): And who knows, my friend, whether those were not the real reasons?] The curtain falls on this paradoxical impasse: that Delia at the same time is and is not what Doro thinks she is. The paradox of life shatters the myth of logic and coherence to which the holder of the *logos* had tried to nail his arguments.

The first *Intermezzo corale* presents us with five critics who argue among one another about the meaning of the first act. Arguments run also through the crowd of spectators whom Pirandello divides into 'Favorevoli' and 'Contrari' [Favourable and Opposed]. Voices are heard from various groups. 'Mi sai dire in che consiste quest'atto? – Oh bella! E se non volesse consistere? Se volesse dimostrare appunto l'inconsistenza delle opinioni, dei sentimenti?' (158) [Can you tell me what the meaning of this first act is? – What a question! And if its meaning were precisely to show the inconsistency of meanings, of opinions?] It is not by chance that Pirandello chose the verb *consistere* where he might have expressed the same idea with a verb such as *significare*. The spectator is, in fact, asking, 'what does the act mean?' but *consistere* has an ambiguous connotation, very relevant in Pirandello's philosophy as expressed by Hinkfuss in the quotation cited earlier in this essay. *Consistere* expresses permanence, form, fixity – that which human beings need in order to function, but which, paradoxically, also kills life by stopping, organizing, and cataloguing it. So the hypothesis expressed by 'Quello che spicca' [the spectator who stands out with his comments] represents the core of Pirandello's philosophy. The same speaker also makes the central statement in the 'Intermezzo corale.'

In the chaos and confusion of plot and characters the only thing that everybody seems to agree on is the truth of the woman, the character of Delia Morello. Public and critics don't understand her; they are divided in their interpretations of her actions, yet they all feel and are convinced that 'il dramma però è vivo, vivo nella donna. Questo è innegabile! Lo dicono tutti.' (159) [the true living drama is in the woman. This cannot be denied! Everybody agrees.] as 'Quello che spicca' remarks. And to the objection of one of the less insightful spectators: 'Ma va' là! Se è tutta una matassa arruffata di contraddizioni!' (159) [But what are you talking about? Can't you see she is a messy bundle of contradictions?], we add: Precisely! Delia Morello is alive and true precisely because she is a bundle of contradictions that cannot be disentangled despite all the ferocious attempts that male reason undertakes. Thus, the act and the whole play consist and have their meaning in the character of Delia Morello – in a character that represents the constant movement between flux and consistency. The logician, who 'a furia di scavare' [by digging] reduces his soul 'a una tana di talpa' [to a mole's hole] (172) has killed every spark of life in himself, and Diego knows it well. This is why he admires and respects Delia. As Luciana Martinelli convincingly argued, speaking about other feminine characters, Delia is the 'magic mirror' that forces men to see their own hidden and repressed selves. She is the force that we met in the powerful page of *L'umorismo* and that Diego here appropriates in one of his more dramatic speeches; she is the force that tears down dams, banks, buildings – constructions into which we channel the torrential flux of our life – and that Serafino Gubbio calls 'la metafora di noi stessi'[26] [the metaphor of ourselves]. Diego's speech, in fact, is the same Serafino used for Aldo Nuti, whose metaphor of himself had become, in the hands of Varia Nestoroff, 'un giocattolo ... un pagliaccetto' [a toy ... a funny doll] to be taken apart.

As the legitimate offspring of Varia – by nature, if not by name – Delia too with her vital force has succeeded in tearing away from men that little clown, 'che ti fabbrichi con l'interpretazione fittizia dei tuoi atti e dei tuoi sentimenti, e ... che non ha nulla a che vedere con ciò che sei o puoi essere veramente, con ciò che è in te e che tu non sai, e che è un dio terribile, bada, se ti opponi ad esso, ma che diventa subito pietoso d'ogni tua colpa se t'abbandoni e non ti vuoi scusare' (176) [that you build with the false interpretation of your actions and feelings, and ... that has nothing to do with what you really are or can be, with what is inside you that you don't know, and that is a terrible god, I warn you, if you oppose him, but he becomes a compassionate one if you let yourself go and do not try to excuse yourself]. Diego, the *raisonneur*, admires the woman who has the courage to destroy all those 'pagliaccetti'; he respects the honesty that makes her act and speak in contrasting ways, without attempting to justify her incoherence. He admires her open acceptance of incoherence and inconsistency as basic characteristics of human nature. He praises her life, one that does not accept the hypocrisy of our fake constructions, but unfolds spontaneously.

Women have this courage, a courage that men lack because centuries of rationalism have denied value to the irrational. Men cannot abandon themselves to the irrational side because 'quest'abbandono ci sembra un "negarci," cosa indegna di un uomo; e sarà sempre così, finché crediamo che l'umanità consista nella così detta coscienza – o nel coraggio che abbiamo mostrato una volta, invece che nella paura che ci ha consigliato tante volte d'esser prudenti' (176) [this letting oneself go seems to us a process of self-negation, something unworthy of a man; and it will always be like this as long as we believe that humanity consists in what we call conscience – or in the courage we had shown once, rather than in the fear that has advised us so many times to be prudent].

The fact that it is once more a male character who exposes man's hypocrisy and so eloquently presents the case should not be interpreted, I would like to argue, as a sign of man's intellectual superiority, but only as a consequence of man's linguistic habits. The same elaborate language that man adopts to impose coherence onto the chaos of existence and to build systems, is here used to bring out his own limitations. Woman already knows it; she does not need the narcissistic satisfaction of listening to her own presumptuous voice. She knows well the limitations and the risks of such discourse. With the exception of one scene in act 1, Delia, who provokes the events and the plot, is constantly present in the others' discourse but is absent from the stage.

Her absence and her mystery, accepted with difficulty by the people around her, prompt all the speeches about her and the attempts at defining her, as happened in *Così è (se vi pare)*. Yet it is not so much the mystery of woman – the mystery of female sexuality – that intrigues Pirandello, but woman as truer to life. If the mysterious characters are always women, the reason is only in part Pirandello's fascination with and curiosity for woman's sexuality. A more important reason, I argue, is that woman is the perfect character to represent the alogical nature of life, since she is a being that does not construct herself as much as man. Delia, in fact, grew up in the country and suffered when she moved to the city 'fra tutto questo finto, fra tutto questo falso, che diventa sempre più finto e più falso' (147) [in the midst of all this falseness, all this fictitiousness, that becomes ever falser and more fictitious]. Her speech exposes the objectifications of women by men, and their total lack of understanding. Men construct women as they wish them to be, just as they build houses and cities, never thinking or caring about their true needs and feelings, as Delia tells Doro.

Delia represents life in its fleeting and absurd essence. She represents the rebellion against man's violence that wants to possess her by force, because he does not understand her, and so fears her. She rebels against those who want to constrain her in the role of wife, whore, or muse and refuses any role. Even the sculptor Giacomo La Vela, like Sirio with Tuda, wants possession. This desire for possession, though sublimated through the artistic creation, still reveals an inability to accept difference, to understand woman; it reveals once more the necessity to imprison her in a familiar form. But this woman does not accept the game of reason; she flees the fixity of form in which man wants to enclose her, thus showing her power as life. It is not by chance that the best role to express such a message is that of the actress. Delia Morello, offspring of Varia Nestoroff, another actress, will develop in the character of Donata Genzi. In *Trovarsi* Donata succeeds in escaping from all roles in which patriarchal reason wants to inscribe her, fleeing society, not in order to be dissolved in nature (as Moscarda does at the end of *Uno, nessuno e centomila* [*One, Nobody and One Hundred Thousand*, 1925–6]) but in order to live, paradoxically, the only possible true life, in the world of art. Only there she will be able to make herself what she wants, and be one and one hundred thousand, remaining thus faithful to that protean and fleeting essence she represents.[27]

The actress will therefore become the perfect metaphor for life. At the end of the play, Donata says: 'Vero è soltanto che bisogna crearsi, creare! E allora soltanto, ci si trova.'[28] [The only truth is that we must create ourselves, and create! And only then we can find ourselves.] Women are aware of the precariousness of their constructions, and accept it. Men, on the other hand, insist on coherence, permanence, and stability; these categories have no part in the incoherent, mutable, and chaotic life. Man is the victim of a tradition that had placed his worth and essence precisely in his skill as a builder of stable and eternal truths. The play *Trovarsi* represents woman's open admission and acceptance of life as a constant construction of infinite masks.

After Pirandello's encounter with Marta, woman was to become protagonist of all his plays; woman as giver of life, woman as living force and energy, woman as art. 'Il mistero d'ogni nascita artistica è il mistero stesso d'ogni nascita naturale,' Pirandello writes in 1934, 'non cosa che si possa fabbricare ma che deve naturalmente nascere, non a caso e tanto meno a capriccio degli scrittori ... ma anzi obbedientissima alle sue inderogabili leggi vitali'[29] [The mystery of an artistic birth is the same as that of a natural birth ... not something that one can construct, but something that must come to life naturally, not by chance or by the artist's caprice ... but obedient to the unbreakable laws of life]. With Marta Abba lending her body and soul to his characters, Pirandello was to succeed in defeating the philosophical discourse of the male *logos* and ascertaining woman's positive force in the world. In a letter written to her from Nettuno in the summer 1928, trying to console her for her aches and tiredness, Pirandello wrote: 'believe me, all your suffering – ... all the pains that seem to be coming from the body but are not, pains of which no physician will ever find the cause – have on the contrary their root in this: that they are Life, all the Life that is in you, all the possibilities of being that are in you and live in you, without you even realizing it.'[30] But Pirandello did. The only salvation for man after the crisis of reason will come from woman. In the end woman is also the embodiment of the three myths that remain after the dissolution of all false values. La Spera, Sara, and Ilse represent the eternal and absolute values of maternity, natural religion, and art, which, though mythical, are by Pirandello identified with the power of the feminine.[31] That power he, as a true androgynous artist, felt in himself, and expressed in a splendid metaphor. 'The sea is immense and always restless; the wave turns into itself, breaks out rumbling and then sucks itself again into a whirlpool, to start over once more turning into itself, without pause ... I, who possess in my soul so many of its swirling waves, always knew!'[32]

NOTES

1 Karen Horney, *Feminine Psychology* (New York: Norton, 1967). The idea of man's envy and dread of woman was further developed by Adrienne Rich in *Of Woman Born* (New York: Norton, 1976). The beginning of the present essay was incorporated and expanded in the introduction of my book, *Pirandello and His Muse: The Plays for Marta Abba* (Gainsville: University Press of Florida, 1998).
2 Hannah Arendt, *The Life Of the Mind* (San Diego: Harcourt Brace Jovanovich, 1978), 10.
3 Hélène Cixous and Catherine Clément, *The Newly Born Woman*, trans. B. Wing (Minneapolis: Minnesota University Press, 1986), 65. The book was originally published in French under the title *La jeune née* (Paris: Union Général d'Editions, 1975).
4 Leonardo Sciascia, 'Pirandello e la Sicilia,' in *Opere*, 3 vols. (Milan: Bompiani, 1991), vol. 3: 1058.
5 I am unaware of any study that has considered Antonietta's madness as possibly provoked by her husband. Long passages from Pirandello's letters to his fiancée are quoted by Gaspare Giudice in his important biography *Luigi Pirandello* (Turin: UTET, 1963), 165–75.
6 As Jean-Michel Gardair remarked, 'Non solo Pirandello è lo scrittore di una Sicilia freudianamente fallocentrica ... è anche uno splendido scrittore della femminilità ... Una femminilità concepita, o piuttosto fantasticata come trasparenza, ossia rifiuto della maschera e di qualsiasi "parte"' [Not only is Pirandello the writer of a phallocentric Sicily – as Freud would define it ... he is also the writer of femininity ... a femininity which is conceived, or rather fantasized, as transparency, that is, as a refusal of the mask and of any 'role.'] See 'Il gioco delle parti: maschile e femminile,' in *La persona nell'opera di Pirandello* (Milan: Mursia, 1990), 117–18. In the course of this essay I hope to demonstrate how the above statement coincides with its opposite. The refusal of any mask will in the end coincide with the acceptance of all masks.
7 Maggie Gunsberg, *Patriarchal Representations: Gender and Discourse in Pirandello's Theater* (Oxford: Berg, 1994), 34.
8 Luigi Pirandello, *Maschere nude* (1958; Milan: Mondadori, 1978), 1:209. Unless otherwise stated, the English translations are mine.
9 Gunsberg, *Patriarchal Representations*, 116.

10 Ibid., 41.
11 *Crisi della ragione* is the title of the book edited by Gargani (Turin: Einaudi, 1979). In it, he states that the rigid and objective logical and linguistic structures we have employed for centuries to understand reality 'have instead drained it of its blood. They have cancelled the unique condition of empirical existence that consists in its irreducibility to logical-conceptual schemes' (p. 15).
12 Rosella Prezzo, 'Il filosofo e il fantasma del femminile,' *Aut aut* 237–238 (May–August 1990): 79. Prezzo here quotes Lévinas.
13 Carlo Sini, *Il silenzio e la parola* (Genoa: Marietti, 1989), 23. In his book Sini does not discuss feminist thought, but, using Merleau-Ponty, Heidegger, and Peirce, he develops a discourse that is very close to that of feminism.
14 *Diotima: Il pensiero della differenza sessuale* (1987; Milan: La Tartaruga, 1990), 25. For the biological studies, see the essay by Sandra Witelson 'Les différences sexuelles dans la neurologie de la cognition: implications psychologiques, sociales, éducatives et cliniques,' in Evelyn Sullerot, ed., *Le Fait Feminin* (Paris: Fayard, 1978), 287–303. For an extensive bibliography on the topic, see Mary Ritchie Key, *Male/Female Language. With a Comprehensive Bibliography* (Metuchen, NJ: Scarecrow Press, 1975) and the volume *Diotima* mentioned earlier.
15 This analysis is developed in *Diotima*, 26. The various authors who wrote this first chapter follow the ideas expressed by Hélène Cixous and Catherine Clément in *La jeune née* and by Julia Kristeva in *Desire in Language* (New York: Columbia University Press, 1980).
16 Prezzo, 'Il filosofo e il fantasma,' 83.
17 There is an interesting, new reading of the play in Lucienne Kroha's 'Behind the Veil: A Freudian Reading of Pirandello's *Così è (se vi pare)*,' in *The Yearbook of the Society for Pirandello Studies*, 12 (1992): 1–23. Kroha sees the core of the play not in the statement of the relativity of truth, but in the disguising of it. Using Freud's 1925 essay, 'Negation,' and its elaboration made for literary analysis by Francesco Orlando, Kroha argues that the philosophical aspects of the play are a defence, a 'copertura' that tries to hide the real core of the issue, which is that of sexual abuse and possibly incest.
18 Mary Ann Witt, 'Modes of narration in *Sei personaggi*,' in *Pirandello: Poetica e presenza* (Rome: Bulzoni, 1987), 607–19.
19 Luigi Pirandello, *Saggi, poesie scritti varii* (Milan: Mondadori, 1960), 1266.
20 The Stepdaughter's disrupting function is also underlined by Rita Verdirame, who reads her through Freud. She is hysteric, Verdirame comments, and 'hysteria is connected with the Oedipus complex of the

child and therefore with the trauma ... of discovering sexual difference, and the violation of the incest taboo.' *Finzione, rassegnazione e rivolta: L'immagine femminile nella letteratura dell'Ottocento* (Enna: Papiro Editrice, 1990), 107. According to Gunsberg's interesting reading of the play, its aim, instead, is 'to reinforce the traditional family/gender hierarchy' (see *Patriarchal representations*, 164). At the end of the play, in fact, only the legitimate family remains. I do not agree, however, with Gunsberg's defeatist interpretation of the Stepdaughter, as I hope to show in what follows.

21 Luigi Pirandello, *Sei personaggi in cerca d'autore*, in *Maschere nude*, 1:56. Further page references from the play are given in the text.
22 Luciana Martinelli, *Lo specchio magico. Immagini del femminile in Luigi Pirandello* (Bari: Dedalo, 1992), 29.
23 Pirandello, *Ciascuno a suo modo*, in *Maschere nude*, 1:128. Further page references to the play are given in the text.
24 'Attrice' and 'pazza' are clearly existential categories that should warn us right away about the importance of this character. On the topic of Pirandello and madness, see: Elio Gioanola, *Pirandello la follia* (Genoa: Il Melangolo, 1983); Giovanni R. Bussino, 'Pirandello's Personal Experience with Madness' in *Canadian Journal of Italian Studies* 6, 22–23 (1983): 21–38; Maggie Gunsberg, 'Hysteria as Theatre: Pirandello's Hysterical Women,' *The Yearbook of the Society for Pirandello Studies* 12 (1992): 32–52.
25 In her enlightening essay 'The Branding of Women: Family, Theatre and Female Identity in Pirandello,' *Italian Studies* 45 (1990): 48–63, Ann Ceasar sees the identity of Pirandello's female characters defined by the male recognition.
26 Pirandello, *Quaderni di Serafino Gubbio* in *Tutti i romanzi*, 2 vols. (Milan: Mondadori, 1973), 2:641.
27 Speaking of Varia Nestoroff, in *Lo specchio magico*, Martinelli writes: 'la professione di attrice diviene la metafora della non appartenenza a sé del personaggio' (130) [the profession of actress becomes the metaphor of the character's not-belonging to herself]. I would like to expand this idea by keeping in mind the last women protagonists of Pirandello's theatre. The profession of actress then becomes the metaphor of human life.
28 Pirandello, *Trovarsi*, in *Maschere nude*, 2:968.
29 Pirandello, *Saggi, poesie scritti varii*, 1038. In one of her last letters to Pirandello written from New York only two months before his death, Marta asked him to write more about women, to create new characters, to enter their souls. See Marta Abba, *Caro Maestro ... Lettere a Luigi Pirandello*, ed. Pietro Frassica (Milan: Mursia, 1994), 387.

30 Benito Ortolani, ed. and trans., *Pirandello's Love Letters to Marta Abba* (Princeton: Princeton University Press, 1994), 21.
31 For an extensive and thorough study of the trilogy of myths, interpreted through a Jungian reading, see Anna Meda, *Bianche statue contro il nero abisso* (Ravenna: Longo, 1993).
32 Ortolani, *Pirandello's Love Letters*, 9. Pirandello is commenting on Ibsen's *The Lady from the Sea*. Marta was at that time studying the role of Ellida. This image will reappear in *Trovarsi*. There, however, the creature of the sea is Elj. Donata, significantly, cannot swim and Elj saves her from drowning. Donata already at the end of act 1 has chosen, though still unaware, art over life.

11

Regicide, Parricide, and Tyrannicide in *Il fu Mattia Pascal*: Stealing from the Father to Give to the Son

THOMAS HARRISON

Sono un germe di quest'uomo che non si muove più; che sono intrappolato in questo tempo e non in un altro, lo debbo a lui! [I am a seed of this man who no longer moves; that I am trapped in this time and no other I owe to him!]

Pirandello, 'La trappola'

Ecco qua: tutto quello che aveva rubato al padre egli lo avrebbe rimesso al figliuolo nascituro. [There you have it: everything he had stolen from the father he would restore to the expected son.]

Pirandello, *Il fu Mattia Pascal*

The power of a father has been usurped, even at the cost of his life. And the son must avenge the act. This is the myth at the heart of Pirandello's richest novel, *Il fu Mattia Pascal* [*The Late Mattia Pascal*, 1904] and the issue at stake in its most commented lines. They are spoken by the character Paleari in the form of a parable. He notes that a marionette theatre in Rome is scheduled to perform the tragedy of Orestes, the avenging son of Agamemnon. What would happen, Paleari wonders, if at the very moment Orestes lifts his hand against the tyrant Aegisthus, the paper sky above them were suddenly to rip? What would happen is that Orestes would turn into Hamlet, he would become incapable of carrying out his act. The anxiety accompanying this hole in the sky would be infinitely more unsettling than the political wrongs requiring his attention.

'Tutta la differenza, signor Meis, fra la tragedia antica e la moderna consiste in ciò, creda pure: in un buco nel cielo di carta' ['That's the whole difference between ancient tragedy and modern, Signor Meis – believe me – a hole torn in a paper sky'].[1] Paleari's words sum up the moral of the tale as it has interested so many of Pirandello's critics: the tear in the metaphysics of life inaugurates modern art, the epoch of the antihero, of the perplexed, self-conscious Pirandellian character, too concerned with the ontological fissure to perform his everyday duties. Yet the question may still be asked: why has Pirandello used an example of tyrannicide to make his point? If he intends to talk about the incapacitating consequences of reflection, what need does he have for a story about two royal sons, both cheated of their rightful patrimony and on the verge of carrying out the most heinous of political crimes?[2] Is there anything in the content of Paleari's fable which helps illuminate the crisis on the level of artistic and existential form?

That the answer is yes is suggested by the reinforcement of the regicidal motif by another important myth in *Il fu Mattia Pascal*: the story of Oedipus. Readers such as Ferrario and Stocchi-Perucchio[3] have shown several ways in which Mattia Pascal, the protagonist of Pirandello's novel, is associated with the Greek hero and parricide: Pascal's wandering eye is surgically altered, leaving him virtually blind for forty days, and his tears mix with blood on at least one occasion. Oedipus, too, is the son of a slain king, pursuing the killer. But unlike Orestes and Hamlet, Oedipus discovers that *he* is the murderer, the tyrant ('Oedipus Tyrannus') who must punish himself for offending against the patriarchal order. There are many other instances of tyrannical, tyrannicidal, or parricidal behaviour in this novel: dramatic cases of stealing another man's property, of sleeping with his wife, of usurping his social or economic place, of struggling to restore a disrupted family order. In light of these prevalent patterns, the Orestes-Hamlet motif in Paleari's fable appears overdetermined. Everything points in the direction of Oedipus: a myth not of restoration (where the proper patriarchal order is re-established following the slaying of the usurper, as with Hamlet and Orestes), but of implacable rivalry – between fathers and sons, and between brothers. It is a story similar to the one that actually originates Orestes' woes: the story of Atreus who kills the sons of Thyestes, his brother, and feeds them to their father.[4] In Pirandello the essence of Orestes and Hamlet is underwritten by this other type of story, only waiting to be brought to consciousness – the story of a vicious and inescapable battle within the patrilinear order.

In Pirandello, though, the Oedipal story does not name the eternal and unchanging nature of the male unconscious as we know it from Freudian psychology. On the contrary, it signals a change – in the conscious rather than unconscious mind. Pirandello's reading of Oedipus signals a historical transformation in human relations by which parricide and regicide run rampant. What is at stake is a vision of modernity, where Orestes becomes Hamlet, and Hamlet turns into the self-knowing Oedipus. The new age is brought about not by the hero's uncertainty as to what to do, but by his recognition of precisely what he is doing, by his recognition that his regicidal behaviour has the form of an ineluctable, historical destiny. The change, of course, is intimately tied to the realization of which Paleari speaks: the higher authority which once enabled humans to live as mechanical, unconscious marionettes is no longer intact; the ethical *logos* dictated by the heavens or the throne has been torn apart. When this happens, no hero can declare in the old, tyrannical way, 'Thus I will it!' No artist or character can say, 'This is the order (the father or truth) I represent.' What inspires the crisis, however, is political evolution. In short, the transformation addressed by Paleari's fable is not primarily psychological or philosophical, but anthropological, and it pervades the poetics of this radically modernist novel.

Few readers will miss the fact that the fictional author of this autobiography introduces himself as a powerless marionette. The only answer Mattia Pascal can give to friends who seek his advice, he states in the first paragraph, is to say, 'Io mi chiamo Mattia Pascal.' (319) ['My name is Mattia Pascal.' (xi)]. He belongs to the same order of puppets as Paleari's Orestes and Hamlet. More interesting than this, however, is the mock dialogue Mattia strikes up with his readers. He imagines them assuming that this fact – that the only thing he knows is his name, and at a certain point not even that – implies that he is an orphan or bastard. The ellipsis in the fourth paragraph resists naming the shameful condition:

Qualcuno vorrà bene compiangermi (costa così poco), immaginando l'atroce cordoglio d'un disgraziato, al quale avvenga di scoprire tutt'a un tratto che ... sì, niente, insomma: né padre, né madre, né come fu o come non fu. (319)

[Some of you may feel like pitying me (it takes so little), imagining the horrible suffering of a poor wretch who suddenly discovers that ... yes, nothing, no father, no mother, no past or present. (xi)]

Mattia's crisis of identity, he imagines his readers imagining, involves a basic confusion about his father or mother. But this reading is thoroughly mistaken in its grasp of the facts:

Potrei qui esporre, di fatti, in un albero genealogico, l'origine e la discendenza della mia famiglia e dimostrare come qualmente non solo ho conosciuto mio padre e mia madre, ma e gli antenati miei e le loro azioni in un lungo decorso di tempo. (319–20)

[In fact, I could draw you a whole family tree, with the origins and ramifications of my line, and I could show you that I not only knew my father and mother, but can name my ancestors also and recount their deeds over a long period of time. (xii)]

Put otherwise, whatever Mattia Pascal's real problem may turn out to be, it has nothing to do with a disruption of the natural order of filiation.

Or does it? Within seven pages Mattia has admitted that the crude intuitions of readers have hit on some truth after all. 'Ho detto troppo presto, in principio, che ho conosciuto mio padre. Non l'ho conosciuto. Avevo quattr'anni e mezzo quand'egli morì.' (325) ['I spoke too soon, at the beginning, when I said that I had known my father. I didn't know him. I was four and a half when he died.' (7)]. Mattia's confusion of identity may indeed involve his father. If not, he would not even construct his autobiography in the traditional way – by spelling out the genealogical ground for his own identity. This ground proves absent. The father is prematurely deceased. And that is where all the family troubles start: 'La sua morte quasi improvvisa fu la nostra rovina.' (326) ['His almost unexpected death spelled our ruin.' (8)].

The next fact that Mattia chooses to relate is no less significant than the first. Upon the death of the father, Mattia's mother entrusts another man with the management of their property, a man who, ironically, had been treated in many ways like a son by Mattia's father (326; 8): Batta Malagna. The 'mole,' as they call him, ends up usurping the family fortune: 'ci scavava soppiatto la fossa sotto i piedi' (328) ['he was secretly digging the graves beneath our feet.' (9)]. Little by little he divests the Pascal family of their holdings.

Every other male introduced in the first ten pages of the novel reinforces the treacherous scenario. There is Mattia's older brother, the better-liked, better-dressed, better-looking Berto; the 'dog faced'

Mattia resents him dearly, and tries to even the score. There is the boys' tutor, Pinzone [Tweezers], whose duplicity is already inscribed in his name.

Mattia relates only one anecdote about Pinzone. One day the brothers bribe him to take them on a country escapade instead of to church, as their mother had wished. The three frolic about happily, increasing their pleasure in and by means of their secret pact. But when they come home and Mattia's mother asks Pinzone what they did, he informs her of every last detail. Pinzone is another back-stabbing father substitute, and the boys learn to avenge themselves 'di questi suoi tradimenti' (331) ['for these acts of treachery' (12)]. Pinzone commands no respect from the sons. He was an authority, says Mattia, in nothing but 'allitterazioni e annominazioni e versi correlativi e incatenati e retrogradi di tutti i poeti perdigiorni' (332) ['alliterations and puns and symmetrical, chained, retrograde verses of all time-wasting poets' (13)]. Instead of teaching the autonomous functions of words, he demonstrates how to make each word parasitic on every other. Pinzone's cannibalizing verses are of a piece with the male behaviour described in these opening pages – especially when we remember that Mattia and his brother preyed on the nests of birds (331; 12) that day when they should have been confessing their sins to God the father. This detail already makes it clear that Mattia himself will offer no exception to the rule this book is proceeding to build: the destruction of the hearth.

The last male described at the outset of this autobiography is the man from whom Mattia's father is reported to have won his fortune: the captain of an English merchant ship who, after losing all his cash at cards, 'si era anche giocato un grosso carico di zolfo imbarcato nella lontana Sicilia per conto d'un negoziante di Liverpool' (325) ['also gambled away a large cargo of sulphur he had taken on in far-off Sicily for a merchant in Liverpool' (7)]. Even the captain is one who appropriates – or expropriates – the property of another. Mattia's father thus builds his wealth out of property usurped from one man by another. To make the paternal associations even stronger, the prototype for this divested proprietor of Sicilian sulphur is the father of the author, Stefano Pirandello senior, the owner of a Sicilian sulphur mine that was ruined by a flood in 1903, the year before the publication of *Il fu Mattia Pascal*. When that happened, his son Luigi lost both his annual allowance and the invested dowry of his wife.

Each baroque twist in the plot of this fiction can be traced to Mattia's efforts to expropriate the power of the prime usurper, Malagna.

To begin with, Mattia sleeps with Romilda, the woman this tyrant is courting. Believing that his wife Olivia is infertile, Malagna is determined to have a son any way that he can, but Mattia beats him to it by getting Romilda pregnant himself. Just after Malagna decides to father this illegitimate child, he discovers that Oliva is also pregnant. The culprit is one and the same (though the seduction of Oliva is an act of correlative vengeance, for she was originally Mattia's before Malagna usurped her). Needing Romilda no longer, Malagna convinces Mattia to marry her. And here his woes double and triple, beginning the true adventures he has set out to tell. Up to this point everything is merely background, merely 'fundamental.'

So dissatisfied is Mattia with his marital arrangement that he seizes on an opportunity provided by the most fortuitous of possible occurrences to flee it. One day he travels to Montecarlo and wins a life's savings at roulette, and on the way back home, he reads in the newspaper that a dead man in his village has been identified as Mattia Pascal. Mattia leaps for joy. Suddenly he is free to assume a new identity. And so he does, adopting the name of Adriano Meis, roaming about for a year, and eventually settling down in Rome. If Mattia had belonged to a properly functioning patriarchal structure – or if he had succeeded in constructing one himself (which he does not, for he is given no son by Romilda) – then none of this would have happened.

Mattia is not the only figure in the book to suffer from a dysfunctional family. The syndrome of a deposed, absent, dead, or irresponsible father pervades the novel. We are told nothing about Romilda's father except that he was an artist, 'morto pazzo, a Torino' (345) ['who died insane, in Turin' (26)]. Here, too, the question arises as to the legitimacy of this paternal figure (or of the child, which is the same). As he contemplates the artist's self-portrait, Mattia cannot help wondering whether this is indeed the man who fathered Romilda: 'Ora io, guardando Romilda e poi la madre, avevo poc'anzi pensato: "Somiglierà al padre!" Adesso, di fronte al ritratto di questo, non sapevo più che pensare.' (345–6) ['A short while before, when looking at Romilda and then at her mother, I had thought: "She must resemble her father!" Now, with his portrait before me, I no longer knew what to think' (26)].

The family from whom Mattia rents a room in Rome has its own deranged or absent father, the theosophist Paleari, who answers the door with his head covered in foam and 'aveva pure così, come di spuma, il cervello' (435) ['whose brain was also more or less made of foam' (114)]. Adriana, his daughter, is continually mortified by Paleari's 'follia' (447) ['madness' (126)]. Her father is so oblivious to all matters of practical existence that he is as good as dead. Thus he is unable to protect his daughter from the preying intentions of the second great tyrant in the book, the son-in-law Papiano. Accompanying the theme of the vulnerable father is once again that of the man who seeks to take advantage of it: the intruder and usurper Papiano, the more powerful 'son.'

Papiano is away in Naples when Mattia rents his room. In that short period Mattia takes his place, adopting the functions of a surrogate son and capturing the affections of both the father and the two women living with him, Adriana and Signorina Caporale. To himself, however, this adopted son – who will eventually be a prospective son-in-law – is an obvious intruder, an impostor of the role he assumes:

Man mano che la familiarità cresceva per la considerazione e la benevolenza che mi dimostrava il padron di casa, cresceva anche per me la difficoltà del trattare ... nel vedermi lì, intruso in quella famiglia, con un nome falso, coi lineamenti alterati, con una esistenza fittizia e quasi inconsistente. (445)

[Thanks to the respect and the affection shown me by the master of the house, I more and more became one of the family; and at the same time, my situation became more and more difficult ... as I saw myself an intruder in their midst, with a false name, altered features and almost non-existent identity. (125)]

Hence there is a mirroring effect when Papiano, who is the original surrogate son, the original, more vicious intruder, returns, since Papiano's own wife, Adriana's sister, died without leaving any children and Papiano is now courting Adriana. If he marries her, he will not have to pay back his first wife's dowry that should rightfully be returned to the father. The stakes, once again, are an illegitimately possessed patrimony.

Pirandello could not make his portrait of Papiano as usurper and tyrant more explicit. When he first sees Papiano, Mattia's thought is that the 'malanimo di quell'uomo' ['the malevolence of the man'] would make it impossible to remain a tenant in a house 'su cui egli – non c'era dubbio – voleva tiranneggiare, approfittando della dabbenaggine del suocero.' (466) ['where he undoubtedly wanted to act as tyrant, exploiting the kindliness of his father.' (143)]. The image of

Papiano as a father-deposing son is reinforced by other, more subtle descriptions. By political sympathy he is a Garibaldino (a secular, populist democrat) yet that does not stop him from working for a marquis who wishes to revive the Kingdom of the Two Sicilies. Papiano thus belongs to the enemy class of the 'borbonico e clericale' (465) ['Bourbon sympathizer and priest lover' (142)] for whom he works – the class of the rebellious sons, but like a typical schemer he dissimulates the fact, serving a cause he secretly wishes to overthrow.

The only detailed portrait of Papiano immediately follows the fable about the two regicidal marionettes, making the narrative function of Paleari's parable primarily that of introducing this treacherous man. Indeed, Mattia transposes the terms from one situation to another:

'E il prototipo di queste marionette, caro signor Anselmo,' seguitai a pensare, 'voi l'avete in casa, ed è il vostro indegno genero, Papiano. Chi più di lui pago del cielo di cartapesta, basso basso, che gli sta sopra, comoda e tranquilla dimora di quel Dio proverbiale.' (468)

['And the prototype of those marionettes, my dear Signor Anselmo,' I went on thinking, 'is here in your house: your unworthy son-in-law, Papiano. Who is more content than he with the paper sky, so low over his head, comfortable and serene dwelling of that proverbial God.' (146)]

This is in fact what we will discover – that Papiano is the efficient, Orestian regicide who will not be distracted from his intentions by a tear in the sky.

Mattia's instinctive reaction to Papiano is to act as Hamlet – to leave the house – but later he is forced to reconsider, largely out of sympathy for the women. He decides to act as the avenging Orestes, to duel with this tyrant and free the victims. Mattia has come to the defence of women before. He rescued his mother from the wrath of his mother-in-law; he protected Romilda from the designs of Malagna; he relieved Oliva of her childless condition; he beat off four ruffians abusing a prostitute in Rome (449; 128). Suddenly the Orestian rivalry looks suspiciously Oedipal, as though the male antagonisms were secretly mediated by desire for a woman. But it also smacks of the story of that self-styled succourer of women, Don Quixote, with whom Mattia is also associated.[5] Does Pirandello mean to suggest that this 'Oedipal' scenario, in which men presumably vie with each other out of an unconscious desire for a woman, is inherently quixotic? The question arises

Regicide, Parricide, and Tyrannicide in *Il fu Mattia Pascal*   197

by virtue of the fact that Mattia fails so miserably, even ridiculously, in his Orestian scheme. Even though he is in love with Adriana (or perhaps primarily because of that), he is forced out of the house by Papiano. The tyrant steals his money and leaves the impostor Adriano Meis with no legal resource. Mattia/Adriano lacks the official and social status required for effective defence. Not sufficiently automatic a marionette, he does not possess the instruments for successful treachery.

Where Papiano and Malagna are confident Orestian schemers, Mattia is doomed to be Hamlet. His intentions throughout the book, quixotic as they may be, are to right an order that has gone awry. The first concrete information Mattia gives about his life consists in the statement 'Fui, per circa due anni, non so se più cacciatore di topi che guardiano di libri nella biblioteca ...' (320) ['For about two years I was a rat hunter, or if you prefer, custodian of books, in the library.' (xii)]. The rats are literal ones, consuming the municipal collection of books, but symbolically they are scavengers on the patriarchal order. They are the rats in the kingdom of Denmark, whom Hamlet, like Odysseus and Orestes, comes home to eliminate. That 'play within a play' by which Shakespeare's prince exposes the conscience of the king has been dubbed 'The Mousetrap.' Later, when Hamlet stabs the 'intruding fool' Polonius, he exclaims, 'How now, a rat?' The first large rat in *Il fu Mattia Pascal* is Malagna, the second Papiano. The two years that Mattia spends as a rat chaser are not simply the years he works as a librarian; they are the years he spends away from home, a time span which Pirandello stresses more often and more clearly. However humorous the forms it takes, the motivation of these two years is nothing less than vengeance: against Mattia's symbolic murder at the hands of his wife and his mother-in-law, who identify the poor suicide's body as his; against Malagna and the debtors; against such tyrants as Papiano, the Spanish painter, and the four hooligans; against Mattia's own impotence and contemptible physical attributes. When Mattia shaves his beard, he notes that the little chin which starts to protrude 'mi parve un tradimento. Ora avrei dovuto portarlo scoperto, quel cosino ridicolo. E che naso mi aveva lasciato in eredità! E quell'occhio!' (406) ['seemed almost a piece of treachery. Now I would have to expose it, the ridiculous little thing. And what a nose he had left to me! And that eye!' (85)].

When Mattia's challenge to Papiano fails, he leaves his new Elsinore to seek vengeance in his original life where his rightful place has been usurped not just by the dead stranger in the graveyard but also by his wife's new husband, Pomino. In this, his third and last life, Mattia is both Hamlet and Hamlet's father. A ghost returned from the dead, he rings the new couple's bell in the dead of night:

M'avanzai, gridando:
 – Mattia Pascal! Dall'altro mondo.
Pomino cadde a sedere per terra, con un gran tonfo, sulle natiche, le braccia puntate indietro, gli occhi sbarrati:
 – Mattia! Tu?!
La vedova Pescatore, accorsa col lume in mano, cacciò uno strillo acutissimo, da partoriente. Io richiusi la porta con una pedata, e d'un balzo le tolsi il lume ...
 – Zitta! – le gridai sul muso. – Mi prendete per un fantasma davvero ? (564)

[I moved forward, shouting: 'Mattia Pascal. From the other world.'
Pomino fell on the floor with a great thud, on his buttocks, his arms thrust back to support him, his eyes open wide.
'Mattia? You!'
The widow Pescatore, who had run in with a lamp in her hand, let out a shrill scream, as if she were in labor. I kicked the door shut and with a bound grabbed the lamp away from her ... 'Shut up!' I shouted in her face. 'Do you really take me for a ghost?' (238)]

The tactics of terror are deliberate, for Mattia's purpose is to 'piombar come un nibbio là sul nido di Pomino' (561) ['swoop down there like a hawk on Pomino's nest' (234)]. This illegitimate new union must be fully undone, reversed by the curse of the dead. 'Il tuo matrimonio s'annulla' (566) ['Your marriage will be annulled' (240)], he shrieks.

Yet in the course of this confrontation, Mattia's resolve strangely weakens. Instead of destroying the family altogether, he decides simply to put Romilda and Pomino into his own position – the uncomfortable, duplicitous position of Hamlet, stopped from identifying himself with his actions by a tear in the sky. His vengeance will consist merely in transmitting his disease. 'Vuol dire,' says Mattia, as he imagines the other alternative,

che se lui non mi vuole più in casa, mi metterò a passeggiare giù per la strada, sotto le tue finestre. Va bene? E ti farò tante belle serenate.
Pomino, pallido, vibrante, passeggiava per la stanza, brontolando:
 – Non è possibile ... non è possibile ...

Regicide, Parricide, and Tyrannicide in *Il fu Mattia Pascal* 199

A un certo punto s'arrestò e disse:
– Sta di fatto che lei ... con te, qua, vivo, non sarà più mia moglie ...
– E tu fa' conto che io sia morto! – gli risposi tranquillamente.
Riprese a passeggiare:
– Questo conto non posso più farlo! (571)

[So if he no longer wants me in the house, then I'll stroll up and down the street, below your windows. How's that? And I'll sing you many beautiful serenades.
Pomino, pallid, trembling, paced up and down the room, muttering:
– That can't be ... that can't be ... At a certain point he stopped and said:
– The fact is that she ... with you, here, alive, wouldn't be my wife any more ...
– And you just pretend that I'm dead! – I answered him calmly.
He started pacing again:
– I can't pretend that any more! (244)]

No anguish could be greater for Pomino than to function as Romilda's husband with the true husband living next door. It is the same discomfort experienced by Matilde in *Enrico IV* [*Henry IV*, 1921] when she is confronted with her duplicity by the victimized Henry. It is the same desperate situation that turns comic when, in *Il giuoco delle parti* [*The Rules of the Game*, 1922], a husband forces his wife's lover to stand up for her virtue. From this point on, Pomino will be forced to live without innocence of gesture. The ease with which he had been used to performing his patriarchal duties will never return. The man is simply incapable of living with the duplicity: 'Vattene via,' he cries, 'poiché ti piacque farti creder morto! Vattene subito, lontano, senza farti vedere da nessuno. Perché io qua ... con te ... vivo ...' (572) ['Go away, since you wanted us to consider you dead! Go away immediately, far away, without letting anyone see you. Because I here ... with you ... alive ...' (245)].

Does this Hamletian revenge, or symbolic tyrannicide of patriarchal pretensions, represent the final stage in Mattia's evolution? It does not. As much as Mattia enjoys torturing Romilda and Pomino, he finally softens even this plan of hounding them with his presence. At a decisive point in their hysterical exchange, his thirst for vengeance is suddenly and unexpectedly slaked. It happens thanks to an entirely fortuitous event: by accident, the new child of Pomino and Romilda is deposited in his arms. She is a girl, and she is inconsolable:

Restai al bujo, nella sala d'ingresso, con quella gracile bimbetta in braccio, che vagiva con la vocina agra di latte ... non dovevo aver pietà di questa, né di loro. S'era rimaritata? E io ora ... – Ma seguitava a vagire quella piccina, a vagire; e allora ... che fare? per quietarla, me l'adagiai sul petto e cominciai a batterle pian pianino una mano su le spallucce e a dondolarla passeggiando. L'odio mi sbollì, l'impeto cedette. E a poco a poco la bimba si tacque. (565–6)

I remained in the dark, in the vestibule, with that frail little girl in my arms, who cried with her voice still bitter with milk ... I was to have no pity for either this child or them. Had she remarried? Well then I, now ... – But the little creature went on crying and crying; and so ... what to do? To calm her, I settled her onto my chest and began to pat lightly with one hand on her little shoulders and to rock her while walking up and down. My hatred died away, my violence vanished. And little by little the baby grew silent. (239)]

The scene casts Mattia into the role of a mother, giving him a responsibility at odds with his masculine pride. And the new duty carries over even into the heat of passion: 'Rassèttati,' he tells his wife some time after giving the baby back, 'guarda, puoi far male alla tua piccina, così' (568) ['Pull yourself together. Be careful, you'll hurt your baby like that' (241)]. As voices grow shrill, he does all that he can to shield the child from the hostilities of this adult generation: 'Andiamo, andiamo di là, – diss'io. – La piccina s'è riaddormentata. Discuteremo di là.' (569) ['Come, let's go into the other room ... The baby's fallen asleep again. We'll discuss things in there.' (242)].

Whether Mattia knows it or not, he is voluntarily abjuring the tyrannical cycle, the compulsive insistence of one male to oust another from his place. It is as though Pirandello wishes to say that in this last and definitive incarnation of life the syndrome of male violence should no longer exist. If the cycle of usurpation is actually terminated, it is because a new balance has been established between masculine and feminine principles of behaviour. More specifically, it is due to a balance between the two bastards birthed in and by means of male rivalry:

Allegro, Pomino! Ti pare che voglia lasciare una figliuola senza mamma? Ohibò! Ho già un figliuolo senza babbo ... Vedi, Romilda? Abbiamo fatto pari e patta: io ho un figlio, che è figlio di Malagna, e tu ormai hai una figlia, che è figlia di Pomino. Se Dio vuole, li mariteremo insieme, un giorno! (568)

Regicide, Parricide, and Tyrannicide in *Il fu Mattia Pascal* 201

[Cheer up, Pomino! You think I want to leave a little child without her Mamma? Come on! I already have a little boy without a father ... You see, Romilda? We're even: I have a son, who's the son of Malagna. And now you have a daughter, who's the daughter of Pomino. God willing, we'll marry them some day. (241)]

This nuptial vision shifts the fantasy from a scene of tragic revenge to one of comic resolution, enabled by the fact that the new child is a girl; the father-son dynamic cannot be perpetuated. On the contrary, this fact enables Mattia to confer legitimacy on the pattern of illegitimate filiation.

If the tyrannical/tyrannicidal syndrome is resolved, it happens not when Orestes turns into Hamlet, but when Hamlet turns into Oedipus – when the modern, ineffectual tyrannicide sees that *he* is the usurper he is seeking to oust, the disrupter of the family, the son coveting both the place of the father and a woman not his by birthright. Hamlet becomes Oedipus when he realizes that tyranny is not a feature of the *other* male, but a principle in which they all participate. In Sophocles' play, the plague besetting Thebes is broken when Oedipus acknowledges that he is the regicide he seeks to punish, abdicating his throne and ripping out his unseeing eyes. By the end of Pirandello's novel, Mattia too gives up his sense of identity and embraces a new role as outlaw: 'Non sono affatto rientrato né nella legge né nelle mie particolarità. Mia moglie è moglie di Pomino, e io non saprei proprio dire ch'io mi sia.' (578) ['I am far from being in a sound legal position, nor have I regained my individual characteristics. My wife is the wife of Pomino, and I can't really say who I am.' (250)]. Where does Mattia sleep, now that he has achieved this paradoxical, negative selfhood? In the same bed in which his poor mother died (577; 250). The late Mattia Pascal, as he now calls himself, is an Oedipus appeased outside the order of all literal, historical accomplishments.

In one perspective, then, *Il fu Mattia Pascal* reads like an allegory: a victimized son plays out the tyrannicidal project to which he is subjected only to discover that it is a perverse, self-propagating process. He ends it through an expiating act of self-sacrifice. But this reading is not complete. To recognize one's participation in parricidal ethics is not necessarily to transcend it. The circle of violence may still remain an ineluctable *giuoco delle parti*, an inescapable fate, even if one follows the Greeks in holding oneself responsible for it.

And so it is with Mattia, as it once was with Oedipus, whose sons Polyneices and Eteocles just continued the male battle. Mattia never really breaks free from the order for which he atones. The first clue lies in his encounter with Oliva, the mother of his illegitimate son, but the wife of Malagna: 'L'ho incontrata per via ... col suo bambino di cinque anni per mano, florido e bello come lei: – mio figlio! Ella mi ha guardato con occhi affettuosi e ridenti, che m'han detto in un baleno tante cose.' (577) ['I met her on the street ... leading a little boy of five by the hand, plump and handsome as herself – my son! She looked at me with affectionate and laughing eyes, which told me many things in a flash.' (250)]. The implication is that Mattia may insinuate himself into a surrogate family at the expense of Malagna. The propagation of the cycle is also suggested by the fact that, by fleeing from Rome, Mattia simply abandons Adriana. Instead of avenging Adriana, her dead sister, and father, he allows Papiano's tyranny to continue its course. There is no restitution here, only avoidance.

Even stronger reasons for believing that the regicidal syndrome will continue beyond the frame of the book can be found in a series of narrative reflections on the society to which its characters belong. In classical days, Pirandello suggests, the possibility of restitution was much easier: one simply killed the usurper and reaffirmed the law against which he had sinned. In the present, however, this law no longer exists. Its hierarchical order has been replaced by 'anarchy,' by political regicide, and by an interminable battle of unfettered egos. How did this change occur? Pirandello explains it on various occasions, beginning with the preface.

Before embarking on his story, Mattia reflects that the age to which he belongs is characterized by a revolution in the status and relationships of human beings. Reflected in the thoughts of the philosopher from whom Mattia takes his name, Blaise Pascal, the revolution is formalized by a simple, factual discovery: that the earth is not, as the Bible taught, the centre of creation. The real casualty of this Copernican revolution, Mattia implies, is the very structure of patriarchy, its cosmic, philosophical support. Before Copernicus pointed his telescope in the direction of the heavens, dwellers of the earth could defer to the judgments of an absolute authority – the Bible in the realm of metaphysics, and the king in the realm of politics. Such authority was upheld by an incontestable word or law or *logos*, allotting each thing its place in a chain of being. At the top of the pyramid stood a monarch or pope, succeeded by expanding tiers of sons and subjects. Here everything was provided with a reason and origin. To legitimate one's worth, all a man had to do was to invoke his social lineage, the status of his father, his place on the political scale. Accompanying the law of the father was a law of truth and a law of identity. Underlying the many lay one. Thus the puppet show of life could proceed with its mechanical course and its cast of imperious heroes, each proud, like a Greek or Roman, of his 'propria dignità' (323) ['personal dignity' (5)].

While such a setup may have appeared tyrannical to aspiring sons, it certainly did not nourish the tyrannical impulse. Regicides, heresies, and other transgressions against authority were swiftly punished. It was actually later in history – in the modern, democratic, 'protestant' age of self-made men – that tyrants and usurpers proliferated in an unprecedented fashion. The seething potential for male rivalry did not flourish until *after* the supreme ruler had been fully disempowered, following that battle of the secular against the sacred about which Pirandello chose to write in *Enrico IV*.[6] The age of male antagonism is in fact the post-Copernican age, where all sons are free to vie for the power relinquished by the despot. Autocratic rule is fully overcome by democracy, the policy by which all persons are equal and the only true authority is the will of the majority. But, of course, this will of the majority is not a will of its own; it is simply a strategy for controlling the potential for aggression contained in these other, numberless wills. In the world of the sons, human qualities or lack thereof are not assigned from the start. They are functions of what one succeeds in achieving – and this usually means by usurping the holdings of someone else, who is no more innately entitled to them, and who can lose them just as easily as he gained them. In this perspective, then, Mattia, Malagna, and Papiano are not exceptions to a rule, but typical representatives of a society where patriarchal authority is forcibly opposed.

Mattia makes this reasoning clear when a happy-go-lucky drunkard causes him to reflect on why he is so discontent:

'Ma la causa vera di tutti i nostri mali, di questa tristezza nostra, sai qual è? La democrazia, mio caro, la democrazia, cioè il governo della maggioranza. Perché, quando il potere è in mano d'uno solo, quest'uno sa d'essere uno e di dover contentare molti; ma quando i molti governano, pensano soltanto a contentar se stessi, e si ha allora la tirannia più balorda e più odiosa: la tirannia mascherata da libertà. Ma sicuramente! Oh perché credi che soffra io? Io soffro appunto per questa tirannia mascherata da libertà ...' (448–9)

['The real cause of all our sufferings, of this sadness of ours – do you know what it is? Democracy, my dear man. Yes, democracy; that is, the government of the majority. Because when power is in the hands of a single man, this man knows he is one and must make many happy; but when the many govern, they think only of making themselves happy, and the result is the most absurd and hateful of tyrannies. Of course! Why do you think I suffer? I'm suffering because of this tyranny masked as freedom ...' (128)]

Everything that Mattia has done in his life has been geared towards achieving such freedom: he struggled against Malagna and Pinzone; he escaped his tyrannical family; he became financially secure; he altered his identity and physical appearance. What had beckoned irresistibly was the idea of remaking himself from scratch, of enacting the dream of the self-made man. At first he even seemed to succeed. With his capital and the prospects of independence it afforded, he liberated himself from all threats to personal autonomy. He became the paragon of the self-governing hero, enjoying the unlimited freedom to do what he wants. Here even the absence of paternal direction appears to be a blessing in disguise.[7]

Yet the irony is that whatever Mattia does to escape tyranny only makes it worse. The ultimate tyranny, he discovers, is not that life of constrictions he tried to elude, but the new life of the self-governing will, in which one is perfectly free to pursue one's desire. For this freedom is shared with others who act as barriers to what one wants, wanting it themselves, contesting one's right to have it, conspiring to possess more, and so on. An egalitarian society allows no one to dictate his rules in the privacy of a lofty 'castle'; it turns every arena for human existence into a 'piazza' (424) ['village square' (103)], a scene of mutually interactive egos and reciprocal influence, where everyone brushes shoulders and no one can do as he might otherwise choose.[8]

The categorical difference between democracy and absolute monarchy is thus reversed: seemingly despotic order is actually freedom (freedom from individual responsibility and from the importunate calls of the will). The apparently libertarian structure of democracy is actually tyranny (tyranny of each against all, each infinitely limited by all). The ostensible reign of egoism is altruistic (where 'one' has the duty to make many happy); the altruistic community is egoistic.

These proliferating, historical threats to personal autonomy are precisely what account for the patriarchal, patrilinear obsessions of the characters in *Il fu Mattia Pascal*. The thief Malagna is intent on having his own son. A male offspring will thus furnish a motive for his stealing. A son will allow the egoistic antagonisms in which his father is caught to be transcended in a bond of wills; the father's property will be fortified against the encroachments of others; thanks to this inherited patrimony, one young man will also have a head start, not having to battle as much as he otherwise would. The procreative impulse is thus motivated by a desire to rebuild the hierarchical, patrilinear order that democracy has abolished, allowing one man or clan to stand above others. That is to say, the tyranny of mutual competition produces a logic of compensation. One steals from the father to give to the son.

Later in his career Pirandello lifts this compensatory logic from a political to an ontological level:

Quando uno comincia a irrigidirsi, a non potersi più muovere come prima, vuol vedersi attorno altri piccoli morti, teneri teneri, che si muovano ancora, come si muoveva lui quand'era tenero tenero, altri piccoli morti che gli somiglino e facciano tutti quegli attucci che lui non può piú fare.[9]

[When a person starts to stiffen, having difficulty moving as before, he wants to see other little corpses around him, so cute and tender, who continue to move as he himself moved when he was cute and tender, other little corpses who look like him and perform all those little acts he is no longer capable of.]

Once upon a time culture was viewed as *Bildung* – a formative process in which parents provided models for their children to follow. That was the time of Mattia's proverbial Greeks and Romans. In the modern age, what is more commonly bequeathed is property and money, or precisely the means by which to be free from everything else. Is this not the hidden, illegitimate law of free market society, where the only practical counter of legitimacy is how much one succeeds in acquiring? All other forms can only be traps, inhibiting one's movement, making one a puppet and eventually a corpse. Once it becomes clear that such traps are more real than all freedom of movement, one simply recreates the cycle.

Is it any wonder, then, that the son harbours parricidal feelings? In 'La trappola' ['The Trap,' 1912], the son wishes to strangle not just his father, but all women, for he views women as the conduits of this murderous scheme. He sees them as demons of vitality, seducing men into thinking they can escape the tyranny in which they are caught (yet only by transposing the condition onto their sons and daughters).

In both this story and 'La distruzione dell'uomo' ['The Destruction of Man,' 1921], the parricidal passion is addressed to the entire charade of creation from which none can escape. In these two works, as in *Il fu Mattia Pascal*, the tyrannicidal impulse is not a timeless feature of the human psyche; it is the offshoot of a historical development that pits the young against older or stronger forces and allows them no freedom but rebellion.

There are other reasons beyond these thematic ones for believing that *Il fu Mattia Pascal* leaves ancient, patriarchal logic permanently disrupted. These reasons are imbedded in the rhetoric of this uncanny novel. The real fable of Paleari is played out in its thick levels of figuration, in its irreducible ambiguities on the level of the letter, in its defiance of credible, naturalistic, narrative logic, and in its critique of hierarchical meanings, many of which have been thoroughly unveiled by the novel's closest reader, Stocchi-Perucchio. The construction of *Il fu Mattia Pascal* undermines the very thinking on which conventional, patriarchal order is based.

Meaning had a linear itinerary in pre-Copernican days, from the *logos* of the father to the *logoi* of the sons, in a network of supported identities. In the nineteenth and twentieth centuries, however, it circulates, divagates, splits, doubles, and turns back on itself. If there is something farcical in Mattia's efforts to trace his own identity back to his father, it is that the father himself is no stable point of reference. He is a moving circle. An itinerant gambler, he achieves his success in a world of play, on the wheel of fortune: 'Sagace e avventuroso, mio padre non ebbe mai pe' suoi commerci stabile sede: sempre in giro con quel suo trabaccolo' (326) ['Wise and venturesome, my father never had a permanent headquarters for his dealings; he was always touring around with that trawler of his' (8)].[10] The world of chance, repetition, substitution, duplicity, and instability that so worried both the historical Copernicus and Blaise Pascal furnishes the narrative and metaphorical basis for Pirandello's novel, displacing all identities and making all fathers absent. When Mattia tries to construct a father figure for the invented childhood of Adriano Meis, he cannot do it. He can only imagine a grandfather. The mechanisms of self-identification force him to overleap the preceding generation. The father stands in a limbo between grandfather (whom he cannot control) and son (whom he imagines he will), a son between his father and his eventual son. The same exclusion is felt in the mute tragedy of the Son of *Sei personaggi in cerca d'autore* [*Six Characters in Search of an Author*, 1921] as well as in an autobiographical note by Pirandello. Reflecting on the pain he experienced when his son Stefano was imprisoned in World War I, Pirandello recognized a symmetry between Stefano and his own father, who also performed his filial duty towards Italy by going to war. The emphasis of Pirandello's remark is all on his own displacement between the two: 'Prima, i nostri padri, e non noi! Ora, i nostri figli, e non noi!' ['First our fathers, and not us! Now our sons, and not us!'].[11] In Pirandello's imaginative world, fathers are not properly connected to the chains of responsibility.

That is why fathers cannot represent real people, even less so than other characters in this book. They only represent representations – shadows, doubles, and mimes, lacking a true index of identity. The suicide at Miragno is merely a substitute for Mattia; Pepita substitutes for Adriana, with whom Mattia can no longer flirt; the painter whom Mattia must duel substitutes for his real antagonist Papiano. Most characters in this book do what they do only because some other, mirror-self is interested in doing it: Mattia courts Romilda because Pomino is in love with her; Aunt Scolastica wants Mattia's mother to marry Count Pomino because she would like him for herself. Instead of expressing autonomous desires, these puppets are motivated by derivative feelings of envy and resentment. They are trapped in an endless, twisting, fortuitous plot, which cannot achieve resolution any more than can its characters. Instead of legitimate, first-born sons, we have bastards and twins. Unique though the events of Mattia's life may seem to be, they reproduce patterns already found in his absent father: gambling and wandering, winning a fortune, abandoning a son. Even the final and most proper name for the hero of this novel (*il fu Mattia Pascal*) takes the form of a bureaucratic idiom used to designate someone as the child of a late father.[12] Although the tyrannicidal syndrome might seem to be broken, Mattia can only remain the nameless son of a father, in a perverse new form of the Oedipal predestination that visits the sons with the sins of the fathers. Only now the 'moral' of this living repetition cannot be fathomed.

On this spinning narrative wheel, all things occupy positions they or their opposites once held before. Dozens of facts turn uncanny, resisting their surface significance. Why, for example, should the two possible names for Adriano Meis's fictional, Turinese father (Francesco and Antonio) be the same as those of Romilda's father, also from Turin? Why should every principle of logic that we feel competent to judge as readers (most obviously, the logic of the thief that does an immediate disservice to others) end up subverting itself? For example, the money Malagna steals from Mattia's father will properly find its way to Mattia's son. The 12,000 lire robbed from Mattia (never really his, of course, but irrationally won from others) will repay Papiano's debt to his father-in-law; if Adriana's dowery is resotred, it will revert to Mattia should he decide to marry her, as Papiano himself expects. Why do the usurpations pervading this book find such appropriate settlements? Is this the strange manner by which the tyrannical/tyrannicidal age achieves its own measure of normalcy? One steals from the father to give to the son; one steals from the son to compensate the losses of the father.

Illogic serves a new type of logic in *Il fu Mattia Pascal*, as mysterious in its nature as the theosophical reflections of Paleari. It is the modern counterpart to that strange union of accident and destiny in *Oedipus Tyrannus*, where the bad 'fortune' by which the young king is victimized is also individually willed. Given these humoristic defiances of the principle of contradiction, nothing in Mattia's story can be made 'instructive' (577; 250). Instruction proceeds in the manner of patriarchal heredity, from the father, the authority, or the model to the son, the follower, or the particular instance. The *logos* that, we are taught to believe, lies at the beginning – like the presumed identity of Mrs Ponza in *Così è (se vi pare)* [*Right You Are (If You Think You Are)*, 1918] – actually stands at the end, still around the corner. What traditionally assumes the role of logic (for example, the speech and knowledge of individuals) actually functions as a mode of oppression.[13] If there is any truth in Pirandello's tales, it can only lie in the fissures *between* these words and beliefs, in those junctures at which they fall silent. And this makes it impossible for even the reader to master the text's meaning.

As it circulates in post-patriarchal society, Pirandellian meaning calls for indefinite reflection. It cannot comfortably issue into mimetic narration, in which things can be known by their signs, desires by their acts, persons by their external demeanours. Instead, it enacts a para-fiction, offering representations and appearances that are simultaneously subverted. Understanding and winning one's place in this world are both efforts like those of the gamblers in Montecarlo – 'estarre la logica dal caso' (375) ['to extract logic from chance' (54)]. Where meaning and power are consistently threatened by usurpation, the logic of the thief is the only sensible one. What was once viewed as the legitimate status of things (X as the property of Y) now lends itself to illegitimate uses, or uses that appear to be so in a conventional perspective. The society of freedom and competition finds its hermeneutical form in fluidity of function and interpretation. The patriarchal Orestian puppet gives way to a puppet with both greater and lesser autonomy, never presuming, like Papiano, to pull his own strings, yet seeing how the strings are attached, and discovering links that the would-be hero does not imagine.

If the puppet show is an ontological trap – robbing one of freedom and turning one's life into a species of death – then the only free life is a posthumous one: a *reflection on* the trap, a life simultaneously inside and outside its law: as with Quixote and Hamlet, or every true reader and writer; as with Oedipus, who not only sees the tyranny in which he participates, but assumes personal responsibility for it, not only guessing at the enigmas of the Sphinx, but acting them out; unlike the life of his sons Polyneices and Eteocles, who kill each other in the attempt to restore a dead order, but like the life of their sister, his daughter Antigone, preparing their burial.

NOTES

1 *Il fu Mattia Pascal* is quoted in Italian from Luigi Pirandello, *Tutti i romanzi*, 2 vols. (Milan: Mondadori, 1985), vol. 1. The corresponding English quotations are taken from William Weaver's translation, *The Late Mattia Pascal* (Hygiene, CO: Eridanos Press, 1987) which, like all English translations cited in this essay, has been freely revised. Henceforth, page references to the Italian and the English texts will be given in the text. Here they are 468, 146.
2 No critic I know addresses this issue directly, even if several navigate around it. Giacomo Debenedetti, for example, in his *Il romanzo del Novecento* (Milan: Garzanti, 1987), characterizes Pirandello's rejection of naturalistic narrative as a gesture of parricide. In her authoritative volume, *Pirandello and the Vagaries of Knowledge: A Reading of 'Il fu Mattia Pascal'* (Saratoga, CA: Anma Libri, 1992), Donatella Stocchi-Perucchio unravels dozens of motifs intimately tied to the tyrannicidal syndrome, including treachery, thievery, vengeance, and the epistemological function of the father. Sources that investigate diverse ramifications of the Oedipus motif in the structures of Pirandello's writing at large include: Michel Gardair, *Pirandello: Fantasmes et logique du double* (Paris: Larousse, 1972); Elio Gioanola, *Pirandello la follia* (Genoa: Il Melangolo, 1983); Jean Spizzo, *Pirandello: Dissolution et génèse de la représentation théatrale. Essai*

d'interprétation psychanalytique de la dramaturgie pirandellienne (Paris: Les Belles Lettres, 1986); Jennifer Stone, *Pirandello's Naked Prompt: The Structure of Repetition in Modernism* (Ravenna: Longo, 1989). In *Patriarchal Representations: Gender and Discourse in Pirandello's Theatre* (Oxford: Berg Publishers, 1994), Maggie Gunsberg examines some discursive implications of patriarchal thought in Pirandello's plays. Maria Valentini's *Shakespeare e Pirandello* (Rome: Bulzoni, 1990) entirely sidesteps *Il fu Mattia Pascal*.

3 Stocchi-Perucchio, *Pirandello and the Vagaries of Knowledge*; Edoardo Ferrario, *L'occhio di Mattia Pascal: poetica e estetica di Pirandello* (Rome: Bulzoni, 1978).

4 The story of Atreus, a rich study of obsessive male rivalry, warrants its own exploration in relation to *Il fu Mattia Pascal*. Briefly – the curse on the house of Pelops, and later the house of Atreus, began when Pelops murdered Myrtilus, the chariot driver who had helped him win a race that awarded him the hand of Hippodamia, daughter of the king of Elis. The curse passed on to Atreus and Thyestes, the two sons of Pelops, who had a violent hatred for one another. They had also murdered their half brother Chrysippus. Later Atreus won a struggle with Thyestes and became king of Mycenae. Atreus first married Aërope the wife of his son Plisthenes. Later he married Pelopia, the daughter of Thyestes; at the time, Pelopia was pregnant by her father. After Thyestes seduced Atreus's wife Aërope, Atreus, in revenge, banished him from the kingdom. Thereupon Thyestes, to avenge himself, sent Atreus's son Plisthenes to kill Atreus. However, Plisthenes fell at the hands of his father who did not recognize his son. It was now time for Atreus to seek vengeance. Atreus killed three sons of Thyestes and served him their flesh at a banquet. Atreus also commanded Aegisthus, the son of Pelopia by Thyestes, to kill his father, but Aegisthus, learning that Thyestes was his father, instead killed Atreus. Some time later, while Atreus's son Agamemnon was away fighting in the Trojan war, Aegisthus seduced Clytemnestra, his wife, and the two joined to kill Agamemnon on his return. The curse on the descendants of Pelops seemed finally to come to an end when the two adulterers, Clytemnestra and Aegisthus, were slain by Agamemnon's son Orestes.

5 One situation finds Mattia out hunting (probably again for nests): 'Un giorno, a caccia, mi fermai, stranamente impressionato, innanzi a un pagliajo nano e panciuto, che aveva un pentolino in cima allo stollo. – Ti conosco, – gli dicevo, – ti conosco ... Poi, a un tratto, esclamai: – To'! Batta Malagna. Presi un tridente, ch'era lì per terra, e glielo infissi nel

pancione con tanta voluttà, che il pentolino in cima allo stollo per poco non cadde.' (335–6) ['One day, when I was out hunting, I saw a haystack, dwarf-like, potbellied, with a saucepan on the top of its center pole. I stopped, fascinated. "I know you," I said to the pile of straw, "Yes, I know you ..." And all of a sudden I cried out: "You're Batta Malagna!" I picked up a pitchfork lying there on the ground and stuck it so zestfully into the stack's belly that the pan on top almost fell down from the pole.' (17)]. The saucepan recalls the basin that Don Quixote mistakes for the helmet of his rival Mambrino.

6 The historical episode on which the plot of Pirandello's play is based is every bit as suggestive as the tyrannicidal structure of *Il fu Mattia Pascal*. Henry IV of Canossa represents the critical, political defence of secular rule against the divine right of Pope Gregory VII. Defying the pope's absolute authority, he begins a rebellion that ultimately culminates in the liberation of *all* subjects from authoritarian rule, or democracy. Incidentally, the rivalry between Henry and the pope is also mediated by a woman – the virtuous Matilda of Tuscany. By contrast, her modern counterpart Donna Matilde is eminently susceptible to the seductive rhetoric of preying males. The contrast between the sacred legislation of the pope and the demands of secular practice is visited again in the chapter of *Il fu Mattia Pascal* called 'Acquasantiera e portacenere' ['Holy Water Stoup and Ashtray'].

7 In numerous places Pirandello gives a positive reinforcement to the distance between fathers and sons. One example is *Uno, nessuno e centomila* [*One, No One, and a Hundred Thousand*, 1925–6], another fictitious autobiography where, on his way to becoming a mystic, Vitangelo Moscarda refuses to walk down any path his father sets out for him. Rather, he follows 'all paths' at whim. The revelant passage in *Uno, nessuno e centomila* can be found in Pirandello's *Tutti i romanzi*, 2: 741. For the English translation, see *One, No One and One Hundred Thousand*, trans William Weaver (New York: Marsilo Press, 1990) 5. A second example is 'La distruzione dell'uomo' ['The Destruction of Man'], where the narrator suggests that we view that 'idleness' of Petix, which so bothers his father, as a condition of thriving potentiality: 'Quest'ozio di Petix,' he writes, 'sarà bene intanto che non venga considerato solamente dal lato del padre, ma un po' anche da quello di lui, perché Petix veramente frequentò per anni e anni le aule universitarie, passando da un ordine di studii all'altro, dalla medicina alla legge, dalla legge alle matematiche, da queste alle lettere e alla filosofia ...' ['Now we would be well-advised to consider this idleness of Petix not only from the point of view of the father, but

also briefly from his, for Petix truly frequented the halls of the university for years and years, moving on from one discipline to another, from medicine to law, from law to mathematics, from mathematics to letters and philosophy ...']. This short story from the collection *La mosca* is cited from Pirandello's *Novelle per un anno*, 1:1045. An English translation can be found in Pirandello's *Short Stories*, trans. Frederick May (London: Quartet Books, 1987), 170. The most compelling defence of the freedom of a son from the compulsions of a father is made in Jean-Paul Sartre's autobiography, *Les Mots* (Paris: Gallimard, 1964). His father's death, which occurred when Jean-Paul was only eleven years old, proved to be the most fortunate of tragedies. It made him the uncontested master of his destiny and the sole companion of his mother.

8 These lines suggest a reassessment of whether Pirandello has really got it right about the Greeks. It is ironic to recall that it was the Greeks themselves who invented the public square (and with it democracy, curtailing the tyrannical impulses recorded in stories like that of Atreus). Nevertheless it is interesting to note that Cyrus, the ancient ruler of Persia, shares the Pirandellian suspicion about the dishonesty of public interaction. Here is his reaction to the military threats of an envoy of Sparta: 'I have never yet felt afraid of people who have a place reserved in the centre of their towns for meeting together and cheating one another on oath. Unless there is something wrong with me, these people [the Spartans] shall soon have troubles of their own to make their tongues wag, without needing the troubles of the Ionians.' Herodotus the historian comments: 'These words of Cyrus were a hit at the Hellenes in general, in allusion to their custom of laying out *piazze* where they buy and sell. The Persians, in contrast, have no use for *piazze* and the institution itself is quite unfamiliar to them' (Herodotus, *The History*, book 1, chapter 153). Trans. Toynbee in Arnold J. Toynbee, ed., *Greek Character and Civilization* (New York: Mentor, 1953), 23.

9 Luigi Pirandello, 'La trappola' (from the collection *L'uomo solo*), *Novelle per un anno*, 1:680–6.

10 The same circularity keeps Moscarda from advancing along any straight path: 'Mi fermavo a ogni passo; mi mettevo prima alla lontana, poi sempre più da vicino a girare attorno a ogni sassolino che incontravo, e mi maravigliavo assai che gli altri potessero passarmi avanti senza fare alcun caso di quel sassolino che per me intanto aveva assunto le proporzioni d'una montagna insormontabile, anzi d'un mondo in cui avrei potuto senz'altro domiciliarmi.' (*Uno, nessuno e centomila*, 741) ['I would pause at every step; I took care to circle every pebble I encountered, first distantly,

then more closely; and I was quite amazed that others could pass ahead of me paying no heed to that pebble, which for me, meanwhile, had assumed the proportions of an insuperable mountain, or rather, a world where I could easily have settled.' (5)].
11 Maria Luisa Aguirre D'Amico, *Album Pirandello* (Milan: Mondadori, 1992), 131.
12 Stocchi-Perucchio, *Pirandello and the Vagaries of Knowledge*, 53.
13 Edoardo Ferrario, *L'occhio di Mattia Pascal*, 82–5.

12
Pirandello in the Discursive Economies of Modernity and Postmodernism

Wladimir Krysinski

Postmodern Vampirandello and the Restless Paradigm

'Je suis un homme lucide, moderne.'

Witold Gombrowicz, *Le mariage* (1947)

One of the most recent textual incarnations of Pirandello is postmodern in nature. In a novel entitled *Larva, Babel de una noche de San Juan* by Spanish author Julián Ríos, Pirandello enters the metaphoric, mocking, and playful field of irony. He takes part in the paralleling of Don Juan's quest with the erotic obsession of a skirt-chasing vampire. In a passage written in the manner of Joyce's *Finnegans Wake*, Don Juan becomes a *vampiropeador*, a womanizing vampire. Julián Ríos offers the following play on words: 'Tú sí que te ibas de pira y te las pirabas de vamp en vampa, vampiropeador! Vampirandello a la busca de sus personajillas.'[1]

Let us leave aside the obvious erotic connotations. If this play on words is untranslatable, it is because the overlapping of portmanteau words makes us hear 'pyromaniac,' 'sweet-talker,' 'tout,' and of course 'banger,' which is the principal interpretant. Pirandello-vampire suffers a surprising fate in this metaphor. Pirandello the author enters into a postmodern order insofar as that term celebrates the game and festival of narrative at the expense of the search for meaning. Thus the nature of the problem – not to say the problematic – of Pirandello finds itself inverted. These are not characters in search of an author. Rather, an author is in search of characters ... and also of cute girls.

Thus there is an erosion of the modern quest for reduced and ambiguous meaning in the Pirandellian fashion. Postmodernism makes of Pirandello an obsessive point of reference, stored somewhere in a seldom-visited historical museum, to be brought out for fun, like a wax work dummy. While this point of view may be exaggerated, postmodernism in its playfulness can only play with Pirandello as a symbol or an outmoded structure. But this postmodern point of view gives us an opportunity to re-read Pirandello's work in the light of a new theoretical, historical, and critical situation of modernity. It gives us the opportunity to reactivate and rethink his works by applying to them a new interpretative framework.

The many celebratory as well as critical retrospectives of Pirandello's work over the last twenty-five years have accustomed us to see in it a limit-paradigm of theatrical modernity. This paradigm accentuates the decentring of the performance, the humorous separation of the two fundamental supports of the mimetic text, that is, of the dramatic story: dialogue and character. It also progressively disintegrates the social, interpersonal ego implied in the confrontations of monologue and dialogue. In 1936, and again around 1945, the Pirandello-paradigm was at once open and closed. It was, in Thomas Kuhn's sense of the word, 'open-ended.'[2] It presupposed a new dynamic that must reformulate the textual and scenic parameters of the theatre as a function of the limit-case in which Pirandello places post-1921 theatrical practice, after an international series of productions of *Sei personaggi in cerca d'autore* [*Six Characters in Search of an Author*, 1921]. The inscription of mimesis in the text and in the performance became ever more problematic. But the novelty of Pirandello's revolution is no longer felt today. It would be naïve to defend the absolute validity of this paradigm. Theatre has followed its evolutionary course, and the Pirandello-paradigm has been reabsorbed and relativized by various theatrical practices. Pirandellism has become widespread – a *fait accompli* of post-Pirandello theatre. It is advisedly that we say 'post-Pirandello,' and not just 'postmodern.' Once an abstraction has been made of 'Vampirandello,' we must attempt a reassessment of this body of work and of its importance within a new epistemological framework.

Pirandello's 'vampirism' will be overcome if we assign to Pirandello the function of a more or less explicit vector and operator in the discursive economies of modernity and postmodernism. In our eyes, these two categories can be no more than heuristic tools that help us to assign Pirandello his place in the evolutionary and involutionary chain of twentieth-century theatre and literature. The concepts modern and postmodern allow us to understand and describe the rhythms and constants, the ruptures and returns, the accelerations, tensions, and intertextualities of literature, theatre, and the arts. By combining historical and theoretical criteria, and by pointing out textual, literary, and theatrical facts, we intend to show how the Pirandello-paradigm functions within them and defines the direction of literary and theatrical evolution. We wish in this way to place Pirandello's works in relation to other works by means of a totalising assessment that recuperates within it the various philosophical, literary and theatrical practises of modernity and postmodernity.

Modernity as the Infiltrating Concept of Crisis and as Positive Project

Let us first of all reconstruct some historical indicators of Pirandello's lifetime and align the significant historic events that determined the future political, economic, social, and cultural world. The period of modern history, from the Paris Commune and the unification of Italy, continuing through the First World War, the October revolution, and the Fascist movements in Italy and Hitler's Germany, up to the end of the Second World War and the Yalta Conference, has been marked by the irresistible rise of the bourgeoisie and the proletariat, and by various crises. It has also been marked by the expansion of the the state and of bureaucratic authorities. The accumulation of significant historical facts, much like the accumulation of capital, creates a saturated state of consciousness – historical, critical, and philosophical consciousness – that is at once certain and perplexed, and that seeks to protect the world from its various entropies by means of a conceptual order. Thus a certain strand of modernity is constituted as the infiltrating concept of crisis. From Nietzsche to Deleuze and Lyotard passing through Max Nordau, Oswald Spengler, Valéry, Ortega y Gasset, and Heidegger, significant concepts include decadence and degeneration,[3] the lack of a sense of history, the death of culture,[4] the decline of the West,[5] the advent of world visions,[6] the schizophrenia of capitalism,[7] and the end of the great narratives.[8]

Opposed to these chiefly negative categories is the opening up of the project of modernity and its possible realization. Jürgen Habermas,[9] the most recent theorist of this project, postulates a differentiation (*Ausdifferenzierung*) of three spheres of values – science, morality, and art – with a view to the rational organization of daily life. In postulating the dialectical development of these three spheres (*Aufhebungsansprüche*), Habermas seems to forget their respective differences in the social praxis of science, morality, and art.[10] Modernity is neither the peak of the crisis nor the project of a harmoniously structured society. Modernity is above all the idea of a radical difference that separates one social formation from another – an excessive artistic practice, an idea or a philosophical system – that is extreme and historically determined, determined by other social formations and artistic or philosophical practices that enter into confrontation with a given historical moment or with repetitive creative modes, experienced as non-current or out-moded with respect to the immediate historical or social moment. The postmodern sensibility modulates modernity and endows it with a new aura, that of a new surpassing. Modernity and postmodernism presuppose a dynamic of surpassing that one can develop in different ways. Seen on the scale of a work of art, surpassing inscribes itself in the aesthetic and in the social resonance of the work. Thus both modern and postmodern imply a tension between the self-regulating aesthetic and the ideological values that transform themselves into the triangular exchange of values between creator, public, and critic.

Pirandello does not escape from these valorizing or depreciating constraints that determine the importance of the 'modern' or 'postmodern' ranking of a work. Thrown back onto the network of negative categories or positive values associated with modernity or postmodernism, Pirandello's works reveal themselves as at once modern in their totality and open to postmodernism. They are modern to the degree that there is in Pirandello a historical consciousness of the change of systems of values and of the transformations of the material and historical conditions of social life. The microcosm of Pirandello's short stories, novels, and theatre condenses a certain negative dialogism of critical attitudes and behaviours pushed to the level of paroxysm. In his works Pirandello signals the crisis of bourgeois values such as individualism, the stability of social institutions such as the family and marriage, as well as the permanence of human nature. Pirandello's whole corpus is based upon a rupture, thematized as much formally as ideologically, of 'the old apparently indissoluble agreement between signifieds and signifiers, between denotation (the real thing indicated) and connotation.'[11] In this rupture Henri Lefebvre sees a distinctive sign of the modern period that gives rise to an inevitable dialectic between daily life and art. If we admit with Lefebvre that 'ideologies ... accompany the crystallisation of mundanity in the modern world,'[12] we are compelled to recognize that Pirandello's dialogism, which presupposes some dominant ideologemes (the crisis of the ego, the multiplicity of masks, the dissolution of the personality, the failure to communicate) is not, for all that, indexed to the dominant ideologies. His dialogism is in a certain sense mono-subjective. His protagonists are sometimes quibbling, sometimes like remnants of Dostoevsky's subterranean psychology. Their monologic attitudes destabilize certain ingredients of bourgeois ideology, especially the idea that an individualism can be achieved and that a world can be made perfect. The fall of language, reduced to the explicative, the curse, and the lament, is produced in Pirandello's work through the inauthenticity of masks and social roles, the validity of which he breaks down.

If decadence is one of the ideological underpinnings of modernity, the decadence of Pirandello's work is not the *Entartung* [degeneration] of which Max Nordau speaks (with its principal ingredients of extreme egotism, selfishness, and individualism). In contrast to Nietzsche, who exalts nihilism, Pirandello's work narrativizes, theatralizes, and discourses upon the shattering of the bourgeois individual in Adorno's sense of the term (as a *Zerfall*, a fall and a division). The *principium individuationis* (the subjective and the particular) enters into conflict with the institutionalized social order. The individual cannot act out his individuation, because he does not have his own space. His interiority, his subjectivity, and his sense of self stumble over the symbolic forms of the institutionalized social order. The internal dialectic of Pirandello's work belongs then to that of Proust, which, according to Adorno's definition, 'breaks down the unity of the subject through the medium of introspection. The subject transforms himself into a scene in which objectivities appear. His individualistic work becomes anti-individual.'[13] Such is also the logic of Pirandello's works from *Il fu Mattia Pascal* [*The Late Mattia Pascal*, 1904] and *Uno, nessuno e cantomila* [*One, No One, and a Hundred Thousand*, 1925–6] to *I giganti della montagna* [*The Mountain Giants*, 1934].

The Project of Pirandello

While it is true Pirandello's work lacks the social project of a modernity that will realize itself through the differentiation of the three spheres of values (science, morality, and art) his work reveals a surpassing of the

The Discursive Economies of Modernity and Postmodernism 219

aporia of bourgeois subjectivity and a strongly thematized crisis of the subject-object relation in the double meaning of the term: subject in its relation with the self as object (Moscarda), and subject in its relation with the Other (Henry IV). Pirandello's modernity projects itself, therefore, onto a new paradigm – that of the individual whose mask does not quite fit. Pirandello's project of de-mythologizing the social game has obvious ethical connotations. The social mask of an individual who is not comfortable with himself is a symbol of a general malaise. The individual tries to free himself from the burdensome weight of the roles he must play. In Pirandello there is much more social tragedy than comedy. Reaching beyond the human comedy, in the manner of Balzac, Pirandello rewrites the social tragedy of the impossibility of being. His take on modernity to some degree impinges upon that of Bergson and Nietzsche. But into *'élan vital'* and 'intuition,' Pirandello inserts an existentialist reflection and an introspection that evoke the 'fear' and 'trembling' of Kierkegaard, the 'concern' and 'dereliction' of Heidegger, and the 'limit-situation' of Karl Jaspers. Pirandello's characters, those spontaneous quibblers, take up their place in a problematic field where great philosophical categories rub shoulders with the literary themes that subsume a modernity, defined as a crisis of values (by Nietzsche), as an ironic discourse (by Musil), and as subjectivity limited by its social determinants (by Proust).

Beyond this uniquely Pirandellian territory is found that which, for the last decade or so, we have called 'the postmodern,' that is to say, according to Jean-François Lyotard, the end of the 'great narratives.' The mental structures constituted in Pirandello's work that interiorize the end of the love-story (in 'La trappola' ['The Trap,' 1912]), of social cohesion (in 'Una giornata' ['One Day,' 1937]) and *Il fu Mattia Pascal*), of the transparency of language (in *Sei personaggi in cerca d'autore* and *Non si sa come* [*One Does Not Know How*, 1935]), and of the cohabitation of alterities (in *Uno, nessuno e centomila*). On the other hand, Pirandello anticipates and signals the possible language of a new beginning based on an awareness of the end of all these narratives. The break that occurs in his work at the time of writing *I giganti della montagna* presupposes this new language.

Pirandello and the Slogans of Modernity

We may not know how to establish a grammar or system of modernity, but we can attempt to specify a certain evolutionary logic of literature and theatre regarding what is at stake in different discursive practices in the economy of the modern and postmodern. This evolutionary logic and these stakes rely upon different definitions of modernity – artistic, literary, or theatrical. Let us recall what Baudelaire, Rimbaud, Barthes, and Baudrillard say about modernity, since their remarks illuminate Pirandello's discursive practices with a convergent and divergent light.

Charles Baudelaire wrote: 'Modernity is the transitory, fugitive, contingent half of art, whose other half is eternal and unchanging.'[14] Pirandello's capture of the transitory is the insistent inscription of the displacement of the ego and of the work in the textual field. In Pirandello, the transitory corresponds to a projection into the thematics and form of acute consciousness of a rupture of the harmony between the characters and their creator himself. In this sense, Pirandello's art is based upon a strategy of 'dialectic images' that, according to Walter Benjamin, define the modern writing of Baudelaire.

Arthur Rimbaud' slogan: 'Il faut être absolument moderne' from *Une saison en enfer*[15] acquires in Pirandello the dimension of an incessant quest for modernity that is nothing other than the quest for meaning – the meaning of life, work, and artistic creation. This quest is played out in the framework of a sociocultural system that implies a permanent conflict of representations. The quest for meaning in Pirandello's work is structured subjectively; each narrative voice creates it through and against the narrated story. The self-consciousness of narrator-characters is constantly destabilized while simultaneously actively supporting a questioning of reality. The quest for meaning is also positioned objectively by the fragmentation and openness of the work. Therefore, the quest for the meaning of theatrical practice reveals itself through a displacement of representational levels and the tension between these levels. In his theatre-within-the-theatre trilogy, Pirandello establishes a dialectic of the subject-object relation that engages the whole system of relations of reflexivity and self-reflexivity of theatre as complex mechanism. The relations between character and actor, character and person, performance and production, life and theatre are thereby imbued with conflict. The quest for the meaning of theatrical practice is infinite and spiral, but its intensity achieves a new, heretofore unheard of theatricality that has been ambiguously described as Pirandellism. In fact, this theatricality consists of a bitter questioning of theatre as social and aesthetic practice. In this way, Pirandello is 'absolutely' modern.

Roland Barthes states that 'modernity begins with the search for an impossible literature.'[16] The 'impossibility' of literature and theatre in Pirandello is yet again the quest for meaning of the anti-mimesis that is a necessary consequence of the conflict of representations. The typically Pirandellian operations of destabilization and doubling of representations find their source in this impossibility that, according to Roland Barthes, defines modernity. But it is in no way an impasse. Rather, it is the horizon of a dialectic whose dynamic is posited as incomplete.

Jean Baudrillard defines modernity in a paradoxical manner as 'recycling of lost subjectivity in a system of 'personalization' in the effects of style and directed aspiration.'[17] In this sense, Pirandello's characters and their subjectivity find themselves at the cross-roads of what can and cannot be represented. Their subjectivity seeks to recycle itself within a system of representations manipulated by society and its institutions. Thus they become 'problematic individuals' and fall back into their masks.

Literary evolution is a serial structure. Correlations established between one work and another, between one series and another, illuminate the tensions between the series and between the texts, just as they reveal the reciprocal overdeterminations between literature and philosophy, art and theatre.[18]

Pirandello's generation witnessed the growth of the trenchant philosophical systems that have marked this century: Nietzsche, Bergson, phenomenology, existentialism. There were also two literary revolutions during Pirandello's lifetime: the 'Copernican' revolution of Dostoevsky that revealed subterranean psychology, and the 'Einsteinian' revolution of Joyce that definitively broke the narrative linearity of time.

The same epoch was home to several historical avant-gardes: futurism, surrealism, and dadaism. How can we situate Pirandello in these different discursive practices? First, we must recall the fact that Pirandello's discourse inscribes itself in the critical interpretative tradition that, according to Gadamer, is at the origin of modernity.[19] In this sense, Pirandello's work is one of the most distinctive signs in the discursive practices of modernity. Like Marx's relations of production, the ideas of life and existence in Hegel and Kierkegaard, and Freud's unconscious, Pirandello's humorism belongs to what Gadamer calls the points of view of interpretation (*Interpretationsgesichtpunkte*).[20] If, after Gadamer, interpretation allows us to unveil the true functioning of the subjectivity of opinion and to achieve knowledge, then the humoristic tradition objectifies itself precisely as critical interpretation and specifies itself on the artistic level to the degree that it is supported by some of the invariants of modernity, notably subjectivity, irony, self-reflexivity, fragmentation, and 'the open work.'

Let us totally rethink the advances of Pirandello's discourse in the perspective of those constants that together underlie modern discursivity. It cannot be denied that Pirandello displaces these constants. Pirandello's prose and his theatre mark a conflict beyond remedy between the monologism of closed interiority and the dialogism of reflexive states of consciousness. Mattia Pascal, Serafino Gubbio, and Vitangelo Moscarda, like the narrative voices of 'Una giornata,' 'La trappola,' and 'La maschera dimenticata' ['The Forgotten Mask,' 1918], reveal the relational and social imperative of conscience. Thus subjectivity is directional and fundamentally dialogical, aimed at a being in the world with others. But it runs up against the Other as difference. Pirandello pushes to its extreme the tension between a perceptive monologism that is critical and subjective in the manner of a confession, and a dialogism that is nostalgic but ineffectual because it presupposes a clash of alterities. The impasse of subjectivity marks the gap between the desire for communication and the obstacle of incommunicability.

Thus, in his own way, Pirandello redefines Dostoevsky's polyphony. It exists only in our intentions. It is positional and fundamentally negative. Society is composed of subjective molecules whose unequal drives and respective degrees of vulnerability create a state of permanent alienation of one from another. Subjectivity that wants to transgress these limitations stumbles over institutionalized society and the Other incarnated by speech and a point of view in conflict. Therefore, Pirandello demonstrates the failure of individualism and radicalizes the breakdown of communication in society through his narrative and theatrical discourse. The cases of Vitangelo Moscarda and Henry IV are particularly significant here. Their stories are the initiatory novels of an impossible society, of a total dispossession of the individual who goes to the limit of his subjectivity. Moscarda formulates it this way: 'muojo ogni attimo, io, e rinasco nuovo e senza ricordi: vivo e intero, non più in me, ma in ogni cosa fuori.'[21] [At each moment I die and am born anew, washed clean of memories in my wholeness and living no longer in myself but in all things outside.] Pirandello radicalizes the non-polyphonic states of subjectivity and creates in all his works a sort of negative allegory of the nonconclusive availability for communication of individuals in a fundamentally deficient society. We know that Proust, Joyce, Musil, Virginia Woolf, Kafka, Jean-Paul Sartre, Jean Genet, and Witold Gombrowicz thematize in a different way this a-polyphony of bourgeois society, but Pirandello makes it the backbone of his art. It is in this way that, on the one hand, naked masks symbolize the end-point of the conflicts between subjective monologism and the impossible dialogism of social intercourse, and on the other hand, they constitute the point of departure for a new post-Pirandellian theatre, based upon the premises of integral Pirandellism that exacerbates incommunicability, role-playing, and irrepresentability of life as a total model of irreproducible subjectivities. This new theatre that we call modern or postmodern appropriates to a certain point Pirandello's discourse and follows the Pirandellian logic of irony, fragmentation, self-reflexivity, and the role of 'the open work.'

Let us try to pinpoint some significant historic, textual, and theatrical moments of post-Pirandellian theatre. First of all, the sense of the Pirandellian logic of modernity is principally humoristic. In Pirandello, the sense of opposites regularizes irony and the other invariants of modernity. From the point of view of humorism, this could be defined as the fulfillment of the opposite of the sense of stability. Pirandello's humorism is a metamorphosis of romantic irony combined with human solidarity. The creator is ironic with regard to his work and his characters, but he allows his characters to speak and he plunges them into an endless existential and philosophical stream of chatter. Thus the character in Pirandello becomes a complex sign of an incommunicable relationship. Humorism drives the author out of his work and his silence. Pirandello puts himself on stage and enters into the semiotic process as the visible sign of a perspective and a point of view. The work is fragmented at once vertically as a superposition of perspectives and points of view, and horizontally as a separation of dialogic levels and structures that support the mimesis. The character is divorced from his role and tries to identify himself with the being who precedes him. The dialogue is disjointed by subjective intensities, and the scenic space becomes an unstable topology in the space of the stage, the room, and the hall. A humorous self-reflexivity is achieved at all the interrelational levels of mimesis. And the work, dislocated in this way, opens itself to the ambiguous interplay of the overlapping of reality and fiction, art and life.

Pirandello and the Evolution of Post-Pirandellian Theatre

In what way does Pirandello's discourse presuppose new evolutionary paths for theatre after 1945? We know that this theatre stems from different textual and staging practices, which are difficult to distinguish in a precise manner. Looking at the way that the Pirandellian matrix announces another theatre beyond its strict reduction to Pirandellism, we should see how the following are affirmed in it: (1) the syncretism of the spectacle, mimesis, and thematics (Peter Weiss); (2) autonomization (Grotowski, Ronconi); (3) socialization (Brecht); (4) performance and 'happening' (John Cage).

The evolution of the theatre since the end of the Second World War has been characterized by a few dominant tendencies. In the first place, there is the destabilization of the theatrical text. The so-called theatre of the absurd, just like the theatre of Bertolt Brecht and Peter Weiss, marks this destabilization in different ways. Ionesco's model makes the dialogue absurd. Brecht's model dialecticizes the text by its structural discontinuity: 'songs' are inserted into the dialogue, the effect of distance establishes a metacommunicative contact with the audience. Peter Weiss's model uses the theatre-within-the-theatre as a means to achieve alienation. In these theatrical quests there is a syncretism, a synthesis of the spectacle and the thematic-mimetic. The message passes through the dialogue, manipulated and displaced, by means of autonomous operators like the absurdity of the dialogue and the scenic situation in Ionesco or like the distance-effect in Brecht and Weiss.

Pirandello's theatre – above all his theatre-within-the-theatre trilogy, which destabilizes the text without, however, making it absurd – presupposes this syncretism. Pirandello engenders in a certain sense the strategic economy of blending and dialectic. The logic of *Questa sera si recita a soggetto* [*Tonight We Improvise*, 1930] consists of calling into question a single hegemonic level of theatrical signs. Distance creeps in between improvization and imitation of life. Pirandello's metatheatre opens up avenues to political theatre and to the theatre of the absurd. The intuitions and centrifugal energies of Pirandello's theatre also open up perspectives on an autonomization of the theatre that is translated by the emphasis on the role of the body and the individual interplay of the actors. The theatre of Grotowski certainly does not derive from that of Pirandello, but the author of *Sei personaggi in cerca d'autore* anticipates it. In *I giganti della montagna*, the discovery of the

The Discursive Economies of Modernity and Postmodernism 225

human body and the autonomy of the stage-place and the stage-play give free reign to the somatic materialization of the spectacle. Cotrone's explanatory monologues aim at rethematizing the human being on the stage as body, fantasy, drive, movement, and gesture.

Contemporary theatre abounds in kinetic, visual, vocal, and bodily manifestations. It is also evolving towards a directional synthesis of game and anti-game, of strategic liberation of the space of both the stage and the actors' occupation of space beside and outside the stage. There is no purely postmodern theatricality, except to define it as a composite structure that signifies by means of variants whose common denominator is probably the irreversible destabilization of the stage space and the dialogico-mimetic game. Present-day syncretic theatricality marks the polyvalence of the practices that we call theatrical. It is the product of what Peter Brook calls 'empty space,'[22] Jerzy Grotowski, 'poor theatre,'[23] Eugenio Barba, 'the contest of opposites,'[24] Fernando Arrabal, 'panic theatre,'[25] and Tadeusz Kantor 'the theatre of death.'[26] All these metaphors have an undeniable cognitive value because they signify a quest for what is possible in the theatre beyond such ancient mimetic requirements as plot, dialogue, character, an Italian-style stage, or a stage circumscribed by a determined space. These possibilities depend upon the theatricality defined by Meyerhold as 'theatre of the fair' and 'theatre of machines,' a geometric materialization of the stage.[27] But they are also indebted to the aesthetic of cruelty. Different theatrical practices produce what Barba calls 'la distruzione del teatro attraverso il teatro'[28] [the destruction of theatre through theatre]. The performance and the 'happening' also play a role in it. They create a theatricality of the untheatrical, of the theatrical in parentheses.[29]

To make a synthesis of the practices of the *Living Theatre*, Grotowski, Ariane Mnouchkine, Ronconi, Barba, Bob Wilson, Alan Kaprow, Peter Brook, the *Bread and Puppet*, and Kantor is above all to recognize: (1) the relativization and the surpassing of the textual; (2) the supremacy of spontaneity and improvization over what is programmed; (3) the synchronization and autonomy of the theatrical, socialization, and politics; (4) the extensive liberation of the threshold of the stage and the visible; (5) the displacement of the mimetic towards the symbolic; (6) the use as signs of the body and the voice, of movement, space, and time, both within and outside mimesis. Is there, then, a Pirandellian matrix common to these different practices? This matrix, if it exists, consists of the structures of dialectically negative doubling that disintegrate the totalization of the theatrical by the mimetic. The confrontation of the *theatrum mundi* with the *theatrum theatri* in the metatheatrical works of Pirandello subverts the signs of representational theatre. If Pirandello's theatre is based upon the conflict of the representations of the subjective and the objective, it is also the necessary convergence-point of the discursive economies of today's theatre.

The return to Pirandello thus confirms the present-day theatrical archaeology of knowledge. This knowledge weaves a web of relations between works and practices. Pirandello's place is significant, because it is thanks to him that theatre assures its self-regulation and transforms itself. Pirandello, more than any other dramatist, has subverted the ideological-aesthetic obstacles that arise against the limitless freedom of the theatre. Thus the surpassing of the existential stage that prepared itself in Pirandello foreshadows the infinite play of the theatre of the world and of the theatre of the theatre at the stage of a new modernity or of postmodernism. Whatever the terms may be, Pirandello unites them beyond masks and performances and within theories.

Translated by Gloria D'Ambrosio and Drew Griffith

NOTES

This essay was first published in French under the title 'Pirandello dans les économies discursives de la modernité et du post-modernism' in Wladimir Krysinski, *Le paradigme inquiet: Pirandello et le champ de la modernité* (Montreal: Le Préambule, 1989), 451–72.

1 Julián Ríos, *Larva, Babel de una noche de San Juan* (Barcelona: Ed. Del Mall, 1984), 18.
2 Thomas S. Kuhn, *The Structure of Scientific Revolutions* (Chicago: University of Chicago Press, 1974), 10.
3 Decadence is one of the ideologemes of modernity. Negatively, it signifies a state of crisis of reason and conscience that is tied to such phenomena as the social alienation of the individual, the degradation of human values in the larger sense, the domination of the state, and the 'process of licensing and mass-marketing the intellectual realm' in the words of Arcangelo Leone de Castris. (See *Il decadentismo italiano: Svevo, Pirandello, D'Annunzio* [Bari: De Donato 1974], 2.) Positively, decadence can be defined as artistic response to the crisis of values and to the critical, historical, and social

The Discursive Economies of Modernity and Postmodernism 227

situation of the individual. Historically circumscribed, decadence was superceded by certain new ways of writing and obsessive themes from Joris-Karl Huysmans and Oscar Wilde to Pirandello and Italo Svevo. Pirandello's work is situated in decadence, because it accentuates the social alienation of the individual and becomes the articulation of the search for a possible escape from the crisis. In this sense, Pirandello's work is 'modern': it is articulated on a dynamic and a thematic of a decadence that is a critical vision of society, and on the postulate of an artistic and thematic radicalism. In addition to works by Carlo Salinari (notably *Miti e coscienza del decadentism italiano: D'Annunzio, Pascoli, Fogazzaro e Pirandello* [Milan: Feltrinelli, 1960]) and Leone de Castris, one must mention Robert Dombroski's *Le totalità dell'artificio: ideologia e forma nel romanzo di Pirandello* (Padua: Liviana Editrice, 1978), a fundamental work that establishes a series of homologies between the structures of Pirandello's work and the ideological and social superstructures of the era that inform the work and whose thematic givens, such as the alienation and crisis of the liberal world-view, this work transcribes. Max Nordau's book, *Die Entartung* [Degeneration] published in 1895 was very successful at that time. For Nordau, degeneration is a biological phenomenon and he studies its social and artistic pathology. Nordau attributes the fault to 'egotists' and 'degenerates' such as Nietzsche, Ibsen, and Zola, and to 'decadents' such as Théophile Gauthier and Charles Baudelaire, but he seems to describe the symptoms much more than the causes; he offers a diagnosis but he does not connect the phenomena that he describes ('psychology of mysticism,' 'psychology of egomania,' 'symbolism,' 'decadence') to social, political, or historic causes. Gösta Andersson, in his important work, *Arte e teoria: studi sulla poetica del giovane Luigi Pirandello* (Stockholm: Almquist & Wiksell, 1966), 92–4, points out the resemblance between the formulas that Pirandello uses in his study 'Arte e coscienza d'oggi' ['Art and Conscience Today,' 1893] ('egoismo, spossatezza morale' [egotism, moral exhaustion], 'sconfinata stima di sé stessi' [unlimited esteem in oneself], 'straordinaria emotività, suggestibilità' [extraordinary emotionality, suggestibility], 'incapacità di volere' [inability to will], 'fantasticheria' [imaginativeness], 'bugiarderia incosciente, facile eccitabilità dell'imaginazione' [irresponsible inclination to lie, facile excitability of the imagination], in Pirandello, *Saggi, poesie scritti varii* [Milan: Mondadori, 1960], 875–6) and those of Nordau in *Die Entartung*. Beyond these resemblances or coincidences in the general picture that Pirandello paints of the moral situation of the world at the time when he wrote his study, it would be unjust to attribute to Pirandello an anticipation of Nordau's arguments and ways of thinking. Pirandello clearly identifies the social and historical causes of the individual's alienation and his art is wrongly attributed to socio-biological pathology. His protagonists are engaged in an objective conflict between society and the individual, a conflict that they interiorize and express subjectively.

4 Paul Valéry's lapidary formula: 'Le temps du monde fini commence' [The time of the ended world begins] as well as his warning: 'Il faut rappeler aux nations croissantes qu'il n'y a point d'arbre dans la nature qui, placé dans les meilleures conditions de lumière, de sol et de terrain, puisse grandir et s'élargir indéfiniment' [One must remind all growing nations that there is no tree in nature that, when placed in the best conditions of light, sun and soil, can grow indefinitely] from 'Regards sur le monde actuel,' in *Oeuvres* (Paris: Gallimard, Bibliothèque de la Pléiade, 1960), 2:923–4.

5 See Oswald Spengler's *The Decline of the West* (1926–9) and his theory of cycles.

6 'The fundamental process of Modern Times is the conquest of the world as a conceived image. The word image now means the configuration (*Gebild*) of the representational production.' See Martin Heidegger, 'The Era of World-Conceptions,' in *Chemins que ne mènent nulle part* (Paris: Gallimard, 1962), 85.

7 See Gilles Deleuze and Felix Guattari, *Capitalisme et schizophrénie, L'anti-Oedipe* (Paris: Éd. de Minuit, 1972), in which the theory of 'desiring machines' is laid out. This book, written against the psychoanalysis of Oedipus and in defence of schizo-analysis, diagnoses in a complex and composite philosophical mode the schizophrenia of capitalism that is unable to liberate the unconscious. Deleuze and Guattari attribute the schizophrenic state to the system of the family.

8 Jean-François Lyotard connects 'great stories' with the problem of the legitimizing of knowledge. 'Le recours aux grands récits est exclu; on ne saurait donc recourir ni à la dialectique de l'Esprit ni même à l'émancipation de l'humanité comme validation du discours scientifique postmoderne.' [To resort to the grand narratives is excluded; one cannot resort either to the dialectic of the spirit or even to the emancipation of humanity as a validation of postmodern scientific discourse.) *La condition post-moderne* (Paris: Éd. de Minuit, 1979), 98.

9 Jürgen Habermas, 'La modernité: un projet inachevé,' *Critique* 413 (October 1981): 950–67.

10 Peter Bürger, 'The Significance of the Avant-Garde for Contemporary Aesthetics: A Reply to Jürgen Habermas,' *New German Critique* 22 (1981): 20.

11 Henri Lefebvre, 'De la littérature et de l'art modernes considérés comme processus de destruction et d'autodestruction de l'art,' in *Littérature et société, Problèmes de méthodologie en sociologie de la littérature* (Brussels: Éd. Université Libre de Bruxelles, Institut de Sociologie, 1967), 116.
12 Ibid.
13 Theodore Adorno, *Noten zur Literatur II* (Frankfurt am Main: Surkamp Verlag, 1965), 165.
14 'La modernité' is the fourth article of a cycle entitled *Le peintre de la vie moderne* written probably in 1859 and published in *Le Figaro* (26 and 29 November and 3 December 1863). See Charles Baudelaire, *Écrits esthétiques* (Paris: UGE, 1986), 372–3.
15 Arthur Rimbaud, 'Adieu,' from *Une saison en enfer*, in *Oeuvres* (Paris: Éd. S. Bernard, 1960), 241.
16 Roland Barthes, *Le degré zéro de l'écriture* (Paris: Éd. Gonthier, 1965), 36.
17 Jean Baudrillard, 'La modernité,' in *Encyclopaedia Universalis* (Paris: Encyclopaedia Universalis France, 1985), 12:424–6.
18 See I. Tynianov 'De l'évolution littéraire,' in T. Todorov, ed., *Théorie de la littérature, textes des formalistes russes* (Paris: Seuil, 1965).
19 Hans Georg Gadamer, 'Die Grundlagen des zwanzigsten Jahrhunderts,' [The Foundations of the Twentieth Century] in *Aspekte der Modernität* (Göttingen: H. Steffern, Vandenhoeck & Ruprecht, 1965), 87.
20 Ibid., 88.
21 Pirandello, *Uno, nessuno e centomila*, in Giovanni Macchia, ed., *Tutti i romanzi* (1973; Milan: Mondadori, 1984), 2:902.
22 Peter Brook, *The Empty Space* (London: McGibbon and Kee, 1968; London: Penguin, 1982). For Brook it is sufficient to take an empty space and call it 'a bare stage'; if one person walks across this empty space while another person watches, 'this is all that is needed for an act of theatre to be engaged.' Brook divides theatre into four principal types: Deadly Theatre, Holy Theatre, Rough Theatre and Immediate Theatre. Deadly Theatre is conventional, commercial theatre, implicitly mediocre. Holy Theatre is 'the Theatre of the Invisible-Made-Visible.' Rough Theatre is close to the people – theatre of marionettes or shadow-puppets – and is usually characterized by a lack of style. Immediate Theatre is a theatre of spontaneity and improvisation. Pirandello's theatrical quest coincides to some degree with a mixture of these four types of theatre. The substance and form of Pirandello's theatre are based on an unstable synthesis of these four theatres. However, in *I giganti della montagna*, he seems to achieve a clear vision of a theatre that conforms to the chief elements of his quest; thus he institutes a theatrical synthesis of Holy, Rough,

and Immediate Theatre. In *I giganti della montagna*, the placement within parentheses of the representation of *La favola del figlio cambiato* [*The Fable of the Changeling Son*] constitutes in some sense a rejection of Brook's Deadly Theatre.

23 Jerzy Grotowski, 'Vers un théâtre pauvre,' in *Cahiers Renaud-Barrault* 55 (May 1956) and *Towards a Poor Theatre* (New York: Simon & Schuster, 1968). To explain the theatre of Grotowski, Raymonde Tempkine polemically cites Lechy Elbernon's statement about the theatre in Paul Claudel's *L'Échange*, and also Mimi's retort in *Questa sera si recita a soggetto*: 'Una sala, una sala grande, con tante file di palchi tutt'intorno, cinque, sei file piene ... un mare di teste; e lumi, lumi da per tutto; un lampadario nel bel mezzo, che pende come dal cielo, e pare tutto di brillanti; una luce che abbaglia, che inebria ... I lumi a un tratto si spengono; ... e il sipario è come una tenda, ma grande, pesante, tutta di velluto rosso e frange d'oro, una magnificenza; quando s'apre ... comincia l'opera ... – Questo è il teatro.' (Luigi Pirandello, *Questa sera si recita a soggetto*, in Manlio Lo Vecchio Musti, ed., *Maschere nude* [1958; Milan: Mondadori, 1978], 285–6. 'A hall, a large hall with all around several rows of balconies, five or six rows full of people ... an ocean of heads; and lights, lights all over; a chandelier in the center, as if hanging from the sky and entirely made of diamonds; a light that can blind and intoxicate you ... All of a sudden the lights are switched off; ... and the curtain is like a drape, but a large and heavy one made of red velvet with golden fringes: a magnificence; when it opens ... the opera starts ... – This is the theatre.') In his volume entitled *Grotowski* (Lausanne: Éd. La Cité, L'Âge d'Homme, 1970), Raymonde Temkine observes that Grotowski postulates a thoroughly new relationship with the audience (77–8), and in so doing, he rejects theatre as the synthesis of all the arts: 'Il en est ... à prôner un "théâtre pauvre" aux antipodes du *théâtre total* qui se jette sur toutes les ressources son-et-lumière nouvelles, avec cette faim dévoratrice bien caractéristique de notre époque technicienne et gadgétomane.' (78) [It is imperative to advocate a 'poor theatre' that is profoundly different from the 'total theatre' that exploits all new audio-visual resources with that devouring hunger so distinctively characteristic of our technological and gadget-maniac times.] Mimi's retort in *Questa sera si recita a soggetto* is not Pirandello's only definition of the theatre, nor is it definitive. It seems to me that in Pirandello's theatre there are some elements of Grotowski's 'Poor Theatre.' In *All'uscita* [*At the Gate*], *L'uomo dal fiore in bocca* [*The Man with the Flower in his Mouth*], and *I giganti della montagna*, Pirandello seeks to rid the theatre of the accoutrements of spectacle. In any case, it is

The Discursive Economies of Modernity and Postmodernism 231

certain that the 'poverty of the theatre,' as Grotowski understands it, is not the univocal destination of Pirandello's theatrical quest.

24 For Eugenio Barba, the formula 'the conflict of opposites' expresses the sense of his theatrical quest. Deriving his inspiration from the idea of 'anatomical theatre,' Barba states: 'Notre théâtre anatomique ne concerne pas seulement le corps de l'homme. Il concerne ses actions et ses rapports à l'intérieur des événements sociaux, à l'intérieur des conflits historiques: les tensions et les oppositions qui constituent les règles profondes des diverses réalités. Il signifie: vision de ce qui se cache sous l'épiderme. Semblable au Théâtre Anatomique est le théâtre auquel nous pensons, à mi-chemin entre spectacle et science, entre didactisme et transgression, entre horreur et admiration' (Eugenio Barba, *L'archipel du théâtre* [Carcassonne: Éd. Contrastes Bouffonneries, 1982], 71) [Our anatomical theatre does not concern only the human body. It concerns its actions and its relationships within social events, within historical conflicts, the tensions and the oppositions that constitute the profound rules of the various realities. This implies the vision of what happens beneath the skin. The theatre we imagine is similar to Anatomical Theatre: a theatre that stands half way between spectacle and science, didacticism and transgression, horror and admiration.]

25 On 'panic' and 'panic theatre,' see Fernando Arrabal, *Le panique* (Paris: Éd. UGE, coll. 10/18, 1973).

26 Tadeusz Kantor states: 'Cette image vivante de l'HOMME sortant des ténèbres, poursuivant sa marche en avant, constituait un MANIFESTE, irradiant, de sa nouvelle CONDITION HUMAINE, seulement HUMAINE, avec sa RESPONSABILITÉ et sa CONSCIENCE tragique, mesurant son DESTIN à une échelle implacable et définitive, l'échelle de la MORT … Les moyens et l'art de cet homme, l'ACTEUR (pour employer notre propre vocabulaire), se rattachaient aussi à la MORT, à sa tragique et horrifique beauté.' *Le théâtre de la mort*, ed. Denis Bablet (Lausanne: Éd. L'Âge d'Homme, 1985), 223. [This living image of MAN exiting darkness, and moving forward, constitutes a MANIFESTO, an irradiating one, of his new HUMAN CONDITION, only HUMAN, with his RESPONSIBILITY and his tragic CONSCIENCE, measuring his DESTINY according to an implacable and definitive scale, the scale of DEATH … The means and the art of this man, the ACTOR (using our own specific vocabulary), are also connected to DEATH, to its tragic and horrifying beauty.]

27 On Meyerhold's artistic approach as a director, see Henri Guilbeaux, *Meyerhold en terre d'Europe, Maïakovsky dans la terre russe* (Paris: Éd. de la Revue littéraire des Primaires LES HUMBLES, 1930), 16.

28 For Barba's remarks on the Odin theatre, see 'Colloquio con Eugenio Barba,' in Franco Quadri, *Invenzione di un teatro diverso: Kantor, Barba, Foreman, Wilson, Monk, Terayma* (Turin: Einaudi, 1984), 83.
29 Michael Kirby remarks that what characterizes the new theatre is above all 'the absence of an information structure,' 'indeterminacy' and 'non-matrixed performing.' See Michael Kirby, 'The New Theatre,' in Richard Kostelanetz, ed., *The Avant-Garde Tradition in Literature* (Buffalo: Prometheus Books, 1982), 324–40.